PRE-CONGRESS SYMPOSIUM:
POPULATION, PRODUCTION AND POWER
JERUSALEM, JUNE 1990

SUPPLEMENT

LAWRENCE E. STAGER
12 GARDEN ROAD
CONCORD, MA 01742

BIBLICAL ARCHAEOLOGY TODAY, 1990

Proceedings of the Second International Congress
on Biblical Archaeology

PRE-CONGRESS SYMPOSIUM:
POPULATION, PRODUCTION AND POWER
JERUSALEM, JUNE 1990

SUPPLEMENT

Israel Exploration Society

1993

EDITORS: Avraham Biran, Joseph Aviram
ASSOCIATE EDITOR: Alan Paris-Shadur

ISBN 965–221–023–4

PRINTED IN ISRAEL by Keterpress Enterprises Ltd., Jerusalem

CONTENTS

SESSION I
POPULATION

OFER BAR-YOSEF, Session Chairman, *Harvard University*

PATRICIA SMITH, *Hebrew University of Jerusalem*
An Approach to the Paleodemographic Analysis of Human Skeletal Remains
from Archaeological Sites
MAGEN BROSHI, *Israel Museum*
The Population of Iron Age Palestine
GIDEON BIGER, *Tel Aviv University*
DAVID GROSSMAN, *Bar-Ilan University*
Village and Town Populations in Palestine during the 1930s–1940s
and their Relevance to Ethnoarchaeology

An Approach to the Paleodemographic Analysis of Human Skeletal Remains from Archaeological Sites

Patricia Smith

Introduction

During the past two decades, paleodemographic studies have become an important feature of archaeological research in Israel, (Broshi and Gophna 1986; Gonen 1984; Gophna 1984; Gophna and Portugali 1988; Finkelstein 1989; Portugali 1988; Shiloh 1980). In these studies the main data sources for estimating population numbers have been size, quantity and density of habitations as deduced from the archaeological findings, and the estimated carrying capacity of the land. While these can provide good estimates of population numbers, they cannot very well discriminate between the various biological factors directly affecting the expansion or contraction of a specific population. As shown by demographic studies of living populations, these factors include life expectancy (especially of females), fecundity and migration (Fig. 1). For

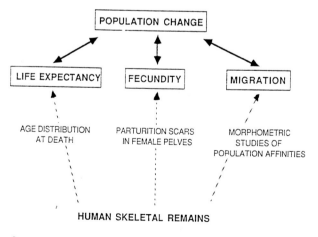

Fig. 1
Flow diagram showing information derived from skeletal analyses

2

archaeological societies with written records, attempts have been made to extrapolate such information from literary sources or funerary inscriptions. However, even where such data are available, they tend to show major internal inconsistencies, and have been deemed less reliable than those derived from examination of the human skeletal remains of the same periods (Ery 1969). Human skeletal remains therefore, provide the only source of information on biological factors associated with changing numbers (Fig. 1) of both prehistoric and archaeological populations.

As we shall detail below, the reliability of the results obtained from examination of human skeletal remains is limited by the extent to which the specimens examined constitute a representative sample of the population under study. This can be checked by reference to standardized population statistics, since cumulative mortality curves can be divided into four major patterns, each correlated with a specific socioeconomic level (Coale and Demeny 1983; Preston 1982). Deviation from one of these standard patterns suggests that a skewed sample of the original population has been recovered. This may be due to any one of a number of factors that include: destruction of part of the site, excavation design, poor preservation limiting age-sex identification, or selective burial treatment of a particular subset of the population. Recognition of such biases is an essential precondition for paleodemographic reconstructions based on human skeletal remains. They have been discussed extensively elsewhere (Acsadi and Nemeskeri 1970; Boddington 1987; Boquet-Appel and Masset 1985; Howell 1976, 1982; Nemeskeri 1989; Waldron 1987). In this paper I will discuss some of the methods that can be used to estimate and compare life expectancy in even biased skeletal samples. For this purpose, case studies from a number of sites in Israel and Jordan will be presented.

Burial Types

Human skeletal remains excavated from cemetery complexes at archaeological sites can be divided into three main types:

A) Primary burials where skeletons are found with all bones in anatomical articulation indicating that they were buried soon after death and remained undisturbed.

B) Mixed burial chambers containing one or more articulated burials. These are usually prominently placed within the burial chamber and surrounded by piled or scattered individual bones. The latter probably represent the remains of earlier primary burials that had been moved to make room for later burials.

C) Secondary burial chambers or containers such as ossuaries containing dry bones probably collected from a separate locality. In these, only disarticulated bones are present while some bones may be absent or duplicated, suggesting that the primary burial site or repository was reused.

Obviously, the probability of bones being damaged or missing increases when they are moved from place to place, as in Type B and C burials. Moreover, the smaller and more delicate the bones, the greater the probability of damage. Thus, even assuming the same burial treatment for all age groups, bones of infants and juveniles are less likely to be preserved than those of adults in secondary burials. The best preservation is likely to occur in the A-type burials, that is primary burials.

Primary burials, identified by the presence of bones in anatomical articulation, characterize only four of the sites discussed here and listed in Table 1. They are the Middle Paleolithic sites of Skhul and Qafzeh (McCown and Keith 1939; Vandermeersch 1981); the late Iron Age site of Tel Mazar (Disi et al. 1983) and the recent Arab site of Dor, excavated by Dauphin (1979, 1981). The remaining sites discussed here are characterized either by secondary burial (or displacement of bones within a burial chamber used over a period of time), or by a mixture of primary and secondary burials within the same cemetery complex (Table 1).

Table 1. List of Sites by Period and Burial Type

Period	Site	Type	Sample size	Source
Mousterian	Qafzeh	A	15	Vandermeersch 1981; Tillier 1989
	Skhul	A	10	McCown and Keith 1939
Neolithic	Abu Ghosh	B	30	Arensburg et al. 1978
Chalcolithic	Shiqmim	B	86	Unpublished data, Hebrew University
	Ben Shemen	B	39	Lacombe 1980
Early Bronze	ʿEin Khuderah	B	45	Bar-Yosef et al. 1977
	Bab edh-Dhraʿ	B	88	Ortner 1979, 1982
	ʿEn Ha-Naẓiv	B	53	Amiran et al. 1986
Middle Bronze I	Jebel Qaʿaqir	C	41	Smith 1982
Middle Bronze II	Tell Beit Mirsim	B	46	Unpublished data, Hebrew University
Iron	Achzib	B	78	Unpublished data, Hebrew University
Persian	Tel Mazar	A	53	Disi et al. 1983
Hellenistic	En-Gedi	B	99	Goldstein et al. 1981
Roman	Jericho	B	192	Arensberg and Smith 1983
Byzantine	Khirbet Shemaʿ	B	197	Smith et al. 1981
Ottoman	Dor	A	166	Unpublished data, Hebrew University
	Beersheba	A	216	Unpublished data, Hebrew University

Key:
A primary burials only
B mixed primary and secondary burials
C secondary burials only

Sample sizes are small for all sites shown, and this is especially true of the two Mousterian samples, which obviously are too small for reliable inferences on paleodemography to be made. The differences in infant mortality (30 percent compared to 53 percent), observed between the two sites is probably due to this cause, since there is no evidence for differences in health status or nutrition between them. They are included here to demonstrate that when soil conditions favor bone preservation, the small delicate bones of infants are preserved even in such early sites. At Qafzeh, now dated at more than 90,000 years (Valladas et al. 1988), skeletal remains of even a newborn infant were preserved.

Model Life Tables

Model life tables provide information on the number of deaths in different age categories of a population of finite number. From these figures the percentage of deaths or survivors in any age category can be calculated. The probability of death in any age category is calculated as the percentage of those dying in that category, divided by the percentage of survivors. The latter calculation forms the basis for estimating life expectancy. This method has been adapted for use in estimating life expectancy of past populations from age estimations of skeletal remains. Obviously, apart from the fact that we are usually dealing with small sample sizes, biases in representation of the different age categories of the original population, for whatever reason, will markedly affect the results obtained.

These biases can be detected by comparing the percentage of individuals in different age categories in the archaeological samples with those calculated for living populations. An alternative method, that is independent of biases introduced through under-representation of infants and juveniles, may then be used to compare relative longevity in different populations. Acsadi and Nemeskeri (1970), and Nemeskeri (1989) have devised an extremely ingenious method of correcting for these biases. They propose that the average number of births can be predicted from the age distribution of adult females in a skeletal sample. The underlying assumption is that the total fertility rate can be calculated by estimating a childbirth frequency in females of some 27 months starting at age 19. This is used to calculate the total number of births which, in turn, provides the baseline data for drawing up "life tables." However, these calculations are based on numerous assumptions and make no allowance, for example, for the effect of infant death on child spacing. We would therefore question their application, especially for small sample sizes.

Living populations show marked differences in life expectancy, and these differences appear even in the first year of life. Thus, the overall frequency of deaths recorded for infants aged 0–12 months by WHO (1976), varied from 1.5 percent for Western populations to 20 percent for developing countries. These differences reflect the harshness of environmental conditions: primarily nutrition and disease load. However, despite these differences in probability of death in this and later age groups, the same overall pattern is maintained. More infants die in the first year of life than in later infancy or childhood. The 1976 WHO survey, reports less than 1 percent infant mortality in England in 1965, versus 28 percent in the first year of life in Egypt (Fig. 2). However these figures represent the country-wide average and this may vary from district to district. In one rural district in Egypt, Dzierzykray-Rogalski (1964) found that over 69 percent of all deaths recorded over a ten year period were of infants under 6 years of age.

As Figs. 2–4 show, populations with high infant mortality are also characterized by a greater risk of death in early adult life. Where infant mortality is high, the probability of death in subsequent years is also higher, with very few adults surviving beyond 50 years. In contrast, in populations with low infant mortality there is a low

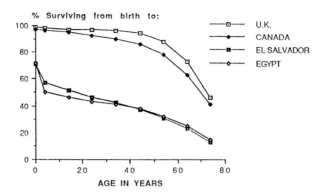

Fig. 2
Survival of different age groups plotted for four populations of different life expectancy: data taken from
WHO Tables

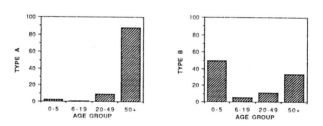

Fig. 3
Age distribution at death in different age categories for two of the populations shown in Fig. 2

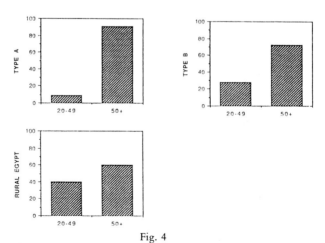

Fig. 4
Relative frequency of old to young adults in populations shown in Fig. 3, together with data calculated
for a rural district in Egypt by Dzierzykray-Rogalski (1964)

probability of death before the age of 50 years. These two types may, of course, be modified if migration is taking place or living conditions alter dramatically. However, since the data we are dealing with here is derived from cemetery complexes that cover at least three generations, we have assumed that they represent stable populations. We may then expect them to fall into one of the two main types presented in Figs. 2–4.

One type is represented by the two populations with long life expectancy (Type A), the second type is represented by the two populations with short life expectancy (Type B). In both types, there is a similar pattern, although the actual figures differ. In both, the first year of life is associated with highest mortality. This drops over the next five years, and falls again during late childhood and adolescence. Thus, while the two populations differ in percentage survival at any one age, the major differences are found in the different frequencies of infants and old individuals. The initial survival rate is highly correlated with subsequent survival. Those populations with high infant survival (Type A), are characterized by relatively low mortality before 55 years, whereas populations with high infant mortality (Type B), show relatively few individuals surviving beyond 55 years. Thus, not only are there fewer surviving adults in Type B population, but relatively fewer survive to old age (Fig. 4). If the skeletal samples deviate from these patterns we may then assume that the samples are skewed.

Archaeological Data

The archaeological sites listed in Table 1 fall into three groups that differ in the percentage of infant deaths. Those with up to 80 percent of all specimens surviving to age 20; those with at least 60 percent of all specimens surviving to age 20, and those with less than 40 percent of all specimens surviving to age 20 (Fig. 5). The extent to which these differences are truly representative of differences in life expectancy, or are biased samples, can best be tested by comparison of the raw data with model life tables obtained from demographic studies of living populations shown in Figs. 2–4. When compared with the model life tables, it can be seen that those populations with a high frequency of adults are, with one exception, those populations showing an opposite trend, with fewer early infant deaths and more deaths in late childhood. These populations then differ from the model life tables by showing a higher frequency of deaths in later childhood than in early infancy. As previously stated, since this contradicts the model life tables, it constitutes a priori evidence for biases in these samples — either because of poor preservation and recovery, or differential burial of adults and infants. This means that these data should not be used to estimate life expectancy, since the relative frequency of adult survivors is artificially inflated by an unknown factor.

If, however, the adults alone are considered, then we can calculate the relative probability of death in any adult age category by dividing the number of deaths in that age category by the total number of adults. This method avoids biases introduced

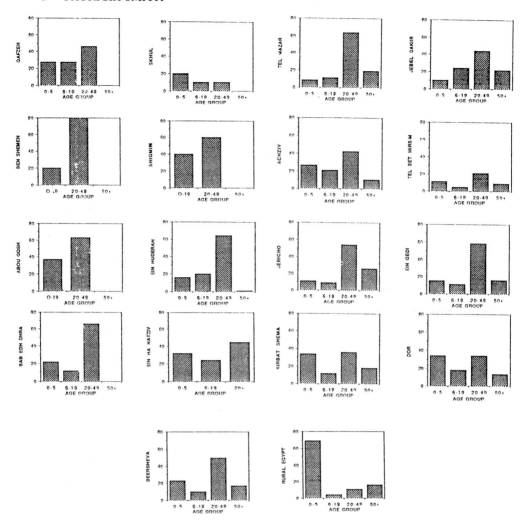

Fig. 5
Age distribution at death of populations listed in Table 1

by the usual method, and provides a more reliable technique for the comparison of relative life expectancy in skeletal samples from different periods and with different burial customs. Similar calculations can also be made for adults in the type A and B model populations as shown in Fig. 4, so that comparisons can be made between the archaeological samples and living populations of known socioeconomic status.

As Fig. 4 shows, the survivorship graph for an entire population can be reproduced from adult death rates alone. In the example given of a population with long life expectancy (Type A), less than 10 percent of adult deaths occur between the ages of 20–54 years, with the remaining 90 percent of adult deaths occurring in the over

55 year age group. In the Type B population, that is one with short life expectancy, 28 percent of all adult deaths occur in the 20–54 age group so that there are relatively fewer survivors to old age. The sample from rural Egypt, with even lower life expectancy, shows how the ratio of young to old adults increases even more as life expectancy decreases.

Fig. 6 gives the relative frequency of early to late adult deaths in the archaeological samples. In contrast to the extreme fluctuations in life expectancy estimated from the entire sample, calculations based on adults alone show much greater consistency between sites studied. In all sites, the percentage of early adult deaths is higher than in even the type B populations, with between 60–70 percent of all adults dying between the age of 20 and 50. This may, of course, represent a systematic bias in our age estimations of older individuals so that our estimates of life expectancy based on adults alone may be too low. They are, however, consistent, with the same criteria applied for all the skeletal samples. The data suggest that life expectancy was highest in the samples from Jebel Qaʿaqir, En-Gedi, Jericho and Meron, and lowest in the samples from Achzib, Tel Mazar and Beersheba.

It can be seen that those populations which conform to the pattern predicted from the model tables in showing a 2:1 or higher ratio of early to late infant deaths also show the predicted ratio of young to old adult deaths. Those sites with a suspiciously low incidence of early infant deaths now differ little from the other sites when the ratio of young to old adults is calculated. This reinforces the hypothesis that the low frequency of infant deaths at these sites is due to sampling biases rather than to greater longevity.

The marked differences found between sites in the relative frequency of infants is not surprising in view of the known differentiation of burials by age, sex and status in different periods. For example, the Neolithic plastered skulls from Jericho (Strouhal 1973) and Beisamun (Ferembach and Lechevallier 1973), together with the decorated skulls from Naḥal Ḥemar (Arensburg and Hershkovitz 1988) all appear to belong to adult males. At the Chalcolithic site of Shiqmim, Levy and Alon (1982) have postulated that grave size and type is associated with status. Cremations in the Iron Age sites studied by us (Achzib, Hazor) are mainly of adults, while separate burial of infants has been reported from most periods since the Neolithic. These factors, as well as poorer preservation of the more fragile infant remains, contribute to their absence or under-representation in most of the sites discussed here. This is especially pronounced at sites characterized by secondary burial. However, even at sites characterized by primary burials such as Tel Mazar (Disi et al. 1983), these considerations obviously apply, and indeed were reported by the excavators.

We propose that the methods discussed here provide a reliable way of assessing such biases in the raw data. It provides a means of correcting for them, and so comparing age profiles in skeletal samples from different sites and periods, without relying on assumptions that cannot be tested regarding infant mortality rates. While the method is less elegant than that proposed by some other paleoanthropologists, we suggest that it is more reliable.

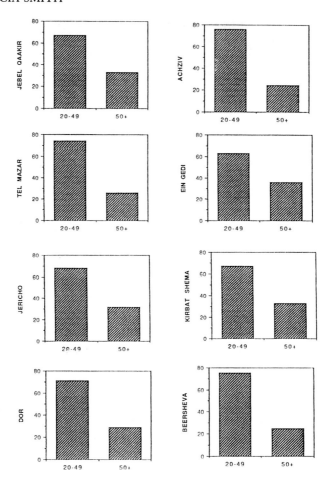

Fig. 6

Relative frequency of old to young adults in those populations listed in Table 1, with detailed information on adult ages

Analysis of the relative frequency of young to old adults in the sites discussed here, indicates that life expectancy at Jebel Qaʿaqir was highest of all sites studied, followed by En-Gedi, Jericho and Meron. Life expectancy was shortest at the Iron Age sites of Achzib and Tel Mazar and the recent sites of Dor and Beersheba. These results indicate that life expectancy in past populations of Israel has fluctuated rather than followed a monotonic trend. This is not an unexpected finding given the marked variations in levels of stress of past populations in this region, as documented both by the archaeological record and the paleopathological data (Smith et al. 1984; Smith and Peretz 1986; Smith 1989). Thus, developmental defects of the bones and teeth indicative of poor health are found in exceptionally high frequencies in those populations reported here as showing the lowest life expectancy, such as Dor and Beersheba

(Goldstein et al. 1976; Smith and Peretz 1986). They are much less frequent at Jebel Qaʿaqir (Smith 1982) and Jericho (Arensburg and Smith 1983), sites with higher life expectancy.

Conclusions

Given the extremely small size of the skeletal samples represented here, any attempt to define in more detail the structure of the populations represented would appear futile. Those who would attempt this are referred to Angel (1970, 1971, 1984) for discussion of the methodology involved in estimating fecundity from female skeletons, and to Howell (1982) for a discussion of the ways in which these more detailed analyses can be tested and the extent to which they are limited by sample size. However, the data presented here support the observations of Howell (1982) and Boquet-Appel and Massett (1985) concerning the systematic bias towards underestimating the age of older individuals. For this reason, I feel that the use of broader age divisions, as used here, may be more pertinent for paleodemographic purposes than attempts to reconstruct life tables in detail. They provide an easy and reliable means of comparing relative mortality in skeletal populations, and I would argue that more sophisticated analyses are unsuitable for dealing with sample sizes of the order dealt with here.

Direct comparison of these age categories in skeletal samples to model life tables of populations with differing life expectancies permits identification of skewing in the skeletal sample, while use of young and old adult age categories for estimation of relative longevity provides a built-in correction factor. However, only careful analysis of the distribution and preservation of bones *in situ*, as well as their removal and laboratory analysis, can determine whether burial practices or soil conditions are responsible for skewing the age distribution of human remains recovered from archaeological sites.

References

G. Acsadi and J. Nemeskeri, 1970. *History of Human Life Span and Mortality*. Budapest.

R. Amiran et al., 1986. "The Excavation of Two Tomb Caves: One in Ancient Arad and One in the Beth Shean Valley," *Israel Museum Journal* 5: 13–18.

J.L. Angel, 1970. "Human Skeletal Remains at Karatas," *American Journal of Archaeology* 74: 253–259.

_____, 1971. *The People of Lerna, Analysis of a Prehistoric Aegean Population*. Washington DC.

_____, 1984. "Health as a Crucial Factor in the Changes in Hunting to Developed Farming in the Eastern Mediterranean," in M. Cohen and G. Armelagos (eds.), *Palaeopathology at the Origins of Agriculture*. New York.

B. Arensburg and I. Hershkovitz, 1988. "Nahal Hemar Cave: Neolithic Human Remains," in O. Bar-Yosef and D. Alon (eds.), *Nahal Hemar. ʿAtiqot* (English Series) 18: 50–58.

B. Arensburg and P. Smith, 1983. "Appendix. The Jewish Population of Jericho 100 B.C.–70 A.D.," *PEQ* 16:133–137.

B. Arensburg, P. Smith and J. Yakar, 1978. "Human Remains from Abou Gosh," *Mémoires et travaux du CNRS de Jérusalem* 2, pp. 95–105. Paris.

O. Bar-Yosef et al., 1977. "The Nawamis near ʿEin Huderah (Eastern Sinai)," *IEJ* 27: 65–88.

A. Boddington, 1987. "From Bones to Population; the Problem of Numbers," in A. Boddington, A.N. Garland and R.C. Janaway (eds.), *Death, Decay and Reconstruction*, pp. 180–196. Manchester.

J.-P. Boquet-Appel and C. Masset, 1985. "Paleodemography: Resurrection or Ghost?," *Journal of Human Evolution* 14: 107–11.

M. Broshi and R. Gophna, 1986. "Middle Bronze Age II Palestine: Its Settlements and Population," *BASOR* 261: 73–90.

A.J. Coale and P. Demeny, 1983. *Regional Model Life Tables and Stable Populations* (2nd edition). New York.

C.M. Dauphin, 1979. "Dor, Byzantine Church," *IEJ* 29: 235–236.

———, 1981. "Dor, Byzantine Church, 1980," *IEJ* 31: 117–119.

W.G. Dever, 1972. "An MB I Necropolis and Settlement on the West Bank of the Jordan," *Archaeology* 25: 231–233.

W. Disi, A.M. Henke and J. Wahl, 1983. "Tell el-Mazar: Study of the Human Skeletal Remains," *Annual of the Department of Antiquities of Jordan* 27: 515–548.

T. Dzierzykray-Rogalski, 1964. "Populational Problems of the Siwah Oasis in the Light of Demographical and Public Health Relations in the Western Desert," *Publications of the Joint Arabic-Polish Anthropological Expedition (1958–1959)*. Warsaw.

K.K. Ery, 1969. "Investigations on the Demographic Source Value of Tombstones Originating from the Roman Period," *Alba Regia: Annales Musei Stephani Regis* 10: 51–67.

D. Ferembach and M. Lechevallier, 1973. "Découverte de crânes surmodelés dans une habitation du VII millénaire à Beisamoun, Israël," *Paléorient* 1: 223–230.

I. Finkelstein, 1989. "Further Observations on the Socio-Demographic Structure of the Intermediate Bronze Age," *Levant* 21: 129–140.

M.S. Goldstein, B. Arensburg and H. Nathan, 1981. "Skeletal Remains of Jews from the Hellenistic and Roman Periods in Israel, III. Pathology," *Bulletin et mémoires de la Société d'Anthropologie de Paris* 8: 11–24.

R. Gonen, 1984. "Urban Canaan in the Late Bronze Age," *BASOR* 253: 61–73.

R. Gophna, 1984. "The Settlement Landscape of Palestine in the Early Bronze II-III and Middle Bronze Age II," *IEJ* 34: 24–31.

N. Howell, 1976. "Toward a Uniformitarian Theory of Human Paleodemography," in R.H. Ward and K.M. Weiss (eds.), *The Demographic Evolution of Human Population*, pp. 23–39. New York.

———, 1982. "Village Composition Implied by a Paleodemographical Life Table: The Libben Site," *American Journal of Physical Anthropology* 59: 263–270.

J.-P. Lacombe, 1980. "Les ossements humains de Ben-Shemen," in J. Perrot and D. Ladiray (eds.), *Tombes et ossuaires de la région côtière palestinienne au IVe millénaire avant l'ère chrétienne. Mémoires et Travaux du CNRS de Jérusalem* No. I.

T.E. Levy and D. Alon, 1982. "The Chalcolithic Mortuary Site near Mezed Aluf, Northern Negev Desert. A Preliminary Study," *BASOR* 248: 37–9.

T.D. McCown and A. Keith, 1939. *The Stone Age of Mount Carmel* II. Oxford.

J. Nemeskeri, 1989. "An Attempt to Reconstitute Demographically the Upper Paleolithic Populations of Europe and the Mediterranean Region," in I. Hershkovitz (ed.), *People and Culture in Change*. BAR International Series 508 (ii), pp. 335–365. Oxford.

D. Ortner, 1979. "Disease and Mortality in the Early Bronze Age People of Bâb edh-Dhrâ," *American Journal of Physical Anthropology* 51: 589–598.

———, 1982. "The Skeletal Biology of an Early Bronze IB Charnel House at Bâb edh-Dhrâ, Jordan," in A. Hadidi (ed.), *Studies in the History and Archaeology of Jordan* I. Amman.

J. Portugali, 1988. "Notes on Socio-Spatial Change in the Region of Israel: Chalcolithic to Iron Age," *Orient* 24: 55–70.

Y. Shiloh, 1980. "The Population of Iron Age Palestine in the Light of a Sample Analysis of Urban Plans, Areas and Population Density," *BASOR* 239: 25–35.

P. Smith, 1982. "The Physical Characteristics and Biological Affinities of the MBI Skeletal Remains from Jebel Qaʿaqir,"*BASOR* 245: 65–73.

—————, 1989. The Skeletal Biology and Paleopathology of Early Bronze Age Populations in Israel," in P. de Miroschedji (ed.), *L'urbanisation de la Palestine a l'âge du bronze ancien: bilan et perspectives des recherches actuelles. BAR International Series* 527 (11), pp. 297–313. Oxford.

P. Smith, E. Bournemann and J. Zias, 1981. "The Skeletal Remains," in E. Meyers et al. (eds.), *Excavations at Ancient Meiron*, pp. 110–118. Chapel Hill.

P. Smith, O. Bar-Yosef and A. Sillen, 1984. "The Archaeology and Skeletal Evidence for Dietary Change during the Late Pleistocene/Early Holocene in the Levant," in M. Cohen and G. Armelagos (eds.), *Paleopathology at the Origins of Agriculture*, pp. 101–136. New York.

P. Smith, L.K. Horwitz and J. Zias, 1990, "Human Remains from the Iron Age Cemeteries at Akhziv, Part 1: The Built Tomb from the Southern Cemetery," *Rivista di Studi Fenici*, 18: 137–150.

P. Smith and B. Peretz, 1986. "Hypoplasia and Health Status: A Comparison of Two Lifestyles," *Human Evolution* 1: 535–544.

E. Strouhal, 1973. "Five Plastered Skulls from Pre-Pottery Neolithic B Jericho. Anthropological Study," *Paléorient* 1: 231–247.

H. Valladas et al., 1988. "Thermoluminescence Dating of Mousterian Proto-Cromagnon Remains from Israel and the Origin of Modern Man," *Nature* 331: 614–616.

B. Vandermeersch, 1981. *Les hommes fossiles de Qafzeh (Israël). Cahiers de paléontologie (paléoanthropologie) du CNRS*. Paris.

T. Waldron, 1987. "The Relative Survival of the Human Skeleton: Implications for Paleopathology," in A. Boddington, A.N. Garland, and R.C. Janaway (eds.), *Death, Decay and Reconstruction*, pp. 55–64. Manchester.

World Health Organization, 1976. *WHO Health Statistics Annual*. I. Geneva.

The Population of Iron Age Palestine

Magen Broshi*

The beginning of the Iron Age was one of the lowest ebbs in Palestinian demography. During the Late Bronze Age, the population of the country dwindled drastically. Rapacious Egyptian rule, the incessant revolts and the recurrent military campaigns conducted within and passing through the country, must have decimated its population. In our estimate, in 1600 B.C.E. the country's population numbered some 140,000.[1] By 1200 B.C.E. the population had diminished to 60,000–70,000.[2]

The decline was mostly in the mountainous regions. In Mount Ephraim there were 81 settlements in the Middle Bronze Age, but only five in the Late Bronze. Drastic decline, though to a lesser degree than in Mount Ephraim, was also noted in the surveys conducted in the Central Hill Country — Manasseh, Judah and Benjamin. There were, on average, in this area 1/10 the former number of settlements (20 out of 220) and 1/5 the former total settled area was inhabited.[3] The demographic growth of the Iron Age was especially marked in these mountainous regions.

The disappearance of the superpowers from the Palestinian scene in the four centuries preceding 734 B.C.E. — the year in which the Assyrian invasions began to cause drastic changes — gave the country the opportunity for intensive growth. This was an extended period of relative peace. Indeed, there were wars: Philistine-Israelite, Israelite-Judahite and Aramean-Israelite, but the hostilities apparently did not prevent intensive demographic growth.

Between David and Hezekiah

We cannot yet draw a map of Western Palestine at the end of the Iron I (ca. 1000 B.C.E.), but we have quite an accurate picture of the Central Hill Country (Judea

---

* This paper is largely based upon one written jointly with I. Finkelstein entitled "The Population of Palestine in 734 B.C.E." (forthcoming).

14

and Samaria). The population of this area numbered approximately 54,000 in 1000 B.C.E. and grew to ca. 165,000 by the mid–8th century. If the population of the other regions grew at the same rate (there is no reason why it should not have), the population of all western Palestine in the year 1000 B.C.E. must have been ca. 150,000.

Such an increase in 250 years would mean an annual growth rate of ca. .4 percent. To us, living in a world with an annual growth rate of 2 percent, such a figure might seem insignificant. However, had this growth rate continued uninterrupted to our own times, the population of the Central Hill Country would have reached the astro-nomical figure of 8.6 billion.[4]

The figure we propose for the year 1000 B.C.E. is similar to the estimates for 2600 B.C.E. and 1600 B.C.E. — two peaks in the demographic history of the country.[5] It seems that during the Bronze Age and Early Iron Age, the sedentary population could not cross the 150,000 threshold. Natural (famine, plague) as well as human (war, misrule) causes created insurmountable barriers to population growth.

The Population of Western Palestine

In 734 B.C.E. there were 1,088 settlements in the country. We reckon that the built up area reached 16,120 hectares. Based upon our calculations, this would mean a pop-ulation of some 400,000. (The precise figure arrived at by multiplying the built up area by a density coefficient of 250 per hectare is 403,000. I prefer to use round num-bers to avoid the deceptive impression of precision).

Size of the Three Political Units

The figure of 400,000 applies to western Palestine, (Palestine of the British Mandate, i.e., Israel and the Occupied Territories), a land area of 26,000 sq. km., 14,000 of which lie north of the Negev and are the subject of our investigation. We can also venture an estimate of the populations of the three political units of this period: Judah, Israel and Philistia.[6] The Kingdom of Judah had an area of ca. 5,000 sq. km. and a population of ca. 110,000. This means a density of 22 per sq. km. The Kingdom of Israel, west of the Jordan, was 7,300 sq. km. With a population of ca. 222,000, its population density would have been 31 per sq. km., greater by half than that of Judah. To this should be added the area of the Gilead, east of the Jordan, 4,200 sq. km.[7] If the population density in the Gilead equaled that of Cisjordanian Israel (quite a plausible surmise — the extensive frontier zones being compensated by the densely populated and lush Jordan Valley), then the kingdom's population would have reached about 350,000. The combined population of the Philistine city-states was ca. 50,000.

Highlands vs. Plains

An interesting phenomenon is the rise in the demographic weight of the hill country vs. the plains. The hill country gradually rose from 35 percent of the total population in the Early Bronze II–III to 40 percent in the Middle Bronze II to 52.5 percent in

Iron II. The rise in the Iron Age was mostly due to the large-scale reclamation of virgin soils, mostly through terrace construction. These modest looking constructions are the *sine qua non* of the intensive demographic growth. As a feat of engineering, they may be likened to the pyramids. Unlike the pyramids, however, these terraces improved the population's standard of living.

The Proportion of Larger Settlements

In the period under discussion there was a decrease in the number of larger settlements. While in the Bronze Age II–III, 63 percent of the population lived in settlements larger than 5 hectares, only 49 percent dwelt in such towns during the Middle Bronze Age II. In the Iron Age II the figure drops to 34 percent. The circumstances of the Iron Age II made possible the existence of a large number of small unwalled settlements, reflecting a feeling of security and stability. The rate of urbanization in both kingdoms was similar — 32 percent in Cisjordanian Israel, 29 percent in Judah.

The Watershed Line — 734 B.C.E.

In the coming third of a century, the country would undergo drastic changes as a result of the onset of the Assyrian invasions. In the year 734 B.C.E., Tiglath-Pileser III conducted his first campaign to Palestine. From that date on, until the end of the 8th century, and perhaps even later, the country suffered from a succession of Assyrian military campaigns that brought about death, destruction, poverty and large-scale deportations — from the country and into it. Samaria was destroyed a dozen years after Tiglath-Pileser's first campaign and the Kingdom of Israel came to an end. Some 20 years later, Judah, under Hezekiah, rebelled against Assyria. Sennacherib's subsequent invasion dealt a terrible blow to the kingdom. Those military campaigns were conducted with typical Assyrian cruelty and exacted a great number of victims, usually ending with mass deportations. The ravages of war, deportation and harsh Assyrian rule resulted in a century of marked decline in the former Kingdom of Israel. Signs of destruction and desertion are discernible at almost every site excavated. Some were deserted following their conquest (e.g. Beth-Shean, ʿEn Gev, Khirbet Marjameh); other sites bear clear signs of decline (Hazor, Shechem, Dothan, Tell el-Farʿah). Even Assyrian administrative centers show evidence of decline (Dor, Gezer).

Judah after Sennacherib's campaign fared even worse. The Assyrian policy in this case was to weaken the buffer state lying between the Assyrian Empire and Egypt. Ruin caused by this war was encountered at Beth-Shemesh, Tell Beit Mirsim, Beersheba, Tel ʿEton and Tel Batash. The most eloquent evidence of Sennacherib's bloody trail was found at Lachish. Jerusalem was saved, but its extramural suburbs were destroyed, many never to be reconstructed. In sharp contradistinction to the havoc wrought in Judah stands Tel Miqneh, the Philistine Eqron. This site grew from 4 hectares in the 8th century into a city of 24–32 hectares in the 7th century.[8] The Assyrian records' figure of about 200,150 Judean deportees is undoubtedly exaggerated (about twice our estimate of the total population of Judah), but the number must have, nonetheless, been very great.

Two Waves of Immigration into Judah

Around 700 B.C.E. Jerusalem mushroomed to more than twice its former size. During the 7th century B.C.E., great numbers of new settlements were founded in Judah. These phenomena can be best explained by presuming two large-scale waves of immigration into Judah: one after the fall of Samaria in 721 B.C.E. and the other after Sennacherib's campaign of 701 B.C.E. The first must have consisted of refugees from the former Kingdom of Israel who preferred living with their brethren in Judah to the harsh Assyrian yoke. The second wave must have included displaced Judeans, leaving the western provinces of Judah that were given by Sennacherib to the Philistine city-states as a punishment to Judah, the rebellion ring leader, and a reward to his loyal Philistine allies. The immigrants from the north and west probably made up for the demographic ravages caused by Sennacherib — but to what extent we cannot yet say for certain.[9]

Ethnic Vicissitudes during the Iron Age

Iron Age Palestine underwent unprecedented changes in its ethnic composition. Lack of space prevents us from doing full justice to the subject, but we would like to point out some of its main features. The period began with the appearance on the local scene of two peoples for which the country would be eventually named: the Israelites and the Philistines. Some five centuries later, the country would receive large contingents of deportees — from the Iranian plateau, Babylonian holy cities and the periphery of Babylonia, northern Arabia, and elsewhere. Great numbers of people from the kingdoms of Israel and Judah were likewise transferred to various provinces of the Assyrian Empire.[10] These deportations continued into the days of Ashurbanipal, about a century after Tiglath-Pileser III. The Bible (Ezra 4) tells us about people exiled to Palestine, but it is quite plausible that, here too, the Assyrians exercised the two-way exile policy, and people were also taken abroad. No less important a phenomenon — and to my mind much more interesting — is the fusion of the motley mosaic of peoples that would ultimately come to constitute the very distinctive entity of Israel. Here, archaeology can contribute very little, and the Bible, virtually our sole source, is not informative. We do, however, possess tantalizing, though insufficient, data enabling us to follow the process of nation-building from many diverse ethnic elements (Canaanites, Edomites, Hurrians, Hittites, and others).[11]

Summary

Due to the wealth of material obtained in recent years, partly in excavations but primarily in surveys, I. Finkelstein and I are able to offer estimates of Iron Age population in Palestine. We believe that in the year 1000 B.C.E. the country numbered ca. 150,000 people, and in 734 B.C.E. 400,000. The population of the Kingdom of Israel (on both sides of the Jordan) reached 350,000, while that of Judah was 110,000 and Philistia only 50,000. These figures highlight processes and require the explanation of various historical and archaeological phenomena. Quantification is not merely a goal in itself: it also helps bring the larger historical picture into high relief.

Notes

1. M. Broshi and R. Gophna, "Middle Bronze Age II Palestine: Its Settlements and Population," *BASOR* 261 (1986): 73–90.
2. Our computation is based on data provided by R. Gonen, "Urban Canaan in the Late Bronze Age," *BASOR* 253 (1984): 61–73.
3. I. Finkelstein, "The Iron Age I in the Land of Ephraim," in N. Na²aman and I. Finkelstein (eds.), *From Nomadism to Monarchy: Archaeological and Historical Aspects of Early Israel* (Jerusalem, 1990), p. 117; S. Bunimovitz, "Cultural Processes and Socio-Political Change in the Central Hill Country in the Late Bronze Age-Iron I Transition," idem, p. 273.
4. Thanks are due to M. Sikron, who assisted us with these calculations.
5. M. Broshi and R. Gophna, "The Settlements and Population of Palestine During the Early Bronze II–III," *BASOR* 253 (1984): 41–53; idem, (see note 1).
6. Philistia was not a united entity, but it was a distinct ethnic, cultural and political unit.
7. Calculated from Y. Aharoni and M. Avi-Yonah, *The Macmillan Bible Atlas* (New York and London, 1968), Map 147.
8. S. Gitin, personal communication; Cf. also S. Gitin and T. Dothan, "The Rise and Fall of Ekron of the Philistines," *BA* 50(1987): 197–222, esp. 212–214.
9. M. Broshi, "The Expansion of Jerusalem in the Reigns of Hezekiah and Manasseh," *IEJ* 24 (1974): 21–26.
10. Cf. N. Na²aman, "Population Changes in Palestine Following Assyrian Deportations," *Cathedra* 54 (1989): 43–62.
11. Much has been written on that subject, however a synthetic monograph is still lacking.

Village and Town Populations in Palestine during the 1930s–1940s and their Relevance to Ethnoarchaeology

Gideon Biger and David Grossman

The findings of archaeological excavations in Israel produce many interesting, but isolated, remnants of rural and urban dwellings. When attempting to estimate ancient population levels, the interpretation of the scattered data is difficult, not only because of the nature of the findings, but also because of numerous methodological problems. The great interest in estimating the population density of single dwellings is understandable. In the absence of reliable census data and given the scarcity of written records, this may be one of the few ways of calculating, though in a crude fashion, the number of people in a given area. Furthermore, even where other sources of information are available, a population density model which is free of intended or unintended bias can provide a relatively objective means for estimating regional population levels.

The effort to use such a model for demographic estimates applicable to conditions of the biblical Land of Israel has led many archaeologists to offer population density coefficients for small units of built-up areas. Such coefficients can then be used for aggregated data to provide regional figures. As will be shown below, the coefficients offered for this purpose have varied widely, and a number of methodological problems have led to difficulties in interpretation.

Because of these difficulties, it was thought that some recent settlements, whose underlying conditions are better known and understood than those of antiquity, might furnish a model for the ancient ones. This is the purpose of the present article. It attempts to supply population density coefficients for rural and urban settlements on the basis of data from Palestine of the first half of the 20th century. The procedure for calculating the coefficient is, however, not without difficulties. An obvious problem is that each society has its own dwelling preferences.[1] A single coefficient may never be satisfactory, even for contemporaneous communities. There are many other problems which will be discussed in some detail following a short review of pertinent literature.

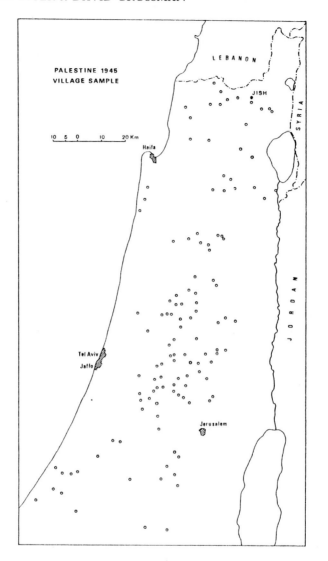

Review of the Relevant Archaeological Findings

Several attempts have been made to calculate a population density coefficient. The results range, in fact, from a high of 460 to a low of eight. Avi-Yonah[2] has suggested a factor of 100, while archaeologists reporting on excavations at Ebla in Syria have raised the figure to 464.[3] An early researcher, J. Garstang[4], suggested a factor of 62.5 per dunam, while, somewhat later, H. Frankfort[5] suggested a density of 30–50 per dunam for Mesopotamian cities. Speaking of the population of Jericho, Kenyon[6] suggested a factor of 49 for the PPNA and 74 for the PPNB. Van Beek[7] calculated the density for ʿAin Ghazal in Jordan at 28–30 per dunam utilizing information from modern tell sites in Yemen (1912). Finkelstein used a factor of 25 when he discussed the population of Iron I,[8] the same factor used by Gophna and Broshi[9] for the Early Bronze Age. Y. Shiloh[10] used the factor of 40–50 for Iron Age settlements.

All of these studies have assumed that there is a fixed and stable coefficient. They did not postulate any modifications over time, or any changes in the coefficient because of variations in the sizes of the built-up area of settlement. A few researchers have noted, however, the methodological problems stemming from dynamic processes in population growth and changes in settlement size.

In an attempt to deal, at least in part, with this problem, Gophna and Portugali[11] have suggested that the coefficient should vary according to the size of settlements and that it should be adjusted to the conditions of specific periods. They assumed that the bigger sites were urban in character, and that the coefficients changed over time. The coefficient was expected, thus, to be progressively lower as the size of the built-up area increased. On this basis they presented coefficients which ranged between 10 and 15 persons per dunam for the largest sites. The urban density for the EB II was calculated by them, using a different set of factors which yielded a coefficient ranging from 15 to 25. The lower figure, 15, was assumed to be associated with non-urban settlements. For the MB they assumed an identical coefficient.

We thus have a wide range of coefficients — ranging from a low of eight to a high of 460. All of them refer to fairly static conditions lasting over many centuries. In our effort to use modern densities in order to draw conclusions concerning archaeological findings, we have adopted the hypothesis that the size of the coefficient should vary according to settlement size. We take into account, however, the possible impact of short-term oscillations, even though we, too, had to use "static" data.

Methods and Methodological Problems

In order to accomplish the task of providing empirically-based coefficients which have a fairly reliable quantitative basis, this paper attempts to measure and calculate the mean density of population in Palestinian villages during the period of the British Mandate. More specifically, the material refers to traditional, non-Jewish, rural and urban settlements as they existed in Palestine in the 1930s and 1940s. However, in order to achieve a broader perspective, and to understand the dynamic processes which account for the observed densities of the study period, data from the late 19th and late 20th centuries were also analyzed.

The data presented here are based on a sample of 130 traditional villages (about 15 percent of Palestine's non-Jewish villages) for which there is reasonable cause to assume continuous occupation from the 16th century. This assumption is based upon a careful comparison of the 19th and early 20th century data with late 16th century Ottoman tax lists.[12] The distribution indicated by the latter was checked and partly amended, using aerial photographs as well as extensive fieldwork. As a result, a "settlement stability map" was produced (Fig. 1). Villages reported in the 16th century and in the Palestine Exploration Fund lists[13] of the late 19th century were considered reasonably stable, and regarded as prime candidates for inclusion in the present analysis.

Additional criteria were applied in selecting the villages. We attempted, insofar as possible, to exclude extreme cases, i.e., villages either too large or too small in size. This was done using the *modal* section of each sub-district as candidates for inclusion, as identified in previous studies.[14]

Another criterion for selecting villages was their relative distance from urban centers and from main roads. It was assumed that the centers affected the rural rates of growth, and as a result, villages close to them would be strongly affected by modernization. This effect can severely distort the results of this study, whose purpose is to focus on traditional densities which, as closely as possible, approximate those of ancient times.

Despite the careful selection process, the major problem remained obtaining data which would reflect ancient conditions. The earliest modern census, conducted by the British in 1922, contains only crude demographic data not considered to be of high quality. The present study utilizes the results of the second Mandatory census, that of 1931.[15]

The basic assumption is, clearly, that the contemporary Arab village was similar to the ancient village of the Land of Israel. Thus, it is assumed that a typical house had only a single story which was divided, as traditional Palestinian Arab dwellings were, into two levels. The ground level was used for keeping animals while the upper level was used for habitation and for indoor activities. Two story buildings probably existed, but they served mainly as the fortresses of ruling families and the handful of rich inhabitants. Higher buildings were probably extremely rare.

The assumption that the traditional Palestinian village is similar to the ancient one is quite common in the literature.[16] However, one cannot totally exclude the possibility that ancient housing was quite different from that of our times. Multi-storied buildings are not totally absent in the rural areas of the Middle East. Their presence in the traditional culture of the Arabian Peninsula, for example, is well documented.

The evolution of the Arab village and the factors resulting in its nucleated character are widely discussed in the literature.[17] Although the exact process of village formation is not known, it is widely accepted that villages initially grew inward, through infilling of enclosed family compounds and yards. This process resulted in the creation of winding, generally narrow, alleys in the inter-compound spaces. But short-term demographic oscillations associated with growth or decline also account for some periodic changes in density. Thus in the 19th century many villages were described as either half-ruined or, occasionally, even totally deserted. In such villages the density must have been low.

It was only toward the last decades of the 19th century that oscillations were replaced by absolute growth. The result was higher densities, but by the 1930s there was already clear centrifugal growth which reduced the density, as the standard of living started to rise and as sanitation and health conditions improved.

To the dynamic forms of village expansion and contraction one must also add the foundation or fixation of *ʿizab* (temporary or seasonal offshoots). The fixation process occurred mainly after 1870, and its impact is neutralized here by avoiding the inclusion of the smallest villages. However, in the Hebron region, and to a somewhat lesser extent, in northern and northwestern Samaria, most of the existing villages belong to the recently-fixed group. Furthermore, the official population of the villages in the Mandate period included the villagers living in the offshoots located outside the confines of the built-up area, even though they did not live within the parent village. Because of this, the density of most of the settlements of the Hebron zone is artificially inflated. This also holds true for many of the large settlements elsewhere (e.g., Yʿabad, Umm al-Faḥm, Tubas, Deir al-Ghussun). The problems created by this exaggeration were removed, to some extent, by avoiding the inclusion of the "head" of the Sub-District village list.

After taking into account these methodological problems, we decided that the only reasonable solution was to rely mainly on data pertaining to the 1930s and the 1940s. Fortunately, this period is fairly satisfactorily covered. The 1931 census[18] is the best demographic source for the pre−1948 period. In addition to a breakdown by sex and religion, the number of settled houses in every village was also counted. A cadastral survey which gave information concerning the size of the built-up area of each village was prepared for the census, but it was not published. In 1938 the first of the "village statistics"[19] was published. It provided population estimates and data on village land use. The latter included the extent of built-up areas. Another set[20] was published in 1945. By then, aerial photographs of the entire country became available for the first time, and these figures were based on east-west flights carried out between December 1944 and January 1945. Shortly afterwards, a series of detailed village maps on scales of 1:1,250 and 1:2,500 were published. We thus have fairly adequate data which can

Table 1: Palestine villages 1938 — Area
(based on sample of 131 villages).

built-up area (dunams)	no. of villages	average density	range of density
up to 10	9	50	30–100
10–20	17	34	22–48
20–30	26	24	8–56
30–40	16	20	8–36
40–50	13	16	10–22
50–60	13	21	6–36
60–70	9	10	6–14
70–80	11	17	6–30
80–100	4	14	6–26
100–150	5	10	6–20
over 150	8	10	6–14

help us to calculate the ratio between settlement size and population. Utilizing all the available sources, the data spans about 15 years, a relatively long period in view of the rapid rate of Arab population growth (estimated at about 2 percent per annum).

Findings and Discussion

On the basis of the data published in the Village Statistics, the overall density of Palestine's rural population in 1938 was about 19 persons per dunam of built-up area. Druze and Christian villages had a lower population density. At that time, the overall Jewish rural population density was five persons per dunam, while the German villages of Palestine had a density of only three. The mean population density of the Arab urban sector was, at that time, rather smaller than that of the Arab rural sector. Nablus had a population density of 4.2 per dunam, while in Hebron it was 8.8. Excluding the open spaces within these towns, the figures are 9 and 14 respectively.

The overall 1938 density coefficient of 19 rose to 22 in seven years when the British published the 1954 Village Statistics. This change may be attributed to a more careful calculation of the built-up areas of the villages rather than to any actual change. Following that, however, the trend reversed. Since the mid–1940s, the population density of the built-up area of the average Arab village fell from 22 persons per dunam to only 4–9 persons in late 1974. Over the last few years, however, another reversal in the overall density has been reported. It appears to have risen to a level of 9–13 per dunam of built-up area. This may be an indication of a renewed centripetal process following a long centrifugal one.[21]

The data presented here (Table 1), based on a sample of 130 villages, reveal that rural population density was partly a function of geographical location and partly a function of the extent of built-up areas.

As expected, the size of the rural built-up area seems to correlate negatively with

Table 2: Palestine villages 1938—Population
(based on sample of 131 villages)

no. of people	no. of villages	built-up mean area	average density
up to 300	7	25.6	18.4
300–400	14	19.8	22.7
400–500	11	33.2	24.7
500–600	18	33.2	21.7
600–700	10	36.8	17.8
700–800	13	46.5	26.8
800–900	14	49.8	23.0
900–1000	9	87.2	18.3
1000–1250	10	60.7	21.4
1250–1500	10	56.4	27.4
1500–2000	6	137.0	25.0
above 2000	9	104.0	23.9

population density. Small villages with a built-up area of up to 20 dunams had a mean population density of about 42 persons per dunam; those with an area of 20–50 dunams — 23 persons per dunam; up to 100 dunams — 17 persons per dunam, and areas larger than 100 dunams — 10 persons per dunam.

On the other hand, there was no discernable correlation between population density and the absolute size of village population. In villages with populations between 300 and 1,250, the density remained approximately the same — in the 18–24 persons per dunam range.

Topography and physical relief, however, did have a clear impact on density levels (Table 3). A careful examination of the table reveals that in the mountain areas of Palestine — Judea, Samaria and the Upper Galilee — population density was 12–20 persons per dunam, while the Coastal Plain and Northwestern Samaria had a population density of 20–30 per dunam. Population density was thus inversely related to elevation.

In order to appreciate the significance of these findings and evaluate them, it was decided to repeat the calculations on one-third of the sample on the basis of village maps and aerial photographs, rather than relying solely on the official statistics. The findings of this independent exercise substantially deviated from those based on the official figures. In most of the villages, the calculated area was found to be smaller than that based on the official data, while for several villages, the opposite was true. The under-estimated size might explain some of the extreme densities (over 100 persons per dunam) in the official data.

If these figures are accepted, then it can be concluded that the density per dunam for Palestine as a whole was 25 persons. The regional differences stand out clearly. In the mountain areas the density was 16–26 while in the Coastal Plain it was as high as 26–40. The effect of the size of the built-up area on density was clearly greater in comparison with the officially-based analysis. However, its correlation with density was consistently inverse. The villages with the smallest area had a population density of 55 per dunam while those whose area was largest had 13 per dunam. The median ranges (the 50–100 dunam levels) had, correspondingly, median densities of about 23 per dunam.

As already stated, these densities do not necessarily reflect stable long-term conditions. The 1930s were characterized by dynamic conditions which generated residential and demographic changes at a scale which probably surpassed those of any previous period.

In addition to the estimation of the mean density for the entire settlement, we also estimated the density per dwelling unit. Y. Shiloh,[22] who used this procedure for his study of findings from biblical times, arrived at a figure of 5.4 dwelling units per dunam. Our estimate for the 1930s, based on the 1931 census, was 4.4. However, according to maps from the late 1940s, there were 3.2 dwelling units per dunam. According to Shiloh, each dwelling housed a family of five, and the calculated density per dunam was 27. There is, thus, no agreement over the most desirable coefficient. The coefficient of five, which seems to be in widespread use, is also controversial.

Table 3: Palestine villages — Geographical density

Area	mean density
Mountains	
Upper Galilee	12.1
Lower Galilee	18.9
Samaria	11.8
Judea	14.5
Plain	
Northern Valley	20.4
Northern Coastal Plain	20.8
Central Coastal Plain	21.6
Shephelah	28.1
Southern Coastal Plain	27.5

Studies based on 19th century data used widely varying coefficients. Ben-Arieh[23] suggested a value as high as seven, while others[24] utilized values as low as four. The higher factor, seven, is preferred by Ben-Arieh, because the Ottoman population data of the circa–1870 "census" suggests that the mean person:house ratio was approximately 3.5. Since the persons counted were males (of all ages) only, the actual ratio must be doubled. Seven would, therefore, appear to be the most adequate estimate.

A detailed but limited survey of five villages in the Ramle Sub-District, conducted in 1944, registered an average of 6.1 per house (i.e., 2.1 rooms per house and 2.9 persons per room). More than three decades later, in 1978/9, according to a survey conducted in western Samaria[25] the density per room was slightly higher: 6.7 per house (2.6 rooms and 2.6 persons per room). The latter is closer to that suggested by Ben-Arieh. It must be borne in mind, however, that, by the 1970s, the economic livelihood was no longer "traditional." Most of the surveyed population derived its livelihood from non-farm sources. A likely explanation for the density variations is that two opposing trends, demographic growth and rising living standards, tended to cancel each other. Net growth during the 1870s was relatively low, but there were more persons per household, including older persons who did not belong to the nuclear family. By the 1970s, the nuclear family was larger, but households consisted primarily of nuclear families.

Interpretation of rural population density data is equally difficult. A likely interpretation must take normal settlement processes into account. The fact that villages which have small built-up areas tend to be very densely populated may be the result of an initial centripetal in-filling process. In such cases, space is intensively utilized, and if no room is left for non-residential facilities (schools, prayer houses, shops and workshops), density is maximized. Where the internal saturation point is reached, outward expansion begins to occur. Some of the old internal dwellings are abandoned, thereby reducing density. In such villages, the only way to verify actual occupancy is house-to-house survey, which could not be conducted in our study areas.

Our study delimited the original, preexpansion, nucleus of each village, and attempted to calculate its population density, but the resulting approximation cannot fully resolve the methodological problems. The discovery that there was a vast range of village densities in each region and in each size-category came as no surprise. This varied range raises serious doubts concerning the validity of the findings: the means may be invalid. Thus, in the Gaza Sub-District, the population density of 46 villages ranged from 5.7 to 94.4 (one village even had an exceptional density of 123.7). Only four villages had values close to the mean (31–33) for this sub-district. In the Hebron Sub-District, too, only four villages (out of 27) had population densities within the mean density range. The average for this sub-district was 21.1, while actual densities ranged from a low as 8.4 to a high of 51.

In the Lower Galilee (Nazareth Sub-District) a mean population density of 31.1 persons per dunam was calculated for 22 villages, only one of which had a density between 30–35, while the actual range was from 7.1 to 55.9. Thus, even one carefully calculated coefficient can bring about an overall picture which, though arithmetically correct, may well be meaningless.

In view of the complexities associated with the rural sector, it is obvious that any comparison of modern urban populations with ancient ones is practically impossible. Rural people predominate in premodern societies, accounting for more than 80 percent of total population, while in modern societies, rural population may constitute less than 10 percent of total population. Even more significant are intra-urban demographic patterns. While in the 1940s parts of Palestine's urban population still inhabited Medieval structures, urban dwellers were already living well within the modern

Table 4: Palestine — Arab settlements 1945
Urban — Rural ratios of built area and population

Sub-district	Total built area	Urban built area	Rural built area	U/R total	Pop.	Urban (U)pop.	Rural (R)pop.	U/R
A) Urban districts
Jerusalem	19100	15990	3110	84/16	147750	68900	78850	47/53
Haifa	15246	12911	2335	85/15	120120	62800	57320	52/48
Jaffa	15177	11697	3480	77/23	134290	55380	78910	41/59
Gaza	16724	13720	3004	82/18	97700	66310	31390	68/32
Total A:	66247	54318	11929	82/18	499860	253390	246470	52/48
B) Rural districts
Safed	3628	1276	2352	35/65	46920	9530	37390	20/80
Acre	5122	1538	3584	30/70	65380	12360	53020	19/81
Nazareth	6270	4988	1282	80/20	39500	14200	24300	37/63
Beisan-Tiberias	3029	1415	1614	46/54	42690	10490	32200	25/75
Jenin	2797	1105	1692	40/60	56880	3990	52890	7/93
Nablus	9783	5571	4212	57/43	89200	23500	65700	27/73
Tulkarm	3965	1672	2293	42/58	71240	8090	63150	12/88
Ramle	7641	5627	2014	74/26	97850	31940	65910	33/67
Ramallah	5435	2812	2614	52/48	47280	7000	41280	13/87
Hebron	5996	2791	3205	47/53	89570	24560	65010	28/72
Total B:	53657	28795	24862	55/46	646510	145660	500850	22/78
Total Palestine:	119904	83113	36791	70/30	1146370	399050	747320	35/65

economy, even where population density was extremely high. Urban slums, squatter settlements and other elements of urban pathology are still widely present in developing countries, but poverty is not a meaningful common denominator between complex modern and ancient societies.

In any comparisons of modern and ancient data, one must consider the impact of the ratio of the size of the urban population to the rural one. It was about 1 to 8 in preindustrial and agricultural societies such as those of the late 19th century. In present-day urban societies, while the ratio varies widely, it is not greater than 1 to 3, even in developing countries.

In 1945 the ratio for the overall population of Palestine was about 1 to 2, but as Table 4 shows, in the urbanized districts it already approached 1 to 1. However, the ratios of the built-up areas were reversed: 4 to 1 in the most urban districts and 1 to 1 in the rural ones.

These findings illustrate the problems facing researchers who do not take sufficiently into account socioeconomic processes. Such processes are most clearly evident in the rural-urban dichotomy, but they also exist in the inter-urban and intra-urban systems. Clearly, then, the complexity of the various human systems, and their dynamic nature, must be taken into consideration.

To illustrate this point, let us assume that the present-day Old City of Jerusalem was abandoned, covered with mud, and later excavated by archaeologists, who found the remains of the Turkish city-wall. We know that during the last 450 years, i.e., since the wall was erected, the number of people living in the Old City has ranged between 8,000 and 40,000. What population density figure would accurately represent this reality? Eighty, or 40, or a mean of 25 would not say anything relevant about the actual population of Jerusalem through this entire period.[26]

Conclusions and Implications

In attempting to make some sense of the findings presented above, we tend to prefer using the mean density level for Palestine, i.e., 25–26 persons per dunam, as the most meaningful for the purpose of the desired comparison with ancient data. This density probably reflects "mature" conditions. Despite the problems outlined here, we think that this density can approximate the desired density coefficient. It applies, however, only to the traditional rural sector, and must be taken to be a very crude approximation of the desired coefficient.

Given seven persons per household, a density of 25 per dunam would be equivalent to about 3.5 households. This is not unreasonable for highly nucleated villages. Clearly, a village of such density may be fairly large. Ten dunams (1 hectare) accommodates 35 households with a total population of 250 persons, but an increasing population may eventually force some reduction of density, not necessarily because of intolerable crowding, but because of growing pressure on available farmland. The inevitable migration of the village overflow or the establishment of new offshoots, if some remote land reserves are still available, can reduce local population density, and create new hamlets where crowding is not lower than in the parent settlement. If the new land is of a lower carrying capacity, which is reasonable to assume, then the size of the hamlet may never reach that of its parent, but this does not necessarily affect its internal density.

For similar reasons, the coefficient of 25–26 cannot be applied to cases such as those associated with the fixation of nomadic settlements. Aside from possible cultural factors, such settlements are clearly affected by the limitations of their resources. Pastoralist encampments must be spread out over large areas in order to provide a minimum amount of grazing area, but even the agriculturally-based settlements which replace the former Bedouin camps or the fixed ʿizab of their fellaḥin neighbors, are adversely affected by meager resources. The new hamlets must, therefore, be widely spaced and of low density. The resulting population density is, consequently, also low. The pattern of settlement which these fixed settlements form tends to resemble loose bunches, such as those which can be seen in the Judean Desert and southern Hebron Hills.[27] It is not surprising, therefore, that such settlements had a density of 2–4 inhabitants per dunam.

Catastrophes, either natural or human-generated, can modify original densities by triggering long distance migration and raising mortality rates. Density is consequently reduced. If, however, we are looking for a "normal" village, then the higher density is a better choice than the lower one. Our conclusion is, therefore, that villages having fairly high population densities represent conditions of "maturity" which are associated with relatively high stability. Such villages are better candidates than others for offering models for cross-cultural and historical comparisons.

Notes

1. R. Gophna and J. Portugali, "Settlement and Demographic Processes in Israel's Coastal Plain from the Chalcolithic to the Middle Bronze Age," *BASOR* 269 (1988): 11–28.
2. M. Avi-Yonah, "Population in Ancient Israel," *Research in Geography of Palestine* (1964), pp. 145–146 (Hebrew).
3. G. Pettinato, *Biblical Archeologist* 39 (1976): 44–47.
4. J. Garstang, *Joshua–Judges* (London, 1931).
5. H. Frankfort, "Town Planning in Ancient Mesopotamia," *Town Planning Review* 21 (1950): 98–115.
6. K.M. Kenyon, *Archaeology in the Holy Land* (4th ed.) (London, 1979).
7. G. Van Beek, "A Population Estimate for Marib; A Contemporary Tell Village in South Yemen," *BASOR* 248 (1982): 61–67.
8. I. Finkelstein, "The Iron I in the Land of Ephraim — A Second Thought," in I. Finkelstein and N. Naʾaman (eds.), *From Nomadism to Monarchy* (Jerusalem, 1990) (Hebrew).
9. M. Broshi and R. Gophna, "Settlement and Population in Palestine during the Early Bronze Age I–III," *BASOR* 253 (1984): 41–53.
10. Y. Shiloh, "The Population of Iron Age Palestine in the Light of Sample Analysis of Urban Plans, Areas and Population Density," *BASOR* 239 (1980): 25–35.
11. See Gophna and Portugali, note 1.

12. W.D. Huetteroth and K. Abdulfattah, *Historical Geography of Palestine, Transjordan and Southern Syria in the Late 16th Century* (Erlangen, 1977).

13. C.R. Conder and H.H. Kitchener, *The Survey of Western Palestine, Memoirs* (London, 1880–1883). Detailed notes on the sources and identification procedure are provided in an annotated list which accompanies a map presented in D. Grossman, "Settlement Expansion and Contraction in Samaria and Judea during the Ottoman Period," in S. Dar and Z. Safrai (eds.), *Shomron Studies* (Tel Aviv, 1986), pp. 303–388.

14. The existence and significance of the modes can be observed in the semi-logarithmic graphs which compare the population records of several mountain and plain sub-districts for the 16th century with those of the present century. The later included the censuses of 1922, 1931, the 1945 Village Statistics, and later estimates. Despite the long intervening period of more than three centuries, most of the rank-size graphs (which were obtained by arranging the villages by their population size) were parallel, indicating the existence of a stable settlement system for most areas. Predictably, only the Hebron area, which is known for its highly dynamic settlement system, had no clear mode. The parallel lines of the modal section revealed, significantly, that the modes themselves were far from uniform. Each period had a different one. Thus, in the 16th century the mode for Samaria was equivalent to a population of 80 to 400 while in 1931 it ranged from 400 to 1,200. The size of the settlements varied, thus, in time. The existence of a definite mode, and the changes which have occurred in its size, must be taken into account in analyzing the densities which we calculated for the present study. See M. Sonis and D. Grossman, "Rank-size Rule for Rural Settlements," *Socio-economic Planning Studies* 18 (1984): 373–380; D. Grossman and M. Sonis, "A Reinterpretation of the Rank-Size Rule: Examples from Western England and Southern Israel," *Geography Research Forum* 9 (1989): 67–108.

15. E. Mills, *Census of Palestine, 1931* (Alexandria, 1932). It may be reasonably assumed, however, that significant population growth occurred in the half century that preceded 1931, i.e., since about 1870. Before this data, village size fluctuated around some constant level. If adequate data, including maps, could have been obtained for, say, 1870, we would have been in a much better position.

16. Y. Hirschfeld, *Dwelling Houses in Roman and Byzantine Palestine* (Jerusalem, 1987) (Hebrew).

17. M. Brawer, "Transformation of Pattern, Dispersion, and Population Density," in D. Amiran et al. (eds.), *Eretz-Israel* 17 (A.J. Brawer Volume) (Jerusalem, 1984), pp. 8–15 (Hebrew).

18. Mills, *Census* (see note 15).

19. Government of Palestine, *Village Statistics 1938* (Jerusalem, 1939).

20. Government of Palestine, *Village Statistics 1945* (Jerusalem, 1946).

21. Brawer, "Transformation" (see note 17); See also R. Hmaisi, "Centrifugal and Centripetal Factors and their Impact on the Structure of Arab Settlements," in D. Grossman and A. Meir (eds.), *The Arab Settlement in Eretz-Israel* (in press) (Hebrew).

22. Shiloh, "Population" (see note 10).

23. Y. Ben-Arieh, "Size and Composition of the Population of Eretz-Israel — Palestine in the 1870s," (paper presented at the conference "Palestine 1840–1948, Population and Migration" held in Haifa in June, 1986).

24. N. Schur, "Historical Changes in the Coefficient of Persons per Household in Ottoman Palestine," *Israel — People and Land* 4 (1986): 251–252.

25. Brawer, "Transformation" (see note 17).

26. D. Grossman, "Settlement Patterns in Judea and Samaria," *Geojournal* 7 (1983): 299–312.

27. In view of the population's access to modern facilities, it is not surprising that 1945 urban densities were much lower than rural ones (Table 4). This finding, however, is by no means self-evident. It is quite contrary to the contemporary European pattern, where rural dwellers have larger and more spacious homes than urban ones.

SESSION II
PRODUCTION

JEAN PERROT, Session Chairman, *C.N.R.S., Centre de recherche français de Jérusalem*

THOMAS E. LEVY, *Hebrew Union College-Jewish Institute of Religion*
Production and Social Change in Protohistoric Palestine
YUVAL GOREN, *Israel Antiquities Authority*
AVI GOPHER, *Hebrew University of Jerusalem*
PAUL GOLDBERG, *Hebrew University of Jerusalem*
The Beginnings of Pottery Production in the Southern Levant:
Technological and Social Aspects
STEVEN A. ROSEN, *Ben-Gurion University of the Negev*
Metals, Rocks, Specialization, and the Beginning of Urbanism in the
Northern Negev
SARIEL SHALEV, *Tel Aviv University*
Metal Production and Society at Tel Dan
ABRAHAM MALAMAT, *Hebrew University of Jerusalem*
Mari and Hazor — Trade Relations in the Old Babylonian Period
A. BERNARD KNAPP, *Cambridge University*
Metallurgical Production and Power Politics on Bronze Age Cyprus

Production and Social Change in Protohistoric Palestine*

Thomas E. Levy

Abstract

The role of metallurgy in the emergence of Early Bronze Age urban centers in southern Palestine, in particular Tel Arad, has recently been explored and emphasized by a number of scholars. However, efforts to investigate the social role of metal working in the preceding Chalcolithic period have only recently been gaining interest among researchers. To date, interpretations of Chalcolithic metal working vary from dismissing it as of little importance to social organization, to viewing it as a key factor in the social integration of some late 5th-early 4th millennia Levantine societies. To reconstruct the role of metallurgy in Chalcolithic societies, a model is presented in which risk management, competition over natural resources and the notion of debt are explored in the Beersheba Valley, where extensive evidence for early metal production has been found. The production of metal objects, especially items which have been interpreted as having had a prestige/cultic function, are viewed as central to the building and maintenance of bonds between members of the Beersheba Valley culture. The discussion focuses on the southern portion of Israel-Transjordan due to the large number of survey and excavation reports and analytical studies of archaeological materials available from the late 5th–4th millennium B.C.E. for this area.

---

* Portions of this presentation have been published as "Production, Space and Social Change in Protohistoric Palestine," in A. Holl and T.E. Levy (eds.), *Spatial Boundaries and Social Dynamics — Case Studies from Agrarian Societies* (Ann Arbor, 1990), pp. 63–82.

The Beginnings of Pottery Production in the Southern Levant: Technological and Social Aspects

Yuval Goren, Avi Gopher and Paul Goldberg

Introduction

The inception of pottery production in the Near East is usually associated with the so-called Neolithic Revolution, and is related to the beginnings of settled life and the development of craft specialization. It is widely accepted that ceramics, when adopted, are associated predominantly with household activities, such as cooking and storage. The development of pottery production is usually designated as a unilinear trend, beginning with domestic fashioning of simply-shaped vessels, and going on to a well-established, full-scale specialism (Rice 1981). In the course of this process, some inventions are adopted, such as the potter's wheel and the pottery kiln. The latter are usually regarded as characteristics of full-time specialism, though several studies have demonstrated that this formula is not so clear-cut (e.g., Nicklin 1971). Since commercial craftsmen are driven mainly by market demands, they tend to produce more products per time-unit, involving better technologies and raw materials for this purpose (Nicklin 1971: 17–24, Arnold 1985: 127–167). Thus, the decreasing amount of time spent on each individual vessel should be considered as an improvement in the methods of pottery production. This model seems to be accepted elsewhere (e.g., Rice 1981, 1984, 1987: 10–12; Feinman et al. 1984; Arnold 1985).

These aspects being of a technological rather than typological nature, were considered to be criteria for the potter's skill and knowledge in producing functional and durable artifacts. Nevertheless, in many cases, pottery serves as a symbolic or artistic item. As Rice (1984: 252) points out, it is sometimes difficult to distinguish between genuine functional and symbolic or aesthetic categorizations since pottery may represent a combination of these. On the other hand, when used for a very specific purpose, with clear social implications (such as ranking expression or cult), pottery may be classed as "socially oriented." In these cases the craftsman's skill may be expressed

33

more in shaping and decorating, and the time spent on each individual vessel may increase (Rice 1984: 251–252). In both cases, a combination of typological and technological studies may assist in determining the vessel's function.

The technologies heralding pottery production in the Levant were originally associated with the production of plaster for architectural use and *"art mobilier"* objects in the Pre-Pottery Neolithic period (8th–7th millennium B.C.E.). Plaster products first appear in the southern Levant inventory of finds as early as the Pre-Pottery Neolithic A (PPNA, late 9th-early 8th millennium B.C.E.) and perhaps even earlier in Natufian contexts (Kingery et al. 1988). In many instances, burnt lime was used in making floors and movable artifacts, together with fired mud and clay. The pertinent technologies entailed the use of bonfires or kilns, and raw materials of flexible nature — all highly relevant to ceramic production (Frierman 1971; Gourdin and Kingery 1975, Aurenche and Maréchal 1985, Kingery, et al. 1988). Such products were first employed in building contexts, e.g. floor plastering or paving of installations. In the Pre-Pottery Neolithic B (PPNB, late 8th and 7th millennium B.C.E.) they became very common as floor covering and were also used for plastering skulls and for producing small quantities of vessels such as bowls and basins. The latter became more common toward the end of the 7th and during the 6th millennia B.C.E. in what had been termed "white ware" or *"vaisselle blanche."* In this context it represents a developing stage in which lime plaster technology is oriented towards the production of vessels (Balfet et al. 1969; de Contenson and Courtois 1979; le Miere 1983; Maréchal 1984; Perinet and Courtois 1983).

During the last two decades, considerable interest has been expressed in the development of lime and lime plaster products in the protohistorical periods of the Near East, particularly the Pre-Pottery Neolithic B (PPNB). Traces of massive plaster production were found at numerous sites, the best known of which include Jericho, Tell Ramad, Mureybet, El Kowm, ʿAin Ghazal, Abu Hureyra, Bouqras and Catal Hüyük (Mellaart 1967; de Contenson 1967, 1969; Dornemann 1969; Moore 1975; Akkermans et al. 1981; Rollefson and Simmons 1986, 1988; Kafafi 1986). These occurrences of lime products have raised questions concerning the methods by which they were produced, their role in the development of craft specialization and their social and economic implications (e.g., Garfinkel 1987).

As a result of the growing interest in this subject, a number of articles have appeared that postulate various methods of Neolithic lime production (Frierman 1971; Gourdin and Kingery 1975, Aurenche and Maréchal 1985, Kingery et al. 1988). The discovery of lime vessels demonstrated a close relationship between PPNB plaster production and later pottery firing methods. A development of the latter from the former was suggested (Balfet et al. 1969; de Contenson and Courtois 1979; le Miere 1983; Maréchal 1984; Perinet and Courtois 1983). The tendency to consider lime plaster manufacture as a complicated, laborious process influenced the interpretations of some archaeologists concerning the socioeconomic development of Pre-Pottery Neolithic societies (Frierman 1971; Garfinkel 1987). The development of modern analytical techniques and instruments, such as the scanning electron microscope

(SEM), X-ray diffraction (XRD), and the electron microprobe, has stimulated some scholars to use sophisticated equipment in the study of early lime plaster technology (Gourdin and Kingery 1975, Kingery et al. 1988). Since both limestone and lime plaster are composed mainly of calcium carbonate ($CaCO_3$), the effectiveness of chemical analysis to distinguish between the two is low. However, since the newly-formed calcium carbonate crystals are much smaller than the ones usually found in limestone or chalk, the differentiation between the two is possible with the aid of an optical (petrographic) microscope.

We are currently engaged in a research project aimed at providing a better understanding of early pyrotechnology as a possible precursor of late Neolithic and Chalcolithic pottery. For this purpose, samples from some of the more important archaeological sites in Israel, including lime products from the PPNB and smaller samples from both earlier and later periods, are being examined. The samples include plastered floors, plastered walls, "white ware", bricks, plaster beads and figurines, as well as pottery assemblages from Neolithic sites. For the reasons discussed above, our results are based primarily on observations of petrographic thin sections using a polarizing optical microscope. Already in the preliminary stages of our work, it became clear that in many cases our results differed significantly from those of Kingery and his colleagues (Gourdin and Kingery 1975, Kingery et al. 1988). Neolithic lime plaster production has been commonly interpreted as reflecting the complexity of Neolithic society. This issue, in our opinion, merits greater emphasis at this time than the study of technological aspects.

Method

All analyzed samples were taken from archaeological sites in Israel. Due to current geopolitical realities, it was not possible to obtain samples from Syrian, Jordanian and Lebanese sites such as Tell Ramad, Bouqras, ʿAin Ghazal, Beidha and Abu Hureyra. Thus, although our results are limited in geographical scope, we are reasonably convinced that similar results can be obtained from artifacts in adjoining regions.

In sampling, we tried to cover a wide range of architectural and non-architectural artifacts from sites ranging from the Pre-Pottery Neolithic A to the Pottery Neolithic cultures (9th–5th millennia B.C.E.). The samples were first examined under a binocular microscope, using magnifications of ×10 to ×40. Petrographic thin sections were then prepared from samples that were impregnated and hardened by polyester resin under vacuum. Large samples (e.g., plastered floors, bricks, etc.) were cut perpendicular to their surface for the preparation of large-size thin sections (7.5 × 5 cm.). Standard-size thin sections (4.5 × 3 cm.) were prepared from smaller samples. The thin sections were examined under a petrographic polarizing microscope at magnifications of ×40, ×100, ×250 and ×400. In some cases alizarin-red stain was used for highlighting non-carbonate components, such as clays.

Results

Our examinations of the Neolithic plaster products revealed that high intrasite and intersite variability existed in the methods of Pre-Pottery Neolithic plaster production. In most instances, similar products were produced differently at each site, and sometimes even within the same site. In most cases, the use of burnt lime was minimal or even absent. This was evident in the presence of numerous microfossils in many of the products, including plastered floors and walls, indicating that the original raw material was never burnt and converted into lime, or at least that the burning process did not reach the temperature needed for decalcination. In some cases, a mixture of marl and small-sized stones together with clay was used in order to form a solid floor or wall pavement, whereas other samples were made of clay with the addition of some burnt lime. Where burnt lime was used in the mixture, it barely exceeded 30 percent of the matrix, while other materials, such as clay, animal manure, marl or soil, were added in larger amounts.

Technological examinations of ceramic vessels of the earliest pottery-using cultures in Israel, namely the Yarmukian and "Jericho IX" entities, point to a clear continuity with earlier PPNB mud and plaster products. A clear dichotomy is pronounced between decorated and undecorated wares, since the former are usually distinguished by the use of highly carbonatic pastes. These materials often contain marl or even burnt lime, though technically and practically inferior to the more accessible clays or soils. On the other hand, undecorated wares are characterized by the use of soils and a greater variety of tempering materials, belying their modification for cooking or storage uses. It may be concluded that in the case of the decorated wares, a white-shaded product was desired rather than a practical vessel. Stylistic analyses of these ceramics show that much time was invested in decorating the vessels. Each individual vessel was treated with both incising and painting (in Yarmukian assemblages), or slipping, painting and burnishing (in "Jericho IX" assemblages). This trend continues, with some modifications, to the mid–5th millennium B.C.E. Wadi Raba culture.

In Wadi Raba contexts, decorated wares continue to be produced of highly carbonatic pastes, providing very bright pottery. Decoration techniques become more sophisticated, yet treatment is less individual. In this case, well-levigated clay, with some content of ferrous oxides, was slipped over the entire "leather-hard" vessel to form a thin film of extremely fine-grained matter. When fired in oxidizing or reducing atmospheres, the iron contents would convert into magnetite or hematite, providing a black or reddish shade. This provides evidence that a pottery kiln was used for producing this decoration style, because the complete control over firing atmospheres cannot be achieved in bonfires. It consequently represents a developmental stage in terms of ceramic technology, yet it decreases the artistic investment "value" of each individual vessel. This technique is well established also in the Halafian assemblages of the Syro-Lebanese horizon (Noll et al. 1975).

Discussion

A primary result of the present study is the demonstration of pronounced variability in production methods of Neolithic wall and floor plasters and smaller objects such as "white ware," beads and figurines, even in a very limited geographical region such as the southern Levant. Technically, these data do not support the view of Pre-Pottery Neolithic society as one characterized by "social interchange and communication over wide regions... fostered by the movement or relocation of skilled craftsmen" (Kingery et al. 1988: 238). In our opinion, Neolithic craft specialization, at least in the case of plaster production, must be considered as rudimentary and by no means a full-time activity. As Blackman (1982: 112) points out, small-scale lime burning is of necessity a summer activity, since rains may cause severe problems in burning and storage of the product. Since calcined and slaked lime must be kept at reasonably low humidity to avoid spoilage, storage problems probably dictated the use of the lime in the same season that it was produced. Thus, scheduling considerations made it a part-time summer activity only. Furthermore, since only a low proportion of burnt lime was detected by us in most of the architectural samples, we are convinced that lime burning was a casual, limited activity which did not require the burning of tons of wood, dung or other type of fuel (in opposition to the interpretations of Garfinkel 1987; Kingery et al. 1988). This low-scale manufacturing activity did not require much labor, since pits and a low-quality fuel (e.g. animal dung, peat or brush wood) were sufficient for this purpose.

The limited geographical region of the study mitigates possible natural causes, such as availability of resources or climate, as an explanation for the high intersite variability in plaster producing technology. The explanation for this variability may therefore be sought in social and economic spheres. Thus, while at some sites very high-quality plasters occur, in others the quality is surprisingly crude. As has been recorded from Arab villages in the Levant, in cases where expensive lime is unaffordable, small amounts of lime are frequently mixed with mud plasters (Canaan 1933: 22; Blackman 1982: 111). The same practice seems to occur in the Neolithic of Israel. The intersite variability may be an expression to some degree of social, economic and functional differences. On the other hand, since most of the *art mobilier* (the non-architectural products) are composed of relatively high proportions of burnt lime, we concur with Blackman's (1982) comment that "the skills required to produce lime plaster bowls and those required in the construction of buildings are obviously quite different in nature. It seems likely that the connection between these two activities did not extend beyond the use of the same starting material." In our opinion, while architectural plasters are basically functional in nature, products such as plaster vessels, beads and figurines were probably more closely associated with decorative or ritual use. The similarities of the technical processes used to manufacture these items and some early forms of pottery raise the possibility that, in many cases, early pottery vessels may have served similar functions.

In some earlier summaries on the beginnings of pottery production in the Levant, scholars such as Amiran (1965) and Kenyon (1969: 62–65) assigned the development of pottery production to a purely functional process, relating mainly to the improvement of the technological properties of the vessel. In their view, Neolithic pottery reflects an innovation in man's cooking and storing methods, and therefore must be evaluated on economic rather than artistic grounds. Against this background, the introduction of a well-established ceramic tradition in the mid–6th millennium B.C.E. in the southern Levant (the Yarmukian culture), was sometimes explained as a result of movement of people (Amiran 1965: 243–247;). This idea stems from the concept, that the earliest pottery to be found in this region was not "primitive" enough in form and decoration, as was the first pottery in other regions, such as Jarmo (Amiran 1965: 243–244). Therefore, these complexes were regarded as inventions diffused from other areas.

The technological and typological analyses of the pottery in question show that this model is oversimplified. The data presented here illustrate that the limited repertoire of lime vessels was augmented by a richer variety of shapes and decorative techniques with the increased use of mud-clay materials. The raw materials of the decorated pottery wares indicate that selection is directed more for the desired shade of the vessel than its technological quality. In later stages (late 5th–4th millennium B.C.E.) a higher standardization of shapes and decorative elements is developed. Only in the 4th-early 3rd millennium B.C.E. the use of selected raw materials intended for specific vessel types is developed and vessels are more functionally oriented. Thus, while the investment in material selection improves through time in terms of the vessel's performance in daily use, the decorative investment decreases concurrently. As opposed to the view of a unilinear trend of ceramic technology, stimulated only by functional improvements, we propose another possible model. This model is related solely to Israel, yet we assume that further research may lead to similar results in other parts of the ancient Near East. Some similarities from other regions, such as Greece (Vitelli 1989), hint at a broader distribution of this practice. According to this model, two regulating mechanisms act simultaneously in the process of ceramic production: one is driven by utilitarian needs such as cooking, storing, etc., whereas the other is affected by non-utilitarian factors. The former sees pottery mainly as functional, whereas the latter categorizes ceramic vessels as intended for consolidation of the social status of members of the society. It would appear that the emergence of pottery in 6th-millennium B.C.E. sites in Israel originated in PPNB traditions of skull plastering, bead and figurine fashioning and other related activities. In this context, "vaisselle blanche" and later decorated wares may be regarded as decorative or ritually oriented artifacts, rather than ones intended for daily use.

In the early pottery assemblages of the southern Levant (mid–6th millennium B.C.E.), an element of lime or lime-like materials continued to be used for the production of decorated wares in which time investment and raw materials selection were intended for decorative purposes alongside the mud-clay materials. Later, a bimodal trend of coexisting technologies for production of either lime-marl or mud-clay raw materials is discerned. The use of both lime and marl as raw materials for architecture, and "*art mobilier*" items declines in time. Concurrently, the relative volume of mud-clay products increases to become the common medium both for the simple utilitarian household products, as well as the formal (social-symbolic) products. Time consumption for producing vessels goes through a conspicuous change from emphasized investment in decorative features and minimal investment in material to a greater investment in functional properties of the vessel, such as impact and thermal shock resistance and lower time consumption on each individual vessel. We may conclude that this is related to the introduction of other exotic raw materials, such as copper and ivory, which replace pottery as the main material utilized for the creation of elite items.

References

P.A. Akkermans, H. Fokkens, and H.T. Waterbolk, 1981. "Stratigraphy, Architecture and Lay-Out of Boukras," in P. Sanlaville and J. Cauvin (eds.), *Préhistoire du Levant*, pp. 485–501. Paris.

R. Amiran, 1965. "The Beginning of Pottery-Making in the Near East," in F.R. Matson (ed.), *Ceramics and Man*, pp. 240–247. Chicago.

D. Arnold, 1985. *Ceramic Theory and Cultural Process*. Cambridge.

O. Aurenche and C. Maréchal, 1985. "Note sur la fabrication du plâtre a Qdeir (Syrie)," *Cahiers de l'Euphrate* 4: 221–226.

H. Balfet, N. Lafuma, P. Longuet and P. Terrier, 1969. "Une invention sans lendemain, vaisselles précéramiques et sols enduits dans quelques sites du Proche-Orient," *Bulletin de la Société Préhistorique Française* 66: 188–192.

J.M. Blackman, 1982. "The Manufacture and Use of Burned Lime Plaster at Proto-Elamite Anshan (Iran)," in T.A. Wertime and S.F. Wertime (eds.), *Early Pyrotechnology, the Evolution of the First Fire-Using Industries*, pp. 107–116. Washington DC.

T. Canaan, 1933. *The Palestinian Arab House, its Architecture and Folklore*. Jerusalem.

H. de Contenson, 1967. "Troisième campagne à Ramad, rapport préliminaire," *Annales Archaéologiques Arabes Syriennes* 17: 17–4.

———, 1969. "Sixième campagne de fouilles a Tell Ramad en 1969. Rapport préliminaire," *Annales Archaéologiques Arabes Syriennes* 19: 31–36.

H. de Contenson and L.C. Courtois, 1979. "A propos des vases enchaux: recherches sur leur fabrication et leur origine,"*Paléorient* 5: 177–182.

R.H. Dornemann, 1969. "An Early Village (El Kowm)," *Archaeology* 22: 69–70.

G. Feinman, S.A. Kowalewski, and R.E. Blanton, 1984. "Modelling Ceramic Production and Organizational Change in the Pre-Hispanic Valley of Oaxaca, Mexico," in S.E. van der Leeuw and A.C. Pritchard, *The Many Dimensions of Pottery*, pp. 295–337. Amsterdam.

J.D. Frierman, 1971. "Lime Burning as the Precursor of Fired Ceramics," *IEJ* 21: 212–216.

Y. Garfinkel, 1987. "Burnt Lime Products and Social Implications in the Pre-Pottery Neolithic B Villages of the Near East," *Paléorient* 13: 69–76.

W.H. Gourdin and W.D. Kingery, 1975. "The Beginnings of Pyrotechnology: Neolithic and Egyptian Lime Plaster," *Journal of Field Archaeology* 2: 133–150.

Z.A. Kafafi, 1986. "White Objects from Ain Ghazal, Near Amman," *ASOR* 261: 51–56.

K. Kenyon, 1969. *Archaeology of the Holy Land*. London.

D.W. Kingery, P.B. Vandiver and M. Pickett, 1988. "The Beginnings of Pyrotechnology, Part II: Production and Use of Lime and Gypsum Plaster in the Pre-Pottery Neolithic Near East," *Journal of Field Archaeology* 15: 219–244.

M. Le Miere, 1986. *Les premières céramiques du Moyen-Euphrate*. (Unpublished Ph.D. dissertation, Lyon, Université Lumière).

R. Malinowski and Y. Garfinkel 1989. *Betongens forhistoria*. Molndal. (Swedish).

C. Maréchal, 1984 "Vaisselles blanches du Proche-Orient: El Kowm (Syrie) et l'usage du plâtre au néolithique," *Cahiers de l'Euphrate* 3: 217–251.

J. Mellaart, 1967. *Catal Hüyük, a Neolithic Town in Anatolia*. New York.

A.M.T. Moore, 1975. "The Excavations of Tell Abu Hureyra in Syria: A Preliminary Report," *Proceedings of the Prehistoric Society* 41: 50–77.

K. Nicklin, 1971. "Stability and Innovation in Pottery Manufacture," *World Archaeology* 3: 13–48.

W. Noll, R. Holm and L. Born, 1975. "Painting of Ancient Ceramics," *Angew. Chem. Internat. Edit.* 14: 602–613.

G. Perinet and L. Courtois, 1983. "Évaluation des températures de cuisson de céramiques et de vaisselles blanches néolithiques de Syrie," *Bulletin de la Société Préhistorique Française* 80: 157–160.

P.M. Rice, 1981. "Evolution of Specialized Pottery Production: A Trial Model," *Current Anthropology* 22: 219–240.

——— , 1984. "Change and Conservatism in Pottery-Producing Systems," in S.E. van der Leeuw and A.C. Pritchard, *The Many Dimensions of Pottery*, pp. 23–293. Amsterdam.

——— , 1987. *Pottery Analysis, a Sourcebook*. Chicago.

G.O. Rollefson and A.H. Simmons, 1986. "The Neolithic Village of Ain Ghazal, Jordan: Preliminary Report on the 1984 Season," *BASOR* Supplement 24: 145–164.

——— , 1988. "The Neolithic Village of Ain Ghazal, Jordan: Preliminary Report on the 1985 Season," *BASOR* Supplement 25: 93–106.

K.D. Vitelli, 1989. "Were Pots First Made for Foods? Doubts from Franchthi," *World Archaeology* 21: 17–29.

Metals, Rocks, Specialization, and the Beginning of Urbanism in the Northern Negev

Steven A. Rosen

The rise of metallurgical technology and its requisite craft specialization, and the concomitant development of redistribution networks, has often been viewed as a primary factor in the rise of early complex societies. In this regard, the administration and control of the distribution of presumably elite metal objects is seen as a significant stage in the development of stratified societies (e.g., Childe 1951: 95–99, 114–142; Redman 1978: 270; Renfrew 1984; Zaccagnini 1983).

With the discoveries of sophisticated Chalcolithic metal technologies, and an elaborate Early Bronze Age production and distribution system, the role of metallurgical production in the rise of complex societies in the southern Levant is being addressed systematically for the first time (e.g., Ilan and Sebbane 1989; Kempinsky 1978, 1983, 1989; Marfoe 1980; Shalev and Northover 1987). Unfortunately, the importance of metallurgy in our civilization may tend to overemphasize its significance in its earliest forms. In order to assess the role of metallurgy in early history more objectively, it is necessary to place it in proper material context by comparisons with other aspects of material culture which may have played similar or complementary roles in the specific cultures under study. The subsequent history of the various technologies is totally irrelevant to understanding the role of a particular technology within a specific culture. The key point here is that metallurgy in the Chalcolithic and Early Bronze Ages does not stand out, either as qualitatively different from other technologies in its functions or roles in these societies, nor as a particularly important factor in the development of these societies.

These points are of import beyond the confines of the Levant. Heskell (1983) has noted the failure, as it were, of metallurgy to emerge from the Neolithic of Catal Hüyük. Apparently the socioeconomic contexts of these earliest experiments in metallurgy were ultimately inadequate to support full-fledged specialization. Significantly, the metals themselves were apparently not of sufficient value to promote that specialization. In a parallel Levantine context, the evidence for full-time, resident craft specialists in the 4th and 3rd millennia B.C.E. is equivocal, despite the use of technologically sophisticated copper/bronze metallurgies. The itinerant trader or specialist tribe models (cf. Betts 1989; also Tadmor 1989) provide alternatives which just as adequately explain the archaeological record, and yet require considerably less "cultural complexity." These models would suggest that metallurgical production specialization *per se*, should best be viewed as a consequence and as a secondary rein-forcing agent in the evolution of complex societies.

Furthermore, besides the actual technical aspects, the craft specialization associated with early metallurgy does not seem to differ from that associated with basalt vessels, some types of flint implements, and perhaps some ceramic types. The leap from the archaeologically demonstrable existence of specialized production to an assumption of elite control and redistribution requires a faith in theory not really sustainable by the actual archaeological evidence. As with metallurgy, an equally legitimate case can be made for a relatively low level of distribution organization for these goods, despite technological sophistication.

Comparisons of Material Culture and its Production and Distribution

Basalt and Phosphorite Vessels

Recent petrographic analyses of basalt vessels from Chalcolithic and Early Bronze Age sites in the northern Negev (Amiran and Porat 1984; Gilead and Goren 1989; Goren 1989) have strongly suggested that the sources for the raw material of these objects are to be found in the highlands of Transjordan, just east of the Dead Sea. The phosphorite from which identical vessels were manufactured, apparently in imi-tation of the basalt, is found in the same general region. No workshop sites have yet been reported. Several scholars (Perrot 1955; Rosen 1986) have noted the total absence of evidence for the manufacture of basalt or phosphorite vessels, in the form of flaking and chipping debris, on the sites at which they were found — demonstrat-ing almost conclusively that they were made elsewhere, presumably at or near the quarries, and that trade was conducted in complete or near-complete vessels. The con-siderable weight of these objects, and the relatively large numbers found at many sites, suggest the likelihood that they were transported by means of pack animals. The pres-ence of donkey and/or horse at Chalcolithic and Early Bronze Age sites (e.g., Angress 1959; Josien 1955; Lernau 1978; Davis 1976: Table 2), and the discovery of animal figurines laden with pots (Epstein 1985; Amiran et al. 1978: 54), support this supposi-tion.

Although most authors have ascribed a ritual and/or elite status to basalt bowls (e.g., Amiran 1969: 24; Amiran and Porat 1984; Levy 1986; Rosen 1986), Gilead (in preparation) has demonstrated their common presence in virtually every residen-tial locus at the Chalcolithic hamlet of Gerar (see Epstein 1982 for a parallel case in the Golan Chalcolithic). As he pointed out, this does not accord well with the use of these artifacts to posit an elite — especially when considering the hamlet nature of Gerar, hardly a set of elite residences. Symbolic significance may still be ascribed to the objects, since to serve their practical function they could easily have been made of local materials (e.g., limestone, ceramics) but were nevertheless imported. The symbolism may well be reflective of household or domestic ritual (cf. Flannery 1976), perhaps extendable to more centralized ritual in specific circumstances. In this context, Perrot (1955: 79) notes the presence of caches of three basalt vessels, deliberately deposited in structures before they were abandoned. He suggests (Perrot 1984) that minor differences in the on-site distribution of these objects may reflect differences in wealth, but is unequivocal in his interpretation of Chalcolithic society as fundamentally egalitarian. The small basalt head recovered from Shiqmim (Levy and Alon 1985), as well as the Golan statues (Epstein 1982) were also clearly not utilitarian objects.

In contrast to the Chalcolithic, the basalt objects — mostly mortars and grinding stones — from the Negev Early Bronze Age sites, as exemplified by Arad (Amiran et al. 1978: 57–58; and other sites, Amiran and Porat 1984) seem to be almost exclusively utilitarian. The typical Chalcolithic basalt bowls are absent from Bronze Age Arad. Workmanship is distinctly inferior, and it seems difficult to ascribe ritual or symbolic function to the crude mortars found at the site, although possibly some of the stone rings may qualify. Although proper evaluation is problematic, there seems to be a quantitative decline of basalt objects from the Chalcolithic to the Early Bronze Age as well. A. Joffe (personal communication) suggests that the Early Bronze Age replacement of Chalcolithic basalt fenestrated vessels by ceramic imitations (Lapp 1968) is indicative of ritual continuity in a context of economic disruption.

Tabular Scrapers
Sourcing flint types chemically or mineralogically is difficult due to the high variability of flint within single sources, and to the great number of exposures all over the Levant. Nevertheless, the Eocene flint which seems to be the major — if not exclusive — raw material in tabular scraper manufacture is relatively restricted in its distribution. The presence of tabular scraper production quarry sites in the central and western Negev suggests that this area may have served as a major source for these tools in the 4th and 3rd millennia B.C.E. (Rosen 1983a, 1989). Similar geological characteristics raise the possibility that other sources may be present in Transjordan (Bartov 1985), although no sites have been reported. Eocene flint exposures are also known from the Shephelah region, and in minor outcrops in Galilee. However, the quantities of these tools are minimal in the north, especially at Early Bronze Age sites, and the geometric decrease from south to north is highly suggestive of a restricted source.

As with basalt objects, with the exception of a secondary workshop at Far'ah site A (Macdonald 1932: 10; Rosen 1986; Roshwalb 1981: 39–45), evidence for the manufacture of these tools (in the form of characteristic debitage or, especially, cores) is totally absent from all Chalcolithic and Early Bronze Age sites. The Far'ah A cache of 77 tabular scrapers, in varying states of completion, along with the general nature of the site as a flint production center (Roshwalb 1981: 88; Macdonald 1932: 10; Rosen 1983a 1987a) suggests preliminary transport in unfinished pieces. The near absence of unfinished pieces (to be distinguished from broken pieces) at other sites implies that the exchange beyond the manufacturing center was conducted in finished pieces. Analysis of the quarry production site at Har Qeren 15 (Rosen 1983a, Rosen and Goring-Morris n.d.) suggests that, in fact, the site was an adjunct to a pastoral encampment. Lithic exploitation at this site is neither particularly intensive, nor is the lithic assemblage restricted to items reflecting the manufacture of tabular scrapers. It rather seems to span a range of utilitarian functions, along with the tabular scrapers.

Microwear analyses of Early Bronze Age tabular scrapers from Bab edh-Dhra᷄ suggest that the pieces may have functioned more as knives than as scrapers, and contextual associations indicate a possible ritual use (McConaughy 1979: 304). The ritual or symbolic aspect of these pieces is supported by: 1) the presence of a tabular scraper in a grave at Shiqmim, one of the rare tabular scrapers recovered from the site (Levy and Alon 1985); 2) the sole flint artifact recovered from the open-air shrine at Biq᷄at ᷄Uvda is a tabular scraper (Yogev 1983); 3) the association of over 400 tabular scrapers with the site of Mizpe Shalem, interpreted by Bar-Adon (1989) and Greenhut (1989) to be a ritual site; and 4) the presence of occasionally repetitive incised designs on Early Bronze Age tabular scrapers which probably reflect symbolic aspects (Rosen 1983a, 1989). Moreover, tabular scraper working edges are easily obtained from non-cortical flakes present in the Chalcolithic and Early Bronze Age tool repertoire, again emphasizing the deliberate stylistic selection of this tool type.

It is important to note here that tabular scrapers from the central Negev and Sinai seem for the most part not to show the same symbolic import. As a rule they are cruder, and incised pieces are rare to absent. They seem to fall more into a general expedient or *ad hoc* tool category than those found further north. For example, no incised tabular scrapers were recovered from any of the excavations at Biq᷄at ᷄Uvda (Rosen 1983b: 206–238), only 1 of 71 pieces from Beit-Arieh's Southern Sinai survey showed incisions (Rosen n.d.), and only 3 of 183 tabular scrapers at Sheikh ᷅Awad showed incisions (Milstein 1981). In contrast, 11 of 30 tabular scrapers from Arad Strata III-IV showed incisions (Schick 1978). On the other hand, the clear association of these tools with tumuli and graves in the Elat region nevertheless indicates some symbolic affinities (Avner 1984; personal communication).

An important aspect in the interpretation of these tools is the apparent difference in tabular scraper distribution between the Early Bronze Age and the Chalcolithic. In the Chalcolithic Beersheba sites (Safadi, Abu Matar, Ḥorvat Beter, Shiqmim) these tools are scarce, although more frequent at Ghassul. In the Early Bronze Age, distribution seems much more regular and widespread, despite the apparent fall-off curve from south to north (Rosen 1983a). Interestingly, the "Ghassul-Beersheba" phase sites around Far᷄ah (E,O) also show an apparent scarcity of these tools when compared to the possibly earlier "Besor" sites (for phasing see Gilead and Alon 1988; for data see Roshwalb 1981). There are fluctuations in the distribution systems of these objects.

It is indicative of our research biases that elite status has never been ascribed to these tools. As with basalt bowls, they are imported, reflect a degree of production specialization, at least partially seem to reflect symbolic functions, and are technologically sophisticated.

Copper

The debate over the source of Chalcolithic copper ores and artifacts has been narrowing; Perrot's (1968: 441) earlier suggestion that the origins of the sophisticated copper artifacts must be sought in Syria or Anatolia has been superseded by a general consensus that the industry is related to Negev or Transjordan sources (Shalev and Northover 1987; Moorey 1988; Shalev et al. n.d.). The two primary possibilities are Feinan and Timnaʿ (e.g., Hauptmann et al. 1985; Hauptmann and Weisgerber 1987; Rothenberg 1972).

Copper metallurgy in the Chalcolithic must be divided into two basic technologies: 1) simple smelting casting, and 2) the lost wax method and other more complex casting techniques (Key 1980; Potaszkin and Bar-Avi 1980; Moorey 1988, Shalev and Northover 1987, Ilan and Sebbane 1989). The choice of the use of pure or near pure copper, or an arsenical copper alloy should be seen in the context of these techniques. According to Key (1980), the alloy pours more easily and congeals more slowly so that it is more suitable for complex casting techniques. In terms of the actual objects, there is a near 1:1 relationship between simple smelting of pure copper on the one hand, and lost wax casting of arsenical copper alloys on the other. One of the few exceptions, a lost wax "standard" of pure copper from the Naḥal Mishmar hoard, is flawed — apparently due to poor congealing of the pure copper (Key 1980; Potaszkin and Bar-Avi 1980).

The basic technologies, in turn, seem to correspond to different production and distribution systems (cf. Shalev and Northover 1987; also Rosen 1986). Although no evidence for the lost wax method or arsenical copper slags has been found at any Chalcolithic site (despite the presence of finished articles at numerous sites), remains of simple crucibles and pure copper slags have been recovered from many sites (e.g., Ghassul, Abu Matar, Safadi-Neve Noy, Shiqmim). That is, while simple objects like axes and awls were probably produced on site (at least occasionally) from imported ores (Perrot 1968: 428–31), technologically complex objects, such as maceheads and standards, were manufactured elsewhere and imported as complete pieces. It is, of course, reasonable to assume that the agent who imported the pure copper ores was also the one who introduced the finished products.

The dual nature of the technologies, ores and production-distribution system, also seems to be reflected largely in function. Whereas such utilitarian items as awls and axes were produced almost exclusively by the more primitive smelting and simple casting techniques, the lost wax method was used to manufacture objects whose utilitarian functions are ambiguous at best, and to which most researchers assign a symbolic or ritual role (Bar-Adon 1980; Levy 1986; Rosen 1986; Ilan and Sebbane 1989; Shalev and Northover 1987; Tadmor 1989, etc.).

The cultic nature of the standards and crowns may be inferred from three lines of evidence: 1) special context in caches (e.g., Naḥal Mishmar) or "foundation" deposits (Shiqmim): 2) complex iconographic aspects, implying high symbolic significance; and 3) difficulties in envisaging utilitarian functions for these artifacts. Although Moorey (1988) has recently suggested that the maceheads were weapons — implying a relatively utilitarian cultural role, the interpretation seems forced since cheap local imitations would have easily served as well as the valuable and sophisticated arsenical copper maceheads. The only requirement was a large enough stone and the ability to haft it to a club. Given the associations between maceheads and such clearly cere-monial or ritual artifacts such as standards and crowns, a ceremonial or ritual function seems the most reasonable interpretation of these objects.

Technologically, the Early Bronze Age seems to show a significant decline in cop-per metallurgy when compared to the Chalcolithic, as evidenced especially by the disuse of the lost wax method. Virtually all of the copper finds from Early Bronze Age contexts can be assigned relatively unambiguous utilitarian functions. Thus at Arad, the entire Early Bronze Age corpus of over 200 copper objects is comprised of awls and axes (Ilan and Sebbane 1989). The artifacts recovered from the Kefar Monash hoard also seem to reflect utilitarian functions (Hestrin and Tadmor 1963), although the lack of clear archaeological context makes interpretation difficult. Ilan and Sebbane (1989) also suggest that forging may have been introduced in this period. This is of some significance since it suggests the possibility of a primitive form of mass production that was probably not present in the Chalcolithic. Although a few crucibles and slags were also recovered, they consider these to represent secondary reuse and indicate that most of the pieces were manufactured off-site.

Hanbury-Tenison (1986: 151–59) has suggested that the disappearance of lost wax casting does not indicate a decline in copper use. Not counting the exceptional Naḥal Mishmar hoard, there seems to have been an increase in copper exploitation in the Early Bronze Age. The dominance of every-day utilitarian objects (awls and axes) suggests that copper may have been relatively accessible — at least to residents of Arad (Kempinski 1989). However, accessibility should not be misconstrued as abun-dance.

Furthermore, Beit-Arieh's (e.g., 1977, 1986) work on the southern Sinai Early Bronze Age has demonstrated both the presence of copper working activities and affinity to the material culture and architecture of Arad. He interpreted these sites as Aradian mining colonies (Beit-Arieh 1981), implying an organized and centralized exploitation of southern Sinai copper resources. Alternatively, de Miroschedji (1986) suggested that they should probably be seen as wilderness trading posts — pastoral camps, manned by local herdsmen with Aradian trade connections. The difference between the two interpretations is of some import since they reflect greater and lesser degrees, respectively, of social complexity at Arad. Evaluation of the competing hypotheses is difficult, but evidence from the Nawamis culture may provide an his-torical context for assessing the problem.

The key point is the apparent chronological and material culture overlap between the Nawamis culture and the "Aradian" sites. In particular, typological and petrographic analysis of ceramics (Bar-Yosef et al. 1977, 1986; Porat 1986) shows close similarity, if not identity, in form and materials between the two types of sites — obviously suggesting close relations. This is further supported by the presence of copper awls in Nawamis tombs. If copper objects were highly valued and produced by export for colonists, their appearance in the tombs of local pastoralists, whose material culture was otherwise limited and rather poor, is anomalous. If, on the other hand, the Nawamis people engaged in mining and working of copper (referred to by Rothenberg [1979] and Kozloff [1981] as the Timnian culture), then the presence of copper is understandable. Thus, de Miroschedji's (1986) suggestion ties these phenomena together. There is little problem in adding the presence of Aradian traders — or perhaps more properly, Canaanite traders or even managers — to this scenario. Indeed, the pastoral population explosion in the central and southern Negev in the Early Bronze II (Rosen 1987b; Haiman 1989: 18–30) may also partially relate to this general trade system and the resulting expansion of a modified Nawamis culture northwards, and of Canaanite culture southward.

Other Realms of Material Culture

Basalt objects, tabular scrapers, and copper objects seem to reflect similar socioeconomic functions in the periods under discussion (Table 1). It is instructive to compare them briefly to other realms of material culture since some clear differences exist.

Sickle blades (Table 1) are the product of (semi-)specialized manufacture in both the Chalcolithic and the Early Bronze Ages (Rosen 1983c, 1987b, 1989; Roshwalb 1981). However, unlike the previously discussed groups, sickle blades are found in abundance at most sites, and the few workshop sites known seem to suggest generally higher intensity of production. Functionally, they are unquestionably associated with agriculture. Although morphological and technological differences exist between sickle assemblages from different periods and regions, once the sickle segments are affixed to the haft, these differences are not visible. Thus, symbolic functions for different sickle styles, as has been claimed for arrowheads (Wiessner 1983), are unlikely. The significant change in sickle manufacture, from Chalcolithic to Early Bronze Age, with the introduction of Canaanean blade technology (Rosen 1983c), may reflect increasing specialization as well as a change in specific raw materials.

Flint axes and drills, beads, shells, and ivory objects also seem to show degrees of specialization and exchange. Bitumen from the Dead Sea (Nissenbaum et al. 1984) was also a trade item. Unfortunately, there is a paucity of information regarding these materials. For example, we have little reliable data on the manufacture of flint axes, although it is likely that they were the products of specialized manufacture (Roshwalb 1981: 22, 45–52). Although large caches of flint drills, probably used in bead manufacture, have been discovered (Burian and Friedman 1987; Macdonald 1932: 8; Roshwalb 1981: 166–7), few beads have been recovered. The general place

Table 1: Comparative Criteria for Cultural Context and Value

Chalcolithic

	Basalt	Tabular Scrapers	Copper Objects	Sickle Blades
Distance	medium to long	medium to long	medium to long	short to medium
Degree of specialization	semi-specialized	semi-specialized	semi-specialized	semi-specialized
Access	restricted	semi-restricted	restricted	readily available
Abundance	not uncommon	relatively rare	relatively rare	abundant
Context	domestic and/or ritual	ritual	utilitarian or ritual*	agriculture

Early Bronze Age

	Basalt	Tabular Scrapers	Copper Objects	Sickle Blades
Distance	medium to long	medium to long	medium to long	short to medium
Degree of specialization	semi-specialized	semi-specialized	semi-full specialization	semi-specialized
Access	restricted	semi-restricted	restricted	semi-restricted
Abundance	not uncommon	not uncommon	not uncommon	abundant
Context	utilitarian	ritual	utilitarian	agriculture

* depending on tool type

of this industry in these protohistoric cultures is not clear. Perrot (1955; 1968) suggested that the carved ivory objects found at Chalcolithic sites indicate semispecialized manufacture. However, the objects are few and there is little evidence for their manufacture. Dead Sea bitumen (Nissenbaum et al. 1984; Amiran et al. 1978: 58) has been found in Chalcolithic and Early Bronze Age loci at Arad and Small Tel Malḥata. This raw material can be used as an adhesive or sealant, and can serve many purposes.

The potentials of economic analysis of ceramics are as great or greater than any of the materials discussed above. Unfortunately, the quantitative descriptions necessary for such studies are rare (but see Commenge-Pellerin 1987; Levy and Menahem 1987). Although large numbers of potsherds have been recovered from most Chalcolithic sites, petrographic analyses (Gilead and Goren 1989) have demonstrated that the vast majority from any specific site were produced within the environs of that site. Gilead and Goren (1989) suggest that this localization of ceramic manufacture, and the village level organization of Chalcolithic society, preclude full-time craft specialization. In the Early Bronze Age, the larger population aggregates may well have been sufficient to support true full-time resident specialization in ceramic production. Obviously, pottery may play either a cultic/symbolic role and/or a utilitarian role in any particular society. Specialized production would be geared primarily toward the utilitarian wares, since they are the ones that would be used in bulk.

The Relative Importance of Copper

In view of the above review of selected Chalcolithic and Early Bronze Age crafts, the relative importance of copper to Chalcolithic and Early Bronze Age societies can be reevaluated. The basic question is whether objective criteria for establishing the relative value of different artifacts, raw materials, or aspects of material culture can be ascertained. More specifically, it appears that the production of copper tools does not differ in any culturally substantive way from other semispecialized realms of material culture.

Establishing a so-called market value of any particular object in a prehistoric society is difficult for a variety of reasons. First, in the absence of a free market economy, value is determined by specific cultural contexts and may vary considerably from group to group, within groups, or even seasonally. Objects of great ritual importance are often simply discarded or deliberately destroyed after ceremonial use. Some objects, intrinsically worthless, accrue immense value only in specific cultural contexts. A classic example is the variable status and value associated with Northwest Indian potlatch copper counters (e.g., Benedict 1934: 164–80).

Clearly, what we view as technological sophistication does not necessarily constitute a means of establishing absolute value. Objects requiring specific skills and technologies must command minimal value, otherwise they would not be produced. However, their relative value with respect to other objects need not be related to the relative complexity of manufacture. Moreover, relative complexity of manufacture is difficult to establish when comparing fundamentally different technologies.

Thus our preconceptions concerning the inherent value of copper objects requires close scrutiny. Moorey's (1988) recent claim that Chalcolithic society was based on a "copper standard" implies an ultimate value for these objects. More objective criteria suggest this to be a significant overstatement.

Archaeologically measurable aspects of the value attributable to specific objects include distance of trade, extent of specialization in production, relative accessibility to raw materials (partly related to distance), abundance in the archaeological record, and cultural context. Obviously, all of these are interrelated, but each is independently measurable. Thus, we may assume that the following features generally reflect greater value: 1) longer trade distance; 2) greater production specialization; 3) limited accessibility to raw material; 4) less abundance in the archaeological record (i.e., greater supply = less demand); and 5) greater symbolic load. But, of course, there are exceptions to these generalities.

Table 1 summarizes the four realms of material culture described above according to these criteria for the northern Negev. Sickles have also been included to exemplify a somewhat contrasting set of attributes. Obviously parameters vary in other regions. The key point here is that there is no discernible difference between the three original technologies and raw materials. Additionally, the table seems to suggest a possible decline in the value of copper during the Early Bronze Age. In short, there seems little reason to assign copper metallurgy a primary role in the emergence of craft specialization, or, concomitantly, the rise of urbanism in the northern Negev.

Production and Distribution: a Partial Model

The craft traditions outlined above all show several outstanding features in common: 1) the import of either raw material or completed items to sites with little or no evidence of local manufacture (excepting the manufacture of simple copper objects); 2) relatively sophisticated techniques of manufacture requiring specialized knowledge and/or tools for production; 3) relatively limited numbers of artifacts at most sites.

These features suggest that the modes of production and distribution in these areas of material culture are similar. Two distinct and contrasting models can be offered to account for these features: 1) full-time, or near full-time craft specialists, each within his own area of expertise, and each supported by the elite of a specific town, village or territory; 2) a system of itinerant pastoral traders/craftsmen whose primary subsistence economy is based on pastoralism or connections to pastoralists, but whose important secondary economy derives from specialized crafts and exchange (Gilead n.d. cf. the Solubba tribe in Arabia [Betts 1989]). Obviously, there could be a range of types of specialization between these two extremes.

Evaluation of the models is difficult because of the ambiguity of the archaeological evidence. Nevertheless, several lines of reasoning suggest that the second alternative, or something akin to it, is to be preferred. First, the almost total absence of local manufacture of basalt vessels, lost-wax copper objects and tabular scrapers, argues against the idea of resident specialists for any of these crafts. The absence of sophisticated copper production is especially telling in light of the on-site evidence for more simple copper technologies. Furthermore, the relatively limited number of all types of objects seems to preclude full-time craft specialization. There simply are not enough basalt vessels, tabular scrapers or copper objects to have kept a full-time craftsman busy, especially considering the long-term occupation of many of the sites (cf. Gilead and Goren 1989 for similar interpretation of ceramic assemblages). Admittedly, the problem of resmelting and reuse of copper may cause us to underestimate the actual number of copper objects in use. However, the very need to resmelt suggests that quantities were limited in the first place. I discount the possibility of later period looting of a site like Arad, for such disturbances on a large scale would surely have been discerned by the excavators.

The itinerant pastoralist model suffers not so much from arguments against it, as from the absence of sufficiently strong arguments in its favor. This is at least partially the consequence of the lesser archaeological visibility of pastoral encampments and the scant attention paid to the subject in general. Still, several lines of evidence can be used to support the model.

As noted earlier, the tabular scraper quarry site at Har Qeren 15 seems best interpreted as an auxiliary site to pastoral encampments in the general area, such as described in the western Central Negev for the Early Bronze Age (e.g., Heiman 1989; Beit-Arieh and Gophna 1976, 1981), or those described in Naḥal Sekher for the Chalcolithic (Gilead and Goren 1986, Goren and Gilead 1986). The Chalcolithic and Early Bronze Age copper mining sites described at Timnaʿ (Rothenberg 1972: 24–62) fit the model well, and a similar interpretation of the Early Bronze Age sites in southern Sinai has already been discussed. With respect to basalt exploitation, it may be noted that the very absence of early basalt quarries in the current archaeological record argues for their low visibility, a characteristic of pastoral exploitation rather than of intensive quarrying. Of course, this is stretching the point.

Conclusions: Craft Specialization and Urbanization in the Northern Negev

In Childe's (1951) classic conception of the rise of urban civilization, reiterated by numerous later scholars (e.g., Kempinski 1978; Tosi 1984; Shennan 1982, and see references therein), craft specialization and urbanization develop together in a mutually reinforcing relationship. The combination of food surpluses and the rise of an elite allow and encourage specialized crafts. On one hand these are supported by the surpluses (controlled by the elite), and on the other, enhance the prestige and power base of the elite. Thus, true craft specialization is listed by Childe (1950) as one of the characteristic attributes of state civilization.

The apparently low level of craft specialization in the Early Bronze Age in the northern Negev (even considering that ceramics are probably specialized products) implies that urbanization there was not of the same order as in Mesopotamia and Egypt. However, it raises the question of what constitutes urbanism and state-level society. Kempinski (1989) is undoubtedly right when he refers to Arad as a town rather than a city. The distinction is important. Cities are attributes of state systems (Adams 1972; Service 1978), with all their attendant ramifications, including craft specialization. The relatively low level of craft specialization is important insofar as it indicates a correspondingly low level of central economic coordination.

If such is the case for the Early Bronze Age, then even lower levels of socioeconomic complexity must be assumed for the Chalcolithic. Levy (1986) has suggested that Chalcolithic societies be seen as "chiefdoms" (Service 1962), implying a redistributive economic system, one of the primary characteristics of chiefdoms. Much of the thrust of Levy's argument has been to stress the socioeconomic complexity of Chalcolithic society, perhaps even toward a level approaching urbanism. Although there can be little question as to the presence of part-time specialists (Perrot 1955), evidence for redistribution is unclear, especially given the itinerant trader model outlined above. If Levy's general interpretation of the Chalcolithic as a chiefdom-level society is correct, the ambiguity of the evidence for redistribution is troubling. Furthermore, Chalcolithic society seems to have remained economically stable for virtually the entire span of its existence. There are no indications of increasing economic intensification throughout the millennium of the Ghassul-Beersheba cultural phase. Such stability is not typical of the feedback growth systems evident in the rise of state societies (e.g., Redman 1978: 215–43; Adams 1966; Wright 1978). In short, analysis of the nature of craft specialization in the 4th and 3rd millennia in the northern Negev suggests that too high a level of cultural complexity should not be attributed to these societies.

On another level it is important to stress that the rise of Early Bronze Age urban society in Israel must be viewed in its proper historical and geographical context. Whereas Chalcolithic societies seem to have been relatively isolated from events and processes occurring in neighboring countries, Early Bronze Age Israel seems to have been much more affected by its neighbors. The significance of Egyptian presence in the southern Shephelah coastal plain in Early Bronze I has been demonstrated by numerous scholars (Gophna 1976; Oren 1989; Hennessy 1967: 26–35; Kempinski 1983; Yeivin 1960; Weinstein 1984; Brandel 1989; Rosen 1988), and the Byblos connection for northern Israel has also recently been emphasized (Ben-Tor 1989). The specifics of the relationship between the Egyptian state and the rise of towns and cities has yet to be fully documented, but that there is a strong relationship cannot be denied. In essence, urbanism in the southern Levant must be seen as a secondary phenomenon.

As such, it is perhaps not surprising to find a lag between economic and political organization (as reflected especially in the huge fortifications of the Early Bronze Age), with the political crystallization occurring first and more rapidly. This is in contrast to the more gradual evolution of primary states (for a recent example of the primary role of trade in pristine state formation, see Algaze 1989). It would explain the apparently low level of the Early Bronze Age economic system, as well as the apparent similarity between Early Bronze Age and Chalcolithic craft organization, despite the major differences in sociopolitical level. I must emphasize that I have deliberately restricted discussion to the southern half of the country, concentrating on Early Bronze I and II. For example, it is clear that the granaries of Beth Yerah reflect a different order of economic organization from that documented here (Esse 1982; Maisler et al. 1952). In the sense that northern Israel is generally more integrated into Syria and the Fertile Crescent, the origins of complex society may be "less secondary," and more an organic (if peripheral) part of developments in Mesopotamia.

The thrust of this essay has been to "demote" the relative importance of copper metallurgy, craft specialization, and indeed the complexity of urbanism in the northern Negev. This does not relegate the phenomena as I have interpreted them to secondary status; indeed the opposite is true. In the vast majority of cases, states and cities arise in secondary contexts. Primary states may not be the ideal models for these occurrences. The detailed archaeological description of the rise of a prehistoric secondary state is of key importance for understanding how this process works on a general level.

References

R.M. Adams, 1966. *The Evolution of Urban Society.* Chicago.
_____ , 1972. "Patterns of Urbanization in Early Southern Mesopotamia," in: P.J. Ucko, R. Tringham, and G. Dimbleby (eds.) *Man, Settlement, and Urbanism,* pp. 735–749. London.
G. Algaze, 1989. "The Uruk Expansion: Cross-Cultural Exchange in Early Mesopotamian Civilization," *Current Anthropology* 30: 571–608.
R. Amiran, 1969. *Ancient Pottery of the Holy Land.* Ramat Gan.
R. Amiran et al., 1978. *Early Arad: the Chalcolithic Settlement and Early Bronze Age City.* Jerusalem.
R. Amiran and N. Porat, 1984. "The Basalt Vessels of the Chalcolithic Period and Early Bronze Age I," *Tel Aviv* 11: 11–19.
S. Angress, 1959. "Mammalian Remains from Horvat Beter (Beersheva)," ʿAtiqot 2: 53–71.
U. Avner, 1984. "Ancient Cult Sites in the Negev and Sinai Deserts," *Tel Aviv* 11: 115–131.
P. Bar-Adon, 1980. *The Cave of the Treasure.* Jerusalem.
_____ , 1989. "Mitzpeh Shalem. Excavations in the Judean Desert by P. Bar-Adon," ʿAtiqot 9: 50–60.
Y. Bartov, 1985. Geological Map in: R. Adler et al. (eds.), *Atlas of Israel,* p. 9. Tel Aviv.
O. Bar-Yosef, A. Belfer, A. Goren and P. Smith, 1977. "The Nawamis near ʿEin Huderah (Eastern Sinai)," *IEJ* 27: 65–88.
O. Bar-Yosef, A. Belfer-Cohen, A. Goren, I. Hershkovitz, O. Ilan, H.K. Mienis and B. Sass, 1986. "Nawamis and Habitation Sites near Gebel Gunna, Southern Sinai," *IEJ* 36:121–165.
I. Beit-Arieh, 1977. *South Sinai in the Early Bronze Age* (unpublished Ph.D. dissertation, Tel Aviv University).
_____ , 1981. "An Early Bronze Age II Site near Sheikh ʾAwad in Southern Sinai," *Tel Aviv* 8: 95–127.
_____ , 1986. "Two Cultures in Southern Sinai in the Third Millennium B.C.," *BASOR* 263: 27–54.
I. Beit-Arieh and R. Gophna, 1976. "Early Bronze Age II Sites in Wadi el Qudeirat (Kadesh Barnea)," *Tel Aviv* 3: 142–150.
_____ , 1981. "The Early Bronze Age II Settlement at Ein el Qudeirat," *Tel Aviv* 8: 128–133.
A. Betts, 1989. "The Solubba: Nonpastoral Nomads in Arabia," *BASOR* 274: 61–70.
A. Ben-Tor, 1982. "The Relations between Egypt and the Land of Canaan during the Third Millennium B.C.," *Journal of Jewish Studies* 33: 3–17.
_____ , 1989. "Byblos and the Early Bronze Age I of Palestine," in P. de Miroschedji (ed.), *L'urbanisation de la Palestine à l'âge du Bronze ancien B.A.R. Inter.* 527, pp. 41–52. Oxford.
R. Benedict, 1934. *Patterns of Culture.* New York.
B. Brandel, 1989. "Observations on the Early Bronze Age Strata of Tel Erani," in P. de Miroschedji (ed.), *L'urbanisation de la Palestine à l'âge du Bronze ancien. B.A.R. Inter.* 527, pp. 357–388. Oxford.
F. Burian, and E. Friedman, 1987. "Chalcolithic Borer Industry at Site 103 — Nahal Nitzana," *Mitequfat Haʾeven* 20: 160–172.
V.G. Childe, 1950. "The Urban Revolution," *Town Planning Review* 21: 3–17.
_____ , 1951. *Man Makes Himself.* New York.
C. Commenge-Pellerin, 1987. *La poterie de Abu Matar et de l'Ouad Zumeili (Beersheva) au IVe millénaire avant l'ère chrétienne.* Paris.
S. Davis, 1976. "Mammal Bones from the Early Bronze Age City of Arad, Northern Negev, Israel: Some Implications Concerning Human Exploitation," *Journal of Archaeological Science* 3: 153–164.

C. Epstein, 1982. "Cult Symbols in Chalcolithic Palestine," *Bolettino del Centro di Studi Preistorici* 19: 63–82.

——— , 1985. "Laden Animal Figurines from the Chalcolithic Period in Palestine," *BASOR* 258: 53–62.

D. Esse, 1982. "Beyond Subsistence: Beth Yerah and Northern Palestine in the Early Bronze Age." (unpublished Ph.D. dissertation, University of Chicago).

K.V. Flannery, 1976. "Contextual Analysis of Ritual Paraphernalia from Formative Oaxaca," in K.V. Flannery (ed.), *The Early Mesoamerican Village*, pp. 333–344. New York.

I. Gilead, n.d. "Farmers and Herders in the Northern Negev in the Chalcolithic Period," in O. Bar-Yosef and A. Khazanov (eds.), *Pastoralism in the Levant*.

I. Gilead and D. Alon, 1988. "Excavations of Protohistoric Sites in the Nahal Besor and the Late Neolithic of the Northern Negev," *Mitequfat Ha'even* 21: 109–130.

I. Gilead and Y. Goren, 1986. "Stations of the Chalcolithic Period in Nahal Sekher, Northern Negev," *Paléorient* 12: 83–90.

——— , 1989. "Petrographic Analyses of Fourth Millennium B.C. Pottery and Stone Vessels from the Northern Negev, Israel," *BASOR* 275: 5–14.

R. Gophna, 1976. "Egyptian Immigration into Southern Canaan during the First Dynasty?," *Tel Aviv* 3: 31–37.

Y. Goren, 1989. "Contacts between Transjordan and Israel during the Chalcolithic Period — Evidence from Petrography of Pottery, Stone and Metal Artifacts," *Mitequfat Ha'even* 22: 148–150.

Y. Goren and I. Gilead, 1986. "Quaternary Environment and Manat Nahal Sekher, Northern Negev," *Mitequfat Ha'even* 19: 66–79.

Z. Greenhut, 1989. "Flint Tools," in P. Bar-Adon, *Excavations in the Judean Desert, 'Atiqot* 9: 60–77.

M. Haiman, 1989. *Shepherds and Farmers in the Kadesh Barnea Region.* Midreshet Sede Boqer.

J.W. Hanbury-Tenison, 1986. *The Late Chalcolithic to Early Bronze I Transition in Palestine and Transjordan.* B.A.R. Inter. 311. Oxford.

A. Hauptmann and G. Weisberger, 1987. "Archaeometallurgical and Mining — Archaeological Investigations in the Area of Feinan, Wadi 'Arabah (Jordan)," *Annual of the Department of Antiquities of Jordan* 31: 419–437.

A. Hauptmann, G. Weisberger and E.A. Knauf, 1985. Archäometallürgische und bergbauarchäologische Untersuchungen im Gebiet von Feinan, Wadi Arabah (Jordanien)," *Die Anschrift* 37 (5–6): 163–195.

J.B. Hennessy, 1967. *The Foreign Relations of Palestine in the Early Bronze Age.* London.

D. Heskell, 1983. "A Model for the Adoption of Metallurgy in the Ancient Middle East," *Current Anthropology* 24: 362–366.

O. Ilan and M. Sebbane, 1989. "Copper Metallurgy, Trade and the Urbanization of Southern Canaan in the Chalcolithic and Early Bronze Age," in P. de Miroschedji (ed.), *L'urbanisation de la Palestine à l'âge du Bronze ancien.* B.A.R. Inter. 527, pp. 139–162. Oxford.

T. Josien, 1955. "La faune chalcolithique des gisements palestiniens de Bir ed-Safadi et Bir Abou Matar," *IEJ* 5: 246–256.

A. Kempinsky, 1978. *The Rise of an Urban Culture: The Urbanization of Palestine in the Early Bronze Age, Israel Ethnographic Studies* 4. Jerusalem.

——— , 1982. "Early Bronze Age Urbanization of Palestine, Some Topics in a Debate," *IEJ* 33: 235–241.

——— , 1989. "Urbanization and Metallurgy in Southern Canaan," in P. de Miroschedji (ed.), *L' urbanisation de la Palestine à l'âge du Bronze ancien.* B.A.R. Inter. 527, pp. 163–168. Oxford.

C.A. Key, 1980. "The Trace Element Composition of the Copper and Copper Alloy Artifacts of the Nahal Mishmar Hoard," in P. Bar-Adon, *The Cave of the Treasure*, pp. 238–243. Jerusalem.

B. Kozloff, 1981. "Pastoral Nomadism in Sinai: An Ethnoarchaeological Study," *Production pastorale et société: bulletin d'écologie et d'anthropologie des sociétés pastorales* 8: 19–24.

P.W. Lapp, 1968. "Bab edh-Dhra Tomb A 76 and Early Bronze I in Palestine," *BASOR* 189: 12–41.

H. Lernau, 1978. "Faunal Remains," in R. Amiran et al. *Early Arad, the Chalcolithic Settlement and Early Bronze Age City*, pp. 83–113. Jerusalem.

T.E. Levy, 1986. "The Chalcolithic Period," *Biblical Archaeologist* 49: 82–108.

T.E. Levy and D. Alon, 1985. "Shiqmim: A Chalcolithic Village and Mortuary Center in the Northern Negev," *Paléorient* 11,1: 71–83.

T.E. Levy and N. Menahem, 1987. "The Ceramic Industry at Shiqmim: Typological and Spatial Considerations," in T.E. Levy (ed.), *Shiqmim I, B.A.R. Inter.* 356, pp. 313–332. Oxford.

E. Macdonald, 1932. *Beth Peleth* II. London.

B. Maisler (Mazar), M. Stekelis and M. Avi-Yonah, 1952. "The Excavations at Beit Yerah (Khirbet Kerak) 1944–1946,"*IEJ* 2: 165ff, 218ff.

L. Marfoe, 1980. Reviews of A. Kempinski "Rise of an Urban Culture" and R. Amiran et al., "Early Arad," *Journal of Near Eastern Studies* 39: 315–322.

S. Milstein, 1981. "The Flint Implements," in I. Beit-Arieh, "Early Bronze Age II Site near Sheikh ʾAwad in Southern Sinai," *Tel Aviv* 8: 119–125.

P. de Miroschedji, 1986."Céramiques et mouvements de populations: le cas de la Palestine au IIIe millénaire," in M.Th. Barrelet and J. Gardin, *A propos des interpretations archéologiques de la poterie*, pp. 10–46. Paris.

P.R.S. Moorey, 1988. "The Chalcolithic Hoard from Nahal Mishmar, Israel, in Context," *World Archaeology* 20: 171–189.

A. Nissenbaum, A. Serban, R. Amiran and O. Ilan, 1984. "Dead Sea Asphalt from the Excavations at Tel Arad and Small Tel Malhata," *Paléorient* 10,1: 157–161.

E.D. Oren, 1989. "Early Bronze Age Settlement in North Sinai: A Model for Egypto-Canaanite Interconnections," in P. de Miroschedji (ed.), *L'urbanisation de la Palestine à l'âge du Bronze ancien. B.A.R. Inter.* 527, pp. 389–406. Oxford.

J. Perrot, 1955. "Excavations at Tell Abu Matar, near Beersheva," *IEJ* 5: 17–40, 73–84, 167–189.

_____ , 1968. "La préhistoire palestinienne," *Supplément au dictionnaire de la Bible* 8: 286–446.

_____ , 1984. "Structure d'habitat, mode de la vie et environnement: les villages souterrains des pasteurs de Beersheva dans le sud d'Israël au IVe millénaire avant l'ère chrétienne," *Paléorient* 10: 75–92.

N. Porat, 1986. "Appendix: Petrography of Sherds from Gunna 100 and Gunna 25," *IEJ* 36: 165–167.

_____ , 1989. "Petrography of Pottery from Southern Israel and Sinai," in: P. de Miroschedji (ed.), *L' urbanisation de la Palestine à l'âge du bronze ancien. B.A.R. Inter.* 527, pp. 169–188. Oxford.

R. Potaszkin and K. Bar-Avi, 1980. "A Material Investigation of the Metal Objects from the Nahal Mishmar Treasure," in P. Bar-Adon, *The Cave of the Treasure*, pp. 235–237. Jerusalem.

C. Redman, 1978. *The Rise of Civilization*. San Francisco.

C. Renfrew, 1984. "The Anatomy of Innovation," in C. Renfrew, *Approaches to Social Archaeology*, pp. 390–418. Edinburgh.

S.A. Rosen, 1983a. "The Tabular Scraper Trade: A Model for Material Culture Dispersion," *BASOR* 249: 79–86.

_____ , 1983b. *Lithics in the Bronze and Iron Ages in Israel* (unpublished Ph.D. dissertation, University of Chicago).

_____ , 1983c. "The Canaanean Blade and the Early Bronze Age," *IEJ* 33: 15–29.

_____ , 1986. "The Analysis of Trade and Craft Specialization in the Chalcolithic: Comparisons from Different Realms of Material Culture," *Michmanim* 3: 21–32.

_____ , 1987a. "The Potentials of Lithic Analysis in the Chalcolithic of the Northern Negev," in T.E. Levy (ed.), *Shiqmim I. B.A.R. Inter.* 356, pp. 295–312. Oxford.

_____ , 1987b. "Demographic Trends in the Negev Highlands: Preliminary Results from the Emergency Survey," *BASOR* 266: 45–58.

_____ , 1988. "A Preliminary Note on the Egyptian Component of the Chipped Stone Assemblage from Tel ʿErani," *IEJ* 38: 105–116.

_____ , 1989. "The Analysis of Early Bronze Age Chipped Stone Industries: A Summary Statement," in P. de Miroschedji (ed.), *L'urbanisation de la Palestine à l'âge du Bronze ancien. B.A.R. Inter.* 527, pp. 199–222. Oxford.

_____ , n.d. "The Chipped Stone Tools from the Sinai Survey," (unpublished manuscript).

S.A. Rosen, and A.N. Goring-Morris, n.d. "Har Qeren 15," (unpublished manuscript).

A. Roshwalb, 1981. *Protohistory in the Wadi Ghazzeh: A Typological and Technological Study Based on the Macdonald Excavations* (unpublished Ph.D. dissertation, London University).

B. Rothenberg, 1972. *Were These King Solomon's Mines?.* London.

———, 1979. *Sinai.* Bern.

T. Schick, 1978. "Flint Implements," in R. Amiran et al., *Early Arad: The Chalcolithic Settlement and Early Bronze Age City*, pp. 58–63. Jerusalem.

E. Service, 1962. *Primitive Social Organization.* New York.

———, 1978. "Classical and Modern Theories of the Origins of Government," R. Cohen and E. Service (eds.), *Origin of the State*, pp. 21–34. Philadelphia.

S. Shalev and P. Northover, 1987. "Chalcolithic Metalworking from Shiqmim," in T.E. Levy (ed.), *Shiqmim* I. *B.A.R. Inter.* 356, pp. 356–371. Oxford.

S. Shalev, Y. Goren, T.E. Levi and P. Northover, n.d. "A Chalcolithic Macehead from the Negev: Technological Aspects and Cultural Implications," (unpublished manuscript).

S. Shennan, 1982. "Exchange and Ranking: The Role of Amber in the Earlier Bronze Age of Europe," in C. Renfrew and S. Shenan, *Ranking, Resource and Exchange*, pp. 33–45. Cambridge.

M. Tadmor, 1989. "The Judean Desert Treasure from Nahal Mishmar: A Chalcolithic Traders' Hoard," in B.B. Williams and A. Leonard, Jr. (eds.), *Essays in Ancient Civilization Presented to Helene J. Kantor. Studies in Ancient Oriental Civilization* 47, pp. 249–261. Chicago.

M. Tosi, 1984. "The Notion of Craft Specialization and its Representation in the Archaeological Record of Early States in the Turanian Basin," in M. Spriggs, (ed.), *Marxist Perspectives in Archaeology*, pp. 22–52. Cambridge.

J. Weinstein, 1984. "The Significance of Tel Areini for Egyptian-Palestinian Relations at the Beginning of the Bronze Age," *BASOR* 256: 61–69.

P. Wiessner, 1983. "Style and Social Information in Kalahari San Projectile Points," *American Antiquity* 48: 253–276.

H.T. Wright, 1978. "Toward an Explanation of the Origin of the State," in R. Cohen and E. Service (eds.), *Origin of the State*, pp. 49–68. Philadelphia.

S. Yeivin, 1960. "Early Contacts between Canaan and Egypt," *IEJ* 10: 193–203.

O. Yogev, 1983. "A Fifth Millennium Sanctuary in the ʿUvda Valley," *Qadmoniot* 16: 118–122 (Hebrew).

C. Zaccagnini, 1983. "Patterns of Mobility among Ancient Near Eastern Craftsmen," *Journal of Near Eastern Studies* 42: 245–264.

Metal Production and Society at Tel Dan

Sariel Shalev

> In answering the question "how was that artifact made?" the archaeologist can go a long way. (Hodder 1982: 92)

Two years ago, in 1988, the results of the symposium: "Bronzeworking centres of Western Asia during the Iron Age," was published by the British Museum (Curtis 1988). In this up-dated presentation of archaeometallurgical data, not even one actual metalworking site was described. This, I think, illustrates better than anything else the striking lack of knowledge concerning metal production sites, especially during the beginning of the Iron Age.

Roger Moorey, in concluding his opening lecture at this symposium (Curtis 1988: 30), stated:

> The bronzeworking centres of Western Asia in the mature Iron Age were an aspect of complex craft interrelationships within a great variety of functioning societies. These centres will never be properly understood unless we strive to set them into the appropriate historical context in all its political, social and economic diversity.

The lack of on-site archaeological knowledge concerning metal working and the theoretical guidelines for its proper interpretation are the *raison d'etre* for this paper on metal production and society at Tel Dan.

Research Methodology

During the excavations at Tel Dan, under the direction of A. Biran, metallurgical industrial remains dating to the 12th–11th centuries B.C.E. were unearthed mainly by R. Ben-Dov. A program of compositional and metallographic research has recently been carried out to address fundamental, yet unanswerable, questions:

1) What exactly was the nature of this activity?

2) How was it conducted?

3) Why was it conducted?

For this purpose, the chemical composition of 13 slag pieces as well as 18 metal samples was analyzed by means of Atomic Absorption Spectrometry [AAS] (at the Institute of Archaeology, Tel Aviv University) and Electron Microprobe Analysis [EMPA] (at the Department of Materials, Oxford University). When possible, metallography and hardness were also recorded.

The archaeometallurgical data recovered from this material is used here to reconstruct the character of this metallurgical activity in order to better understand its role in the Iron Age I society of Tel Dan.

Archaeological Evidence

To date, remains of metalworking have been unearthed mainly in Area B on the southern part of the Tel (for details of the archaeological stratification and pottery typology see: Biran 1989).

The archaeological data consists mainly of several stone circles and ash pits in an open area. In association with these structures, remains of over 10 tuyères, 20 crucibles, slags and approximately 20 metal pieces and numerous small finds were discovered.

The earliest evidence for metallurgical activity dates to the 16th century B.C.E. In a limited excavated zone, a small *tabun* was revealed in an open courtyard of a building. Crucible remains, broken tuyères and small metal objects were found in its vicinity. The main archaeological evidence belongs to the beginning of the Iron Age, 12th–11th centuries B.C.E. At that time, Tel Dan was a small unfortified village. Its inhabitants left behind remains of simple pottery of local types, as well as some collared-rim jars and Philistine pottery known mainly in the south (Frankel 1990: 30). This Iron Age community used Area B for open air metal workshops.

The earliest remains from that period (Stratum VI) are stone circles and ash pits in an open area defined by the ruins of Late Bronze Age buildings. Later in Iron I (Strata V–IV), Building 7082 was constructed. The metal installations were at that time built mainly in the open courtyards in the vicinity of this structure. Crucibles and tuyères, as well as metal pieces and objects, were found mainly in and around these installations and in several of the rooms (for further details see: Biran 1989).

The following Iron I remains were sampled for metallurgical analysis:

Table 1A
Crucible Slags

No.	Locus	Description	Stratum	Reference
1.*	7060	crucible remains	IV	first publication
2.	7015	crucible (thin slag)	IV	Biran 1989:128
3.	7176	bottom of crucible	IV	first publication
4.	7068	bottom of crucible	V	Biran 1989:125
5.*	7125	ash near crucible	V	first publication
6.	7131	near crucible remains	V	first publication
7.*	7126	crucible in ash pit	V	first publication
8.*	7119	bottom of crucible	V	first publication
9.	7115	inside crucible	V	first publication
10.	7115	outside crucible	V	first publication
11.	7160	bottom of crucible	V	first publication
12.*	7079	edge of crucible	VI	first publication
13.	7169	crucible remains	VI	first publication

* Metal prills found during the preparation of slag sample
Nos. 1,5,7,8,12 were analyzed separately.

Table 1B
Metal Objects (weight in gm. and measurements in cm.)

No.	Locus	Object	Condition	Weight	Length	Width	Thick.	Stratum
1.	7060	strip	broken	+13	+16.80	0.85	0.26	IV
2.	7060	plaque	broken	+0	+1.37	+0.86	0.04	IV
3.	7060	small awl	intact	1	2.29	0.44	0.26	IV
4.	7015	handle(?)	broken	+40	+8.53	1.88	0.72	IV
5.	7122	ingot	broken	+64	+4.53	+4.21	1.35	IV
6.	7114	awl/spatula	damaged	15	13.26	0.78	0.51	IV
7.	7052	awl	broken	+5	+4.08	0.43	0.43	IV
8.	7133	sock. point	intact	120	16.00	2.67	2.20	V
						1.64	1.00	
9.	7125	sock. point	intact	38	6.94	2.41	1.95	V
						1.30	1.01	
10.	7131	flat axe	intact	324	13.00	4.50	1.17	V
11.	7126	hook	intact	3	4.50	0.60	0.36	V
12.	7117	pin	intact	4	12.86	0.20	0.20	V
13.	7020	needle	intact	10	14.60	0.86	0.56	V
14.	4202	handle(?)	broken	+14	+3.56	+2.13	0.69	V
15.	4202	arrowhead	damaged	10	9.50	2.00	0.40	V
16.	7065	arrowhead	intact	8	9.50	1.50	0.40	VI
17.	7079	lump	amorphic	9	3.58	1.69	0.92	VI
18.	7169	awl/spatula	broken	+10	+6.79	0.62	0.52	VI

In addition to this Iron I material, one metal object (a pin) and one piece of LB I slag were analyzed for comparison.

Metallurgical Data

Chemical compositions are shown in the following table. For a detailed description of the methodology and detection limits see: Shalev and Northover (in press).

Table 2A

Elemental analysis of samples from crucible slags by AAS (values in wt.-percent). (Metal prills from slag sample Nos. 1, 5, 7, 8 and 12 are presented separately in Table 2B).

No.	Fe₂O₃	Co	Ni	Cu	Zn	As	Ag	Sn	Sb	Au	Pb	Bi	SiO₂	CaO	MgO	MnO	Al₂O₃
1.	6.8	0.03	0.02	62.7	0.02	0.07	0.02	1.35	n.d.	0.01	0.07	n.d.	16.8	4.13	0.36	0.11	2.87
2.	32.7	0.30	0.02	25.2	0.15	0.02	0.01	0.28	0.01	0.01	1.20	n.d.	19.8	8.00	0.54	0.60	6.40
3.	11.6	0.03	0.02	27.2	0.02	0.14	0.01	1.13	0.01	0.01	0.15	0.01	16.7	7.86	0.96	0.06	4.20
4.	21.4	0.15	0.04	46.8	0.11	0.06	0.01	0.65	n.d.	0.01	0.27	n.d.	13.3	7.00	0.74	0.74	3.50
5.	1.6	tr.	0.02	66.5	0.02	0.14	0.02	0.10	0.02	0.01	0.13	n.d.	7.4	1.25	0.12	0.01	0.46
6.	16.5	0.08	0.03	31.4	0.03	0.06	0.01	0.52	0.01	0.02	0.19	0.01	8.7	6.10	0.67	0.60	1.30
7.	2.8	0.01	0.01	43.6	0.02	0.11	0.01	0.55	0.01	0.01	0.14	n.d.	7.8	2.85	0.23	0.03	0.56
8.	6.8	0.01	0.02	40.6	0.08	0.13	0.01	1.66	0.02	0.01	0.11	n.d.	14.6	7.75	0.63	0.09	2.78
9.	12.6	0.08	0.01	18.1	0.15	0.06	0.01	0.14	0.01	0.01	0.08	0.01	25.8	12.2	1.46	0.64	7.33
10.	1.8	tr.	0.01	44.5	0.01	0.33	0.01	0.07	0.01	tr.	0.25	n.d.	12.1	1.20	0.14	0.01	1.57
11.	7.5	0.01	0.02	23.8	0.02	0.11	0.01	0.11	0.01	0.01	0.14	0.01	35.2	2.60	0.46	0.14	12.8
12.	9.1	0.02	0.01	12.3	0.03	0.02	0.01	0.05	n.d.	0.01	0.10	n.d.	48.5	10.6	0.68	0.21	15.3
13.	44.9	0.16	0.03	7.4	0.24	0.10	tr.	0.93	0.01	0.01	0.10	0.01	20.6	12.6	1.52	0.55	7.06

Table 2B

Elemental analysis of metal prills from crucible slags by AAS (values in wt.-percent)

No.	Fe	Co	Ni	Cu	Zn	As	Ag	Sn	Sb	Au	Pb	Bi	total
1*	1.60	0.01	0.04	91.0	0.03	0.28	0.10	4.73	0.06	0.01	0.11	n.d.	98.0
5*	0.27	n.d.	0.02	94.5	0.04	0.50	0.02	0.14	0.12	0.01	0.15	n.d.	95.8
7*	0.42	0.01	0.03	85.0	0.05	0.26	0.04	6.77	0.04	0.01	0.16	n.d.	92.8
8*	0.84	0.01	0.02	84.6	0.04	0.34	0.03	1.85	n.d.	n.d.	0.10	n.d.	87.8
12*	0.20	n.d.	0.02	96.5	0.05	0.08	0.10	0.18	n.d.	0.01	0.08	n.d.	97.2

Table 2C

Elemental analysis of metal objects by AAS (1–5, 8–10, 17–18) and EMPA (6–7, 11–16) (values in wt.-percent). To relate AAS to EMPA data, nos. 2, 3, 5, 10, 17 were analyzed by both techniques.

No.	Fe	Co	Ni	Cu	Zn	As	Ag	Sn	Sb	Au	Pb	Bi	total
1.	0.09	0.01	0.05	92.4	0.06	0.63	0.07	4.50	0.09	0.01	0.33	n.d.	98.2
2.	0.66	n.d.	0.02	69.8	0.08	0.36	0.08	1.40	0.04	0.01	0.09	n.d.	72.5
	0.43	n.d.	0.03	97.7	n.d.	0.61	0.03	0.95	0.03	n.d.	0.18	0.03	EMPA
3.	0.18	tr.	0.02	76.0	0.03	0.31	0.06	2.81	0.14	0.01	0.25	n.d.	79.8
	0.08	tr.	0.02	97.6	n.d.	0.20	0.04	2.30	0.12	tr.	0.27	n.d.	EMPA
4.	0.09	0.01	0.04	90.4	0.04	0.46	0.09	7.95	0.08	0.01	0.39	n.d.	99.6
5.	2.43	0.03	0.02	90.3	0.10	0.13	0.01	n.d.	n.d.	0.01	0.53	n.d.	93.6
	3.50	0.05	0.03	94.8	0.08	0.29	tr.	n.d	tr.	n.d.	1.29	n.d.	EMPA
6.	0.04	n.d.	0.01	94.2	n.d.	0.33	0.03	4.69	n.d.	n.d.	0.69	0.02	EMPA
7.	0.31	0.01	0.03	92.5	n.d.	0.32	0.04	6.26	0.21	tr.	0.35	n.d.	EMPA
8.	0.22	n.d.	0.01	74.7	0.03	0.67	0.05	1.57	0.03	n.d.	0.34	n.d.	77.6
9.	0.55	n.d.	0.01	67.7	0.09	0.52	0.10	4.24	0.06	0.01	0.42	n.d.	73.7
10.	0.24	0.01	0.02	98.4	0.05	0.50	0.09	0.42	0.04	tr.	0.17	n.d.	99.9
	0.28	tr.	0.02	99.0	0.01	0.18	0.05	0.32	0.02	n.d.	0.13	n.d.	EMPA
11.	0.44	0.02	0.06	97.1	n.d.	1.06	0.08	1.15	0.03	n.d.	0.06	0.01	EMPA
12.	0.65	0.02	0.04	95.2	n.d.	0.59	1.06	1.76	0.13	0.12	0.44	n.d.	EMPA
13.	0.36	0.01	0.04	97.0	n.d.	0.46	0.02	2.05	0.01	n.d.	0.02	0.02	EMPA
14.	0.14	0.03	0.03	88.2	n.d.	0.31	0.02	11.0	0.01	n.d.	0.21	n.d.	EMPA
15.	0.56	0.01	0.03	95.6	n.d.	0.45	0.07	2.80	0.04	0.05	0.43	n.d.	EMPA
16.	1.14	0.02	0.07	96.7	n.d.	1.40	0.07	0.34	0.08	n.d.	0.13	0.01	EMPA
17.	0.05	0.05	0.02	94.8	0.03	0.06	0.05	4.38	0.03	0.02	1.12	n.d.	99.6
	0.06	0.01	0.04	93.7	n.d.	tr.	0.04	4.90	0.02	n.d.	1.15	tr.	EMPA
18.	0.11	0.04	0.07	75.0	0.08	0.46	0.07	8.91	0.05	n.d.	0.25	n.d.	85.0

The total for EMPA is normalized to 100 percent, not taking into consideration the presence of sulfide in the range of .1–.3 percent (except in No. 5 where it reaches 2.13 percent).

Metallographic Descriptions of Artifacts

1. Metal plaque (Table 1B, 2) surface of whole object. Heavily corroded; very extensive intergranular corrosion; some elongated sulphide inclusions. Fully recrystallized equiaxed grain structure with annealing twins; grain dia.= 20–30$^{\mu}$; undeformed, no slip traces or coring etched. Plaque area has been cold worked and annealed with very little, if any, final cold work; total reduction ≈ 60–70 percent; annealing time and temperature have been sufficient for homogenization; annealing temperature ca. 700°C. Object too thin and corroded for hardness test.

2. Small awl (Table 1B, 3) surface of whole object. Surface corrosion mainly at tips; some intergranular corrosion; numerous elongated small sulphide inclusions. Fully recrystallized equiaxed grain structure with annealing twins; grain dia.= 15–20$^{\mu}$; slightly deformed. Grain deformation and slip traces vary across the awl section and tips; from undeformed grains with few slip traces to elongated grains with a distorted pattern of duplex slip. Awl area has been cold worked and annealed with final cold work varying between 10–15 percent at one surface to 35–40 percent at the other and 50–60 percent at one tip; total reduction ≈ 70–80 percent; annealing time and temperature have not been sufficient for total homogenization; annealing temperature ca. 550°. Hardness = 140 (center) — 174 Hv2.5 (edge).

3. Ingot piece (Table 1B, 5) sample of whole section. Thick corrosion layer on convex surface; heavily pitted surfaces and interdendritic corrosion; numerous sulphide inclusions up to 65$^{\mu}$ in dia. As-cast; grain dia.= 125$^{\mu}$; thick α phase dendrites; coring; no interdendritic phase visible. Hardness = 104 (near convex edge) — 115 (center) — 121 Hv2.5 (near straight edge).

4. Awl (Table 1B, 7) sample of middle section. Heavily corroded; very extensive intergranular corrosion; some sulphide inclusions. Fully recrystallized equiaxed grain structure with annealing twins; grain dia.= 30$^{\mu}$; undeformed grain structure; no coring. Sample area has been cold worked and annealed with very little, if any, final cold work; annealing time and temperature have been just sufficient for homogenization; annealing temperature ca. 650–700°C. Hardness = 95.8 Hv2.5.

5. Flat axe (Table 1B, 10) sample from angle of side. Corroded; heavily pitted surface. The pitting follows interdendritic lines; evenly distributed sulphide inclusions varying in size and shape. As-cast; grain dia.= 100$^{\mu}$; thick α phase dendrites; coring; no interdendritic phase visible. Hardness = 51.5 Hv2.5.

6. Pin (Table 1B, 12) sample from the bent head. Heavily corroded; very extensive intergranular corrosion with transgranular branching; very few sulphide inclusions. Fully recrystallized equiaxed grain structure with annealing twins; grain dia. = 10$^{\mu}$; straight slip traces and very limited grain deformation; no coring. Sample area has been cold worked and annealed with some subsequent cold work; final cold work ≈ 20 percent; annealing time and temperature have been sufficient for homogenization; annealing temperature above 650°C. Hardness = 125 Hv2.5.

7. Metal lump (Table 1B, 17) sample of whole cross-section. Heavily corroded; pitted surface and interdendritic corrosion; several gas holes in the cast. As-cast; uneven

dendritic structure: mainly thick α dendrites, 4 μ arms spacing and interdendritic gray (high tin) phase with lead segregation; some cavities of thin α dendrites in wider inter-dendritic matrix, mainly corroded. Hardness = 95.8–96.7 Hv2.5.

Discussion

The analysis of slags and metal prills in slags is not a reliable guide to the actual composition of the melted bronze. Copper and tin will diffuse into the slag zone at different rates, and also bear different potential for oxidation, aside from consideration of the decomposition of molten bronze in oxidizing conditions. The degree of metallurgical quality control exercised in terms of alloying and finish can only be accurately determined from known products of the industry.

Taking these guidelines into consideration, the analyzed slags (Table 1A, 1–13) represent mainly a bronze-working industry of copper with varying amounts of tin. Although a great variability in the tin content can be detected in different areas of the same slag (as determined by means of EMPA in Table 1A 1, 2, 6, 7, 9, 13), the overall diversity (as presented in the AAS analyses) seems to reflect a bronze industry with an uncontrolled amount of tin in the metal.

Tin is detected in all samples; five have tin <.15 percent, while the remaining eight have tin >.25 percent, with four values >1 percent. The low tin content in prills is equally evident by low tin in slags and therefore enables us to present the prills analyses separately. Comparing the bulk analyses of the slags with the AAS analysis of the metal prills and the EMPA of five of the samples cited above, shows mainly tin bronze as well as some copper (up to .14 Sn) production. It is worth mentioning here that in cases where tin is not present as an alloying element, it is still there as one of the major impurities.

A good example of the tin content variation within one slag is A 6. Although the average tin content detected by AAS is relatively low, a microanalysis reveals small bronze prills with up to 40 percent Sn that were "trapped" between the crucible and the slag.

The same situation, although not so extreme, was detected in other samples. Slag A 13 reveals in the AAS analysis an average of less than 1 percent Sn while the tin content in some small metal prills is more than double this. The average amount of tin detected in slag A 2 was also relatively low (.3 percent Sn) while microanalyses of some bronze prills in this slag reveals up to 5 percent tin. In various slags (e.g. A 1, 2, 7) the amount of tin and iron in the metal prills was significantly enriched by the corrosion.

The copper and iron oxides as well as calcium iron olivines (in slag A 7) represent a temperature of ca. 1200°C. The low amount of iron oxide in the silicate matrix of the slags (≈ 1 percent in A 7) could represent a melting process. The exceptionally high iron oxide content in slag A 13 could result from melting metal with some iron, like the piece of ingot B 5.

The relatively high amount of copper and copper/bronze prills in the slags as well as the varying amount of tin could reflect a melting/remelting process as opposed to the first stages of metal production (smelting and refining).

The results of previous laboratory simulations of bronze-making (Wayman et al. 1988) show that similar slags could be formed by the attack of the melt on the crucible (or furnace) lining. This could be achived by co-fusion of metallic copper and tin ingots as well as bronze scrap remelting.

The metal finds were scattered at the production area, within and in the immediate vicinity of the metal working installations that could serve as the main metal source for this local industry, which was most probably based upon the remelting of scrap.

The metal analyses (B 1–18) represent (with the exception of B 5, 10 and 16) a bronze production of copper mixed with different amounts of tin (1.2–11 percent Sn). This kind of chemical composition with such tin variation is not exceptional among the known data of metal composition of finds from Iron I sites in the eastern Mediterranean (Waldbaum 1989). Here the variability in the tin content as well as the amount of impurities (mainly: arsenic, lead and iron) point, as in the case of the slags, to an uncontrolled bronze production.

Up to now, eight intact objects were found in the immediate vicinity of the Iron I metal production installations on the tell. They include small objects like a pin, needle, hook and arrowheads, as well as three larger items.

Of the two arrowheads, one (B 15) could be a product (according to its metal composition) as well as a source material (due to its size) in this local industry. The metal composition of the second arrowhead differs from all the others. This small object (B 16) was made of arsenical copper (1.4 percent As) with tin only in the trace level (.3 percent Sn) and more than 1 percent iron. It bears a close resemblance to the metal composition of an LB I pin from L.4647 in the same area on the tell (95.7 percent Cu, 1.5 percent As, .1 percent Sn and 1.3 percent Fe). Therefore, it could have originated in an earlier context and been left for recycling in the Iron I local production.

The arsenic content of all analyzed objects does not exceed .6 percent, except in the aforementioned case and in the metal composition of a small hook (B 11). The 1.1 percent of arsenic as well as 1.2 percent of tin could result from a source-metal containing some earlier pieces (like B 16) in the molten metal scrap.

The two socketed points (B 8–9) were made of low tin bronze (4.2 percent, 1.6 percent Sn). Their metal compositions (low Sn and impurities of As, Pb and Fe) fit well with the analyses of the metal scrap and slags and therefore could well be the end-product of this local industry.

Objects of this type are known also from several other sites, including Hazor, Tell Qasile, Tel Ḥefer, Tel Zeror and Timnaʿ, and could be interpreted as weapons (a spear butt) according to Yadin (1963: 352) or as agricultural tools (the point of a hand pick or a planting stick) according to ethnological parallels (Shalev [forthcoming]).

The unfinished copper flat axe (B 10) is also commonly known at Hazor, Megiddo, ʿAfula, Tell Qasile, and Tel Masos). This object could serve as a nice example of the local metal production at Tel Dan. It was cast from copper with only .4 percent tin into an open mould and was left unfinished, most probably due to its missing edge. It appears that an insufficient amount of metal and the decreased fluidity of molten copper with such a low amount of tin could cause such a casting defect. The metal composition of Sn, As, Pb and Fe coincides with the described data concerning this local industry. It seems that this unfinished cast was left for remelting.

Only two metal objects could not be defined as actual artifacts or fragments thereof. The first (B 17), is a small lump of bronze, presumably left from a local tin bronze cast and saved for remelting. The second (B 15) is a small slice of a round shaped ingot. Its unique metal composition of pure copper with no trace of tin and a high content of iron (2.4 percent) and sulphur (2.1 percent) as well as typological and technological resemblence to finds from sites near the copper mining area in southern Israel (Yotvata and ʿEn Yahav) all testify to a non-indigenous metal product of smelting which was brought to the site probably to be used in the local manufacturing process.

Conclusions

The analytical results may be utilized to answer the questions asked above concerning:
1) the nature of metallurgical activity; 2) its reconstruction; and 3) its interpretation.

1) The metallurgical industry at Tel Dan at the beginning of the Iron Age, consisted mainly of the production of copper-based tin-bronze objects. The appearance of numerous broken bronze artifacts in the immediate vicinity of the crucibles as well as their tin content as compared to the tin content in the slags, all exemplify a local industry based on the remelting of scrap. The bronzesmiths at Tel Dan did not control tin content and therefore could not achieve a steady and optimal percentage of tin in the melt. This is reflected in the varying and relatively low amounts of tin detected. The presence of tin in the metal is, therefore, not the result of deliberate addition, but rather due to its presence in the source material for the melt.

2) The manufacturing process may be reconstructed as follows: The broken metal objects were gathered inside a clay crucible which was placed within a stone circle. It was then covered with wood charcoal and/or other combustible, the remains of which appear as light gray ash. The required temperature was achieved by blowing air through bellows connected to clay tuyères, some of which were found while excavating these installations. The melted bronze was then poured into an open mould, probably made of clay or sand. These casts were then shaped into their final forms through cycles of annealing and hammering.

3) The simple manufacturing process practiced at Tel Dan to a certain extent reflects the socioeconomic situation in this village society during the end of the 2nd

millenium B.C.E. It would not appear to have been a sophisticated and complex industry based upon imported metal ingots for the manufacturing of prestige and/or luxury products. The reconstruction of the metallurgical activities at Tel Dan reflects production based mainly on a local, limited recycling of broken and defective bronze objects as the main raw material in a remelting crucible process. This local village industry not only met local needs, but also supplied a limited marketing area with simple commodities, primarily tools and, to a lesser extent, weapons.

References

A. Biran, 1989. "The Evidence for Metal Industry at Dan," *Eretz-Israel* 20 (Yigael Yadin Memorial Volume): 120–134 (Hebrew).

J. Curtis, (ed.), 1988. *Bronzeworking Centres of Western Asia c. 1000–539 B.C.* London.

G. Frankel, 1990. "Upper Galilee in the Late Bronze-Iron I Transition," in N. Naʾaman and I. Finkelstein (eds.), *From Nomadism to Monarchy*, pp. 16–33. Jerusalem (Hebrew).

I. Hodder, 1982. *The Present Past.* London.

S. Shalev and J. Northover, (in press). "Metal Objects from Shiloh."

S. Shalev et al., (in press). "A Chalcolithic Mace Head from the Negev: Technological Aspects and Cultural Implications."

J.C. Waldbaum, 1989. "Copper, Iron, Tin, Wood: The Start of the Iron Age in the Eastern Mediterranean," *Archeomaterials* 3: 111–122.

M.L. Wayman, M. Gualtieri and R.A. Konzuk, 1988. "Bronze Metallurgy at Roccagloriosa," in R.M. Farquhar, R.G.V. Hancock and L.A. Pavlish (eds.), *Proceedings of the 26th International Archaeometry Symposium*, pp. 128–132. Toronto.

Y. Yadin, 1963. *The Art of Warfare in Biblical Lands.* Norwich.

Mari and Hazor — Trade Relations in the Old Babylonian Period

Abraham Malamat

The excavations at Mari, located on the Euphrates to the north of the Syrian-Iraqi border, have yielded some 25,000 tablets in Akkadian cuneiform from the Old Babylonian Period (the 18th century B.C.E.). By now, some 6,000–odd tablets have been published in over 20 volumes (*ARMT*; the latest is vol. 26/1–2).[1] So far 15 letters and administrative/economic documents mentioning Hazor in northern Palestine have been found at Mari.[2] This is a considerable number, taking into account the vast distance between the two sites. Hazor is the southernmost western locality documented at Mari. True, there may be a reference to a site further south, in central or southern Palestine, but the document is damaged where the toponym in question appears.[3] Thus, Hazor remains at the edge of Mari's economic sphere of influence, but seems to have been politically independent, unlike its northern neighbor Qatna in middle Syria. Aleppo, still further north, held a measure of supremacy over Mari. We can view the relationship between Mari and Hazor as both central and peripheral and as having all the sociological ramifications inherent in such a constellation.[4]

Of the 15 documents attesting to ties between Mari and Hazor, six are letters sent by Zimri-Lim, the last king of Mari, or by his royal officials. These documents testify to the exchange of messengers, some of them having no doubt acted also as merchants. Once or twice a messenger from Hazor was entertained at the palace of Mari together with emissaries from other important cities, but unfortunately we do not know if the person's mission was diplomatic or economic.

The real significance of these documents is their revelation of all the major export goods dispatched from Mari to the West and vice-versa contained in the economic texts. As is well known, the major export to the West was tin, vital for the manufacture of bronze. Bronze is produced by alloying copper with tin at a ratio of 1:7–10. Bronze is much stronger and more practical than pure copper, particularly for the manufacture of tools and weapons. There was a great increase in the use of bronze during the corresponding MB II period in Palestine. Thus, Mari's tin trade with the West flourished. Mari received the tin from the East via Iran, perhaps from Afghanistan and Pakistan. (The recent theory that the Taurus Range in southern Anatolia[5] was the ancient Near East's source of tin remains without decisive proof.) In Syria-Palestine, copper was readily available, but tin — like crude oil in recent times — had to be brought from afar. Two economic texts from Mari relate to shipment of this strategic commodity to Hazor. In one of these documents (*ARMT* 7, 236), Hazor is mentioned together with the land of Yamḥad, whose capital was Aleppo, as the destination of a shipment of about 5 kg. of tin — sufficient to yield 35 to 45 kg. of bronze. The other text, which we call the "tin document"[6] is of considerable significance in several respects. After stating the amount of tin reserves at Mari at the time, it specifies the consignments of the metal to be sent from Mari to various destinations in the West. Certain points of the original reading by Dossin have recently been collated anew, and we base our interpretation on the latter study (*ARMT* 23, 556: 18–32). After recording the largest consignment, which was sent to Aleppo, we read of "8 1/3 minas" or approximately 5 kg. for Ewri-Talma, ruler of Layašim (or Layišim). It is difficult to identify. It is mentioned just before Hazor in our tablet and was first identified with the biblical city of Laish (later Dan),[7] some 30 km. north of Hazor. Indeed, Laish was an important city during the Mari period. However, in a new text, a similar toponym appears in a context in the far north, between Aleppo and Ugarit (*ARMT* 23, 535: iv, 27). The close association of Laish with Hazor in our document may suggest the existence of two cities with the same name, one in northern Palestine and the other far to the north in Syria — a phenomenon of homonyms well known in the Amorite sphere.

The most important city mentioned in the "tin document" is undoubtedly Hazor, which was to receive three tin consignments totalling over 50 minas, that is a quantity sufficient for some 400 kg. of bronze. Although to date excavations at Hazor over an area of 16 acres have yielded very few bronze utensils,[8] we must assume that intensive bronze production took place there in the MB II period. From the "tin document" we learn for the first time the name of Hazor's king: Ibni-Adad, which is an Akkadian form of the local West Semitic name Yabni-Addu. Perhaps another person of Mari's royal dynasty is mentioned, namely Atar-Aya, one of Zimri-Lim's wives. On the basis of as yet unpublished material from Mari, it has been surmised that Atar-Aya was a princess from Hazor — revealing dynastic ties between Mari and northern Palestine, an unanticipated windfall for the historian. The next entry in our document deals with a tin consignment to Qatna in middle Syria. A Caphtorite (a merchant from Crete) is then mentioned and after him a dragoman, who served as the spokesman or chief merchant in the Cretan commercial colony at Ugarit. The seaport of Ugarit cultivated close ties with the Aegean throughout its history, and there is clear archaeological evidence at that site of commerce with the Aegean during the Mari period (Middle Minoan II pottery), such as Kameres ware, a degenerate piece of which was also discovered at Hazor. In short, it seems likely that Mari, especially in the days of Zimri-Lim, was responsible for the intensification of bronze manufacture, or in modern parlance, industrialization — encountered in the Canaanite sphere.

Now let us consider products shipped from Hazor to Mari. In this connection, the economic tablets at Mari are quite laconic and at times vague. There is mention of a three-jar shipment of wine at the Mari palace witnessed by a messenger from Hazor (*ARMT* 24, 75). There is no express statement that the wine jars came from Hazor, but this was most likely the case, as Syria-Palestine was well known for its wine exports and, moreover, wine of the best quality. There are many references to caravans from various places in the West, such as Aleppo or Carchemish, shipping scores of wine and olive oil jars to the palace of Mari.[9] Another export from Hazor was precious objects, sent as gifts to the king of Mari, a diplomatic gesture commonly made by the rulers of this and later periods. Among the precious items from Hazor[10] were gold and silver vessels and gold jewelry (*ARMT* 25, 43, 103, 129), including a ring or, perhaps, a necklace, judging by its weight. Interestingly enough, most of these gifts were sent to Zimri-Lim during his grand journey to Aleppo and further on to Ugarit. The items from Hazor were stored in various depots in distant regions, such as that in Ugarit, which were maintained by the king of Mari.

Relevant to these precious objects is a most intriguing Mari letter which I had the privilege to transliterate and translate.[11] The letter, written by Zimri-Lim, was addressed to his father-in-law Yarim-Lim, king of Aleppo, and pertains to relations between Mari and Hazor. A Mari official or craftsman was dispatched all the way to Hazor to obtain "silver, gold, and precious stone(s)," either as raw materials or as finished products. The Hazorites claimed that the emissary made off without paying for the goods, and thus they detained a merchant caravan from Mari. This document proves that precious metals were commodities *per se* in Canaanite cities in MB II. They are otherwise attested only rarely by such evidence as an Akkadian legal document from Hazor ("200 pieces of silver") and by sporadic finds of gold and silver objects in contexts of this period, mainly in tombs at such sites as Gezer and Megiddo and from a little later at Tell el-ʿAjjul. A few centuries later, large quantities of gold and silver were listed among the booty seized by Thutmose III in northern Palestine, but surely neither Hazor nor any other site within Canaan was the ultimate source of these materials: We must assume that at least the gold was brought from Egypt, the major supplier of this material in antiquity.

Another important aspect reflected in the document under discussion relates to trade customs. The messenger who allegedly stole the precious objects testified that he had received a "bill of sale"[12] but was robbed of it together with the goods at Emar on the Great Euphrates Bend, thus being left without proof of his innocence. In this letter, Zimri-Lim was clearly seeking to prod his father-in-law, the king of Aleppo, into recovering the stolen property, hence, Yarim-Lim was sovereign of northern Syria, including Emar.[13] The major theme underlying the whole episode pertains to international law regarding merchants or agents in trouble on foreign soil. No doubt, this sort of incident led to interstate agreements guaranteeing the protection of merchants abroad, as exemplified at Ugarit, at Babylon and in Egypt.

Finally, we will relate to another item from Syria-Palestine exported to Mari and

Mesopotamia. The Mari documents frequently mention products characteristic of Syria-Palestine from places like Aleppo, Qatna, or the seaport of Byblos or Gebal (Gubla).[14] Among the more important items were different kinds of precious trees and timber, most significantly, cedar. Likewise, horses from Amurru,[15] which had the prestige of modern-day Arabian horses, were exported. Of the greatest significance, however, were the foodstuffs, especially wheat, olive oil, and wine, as well as honey (we are not certain if the latter refers to figs and dates or to honey produced by bees). The above indicate stability in settlement over a long period. The Syro-Palestinian species of the above foodstuffs were considered to be of excellent quality and were highly esteemed in Mari and Mesopotamia in general. Large quantities were shipped to the East. It is noteworthy that the main exports from the West conform to the so-called "seven varieties" of plants in which, according to Deuteronomy 8:8, Canaan excelled: "A land of wheat and barley [grown also in Mesopotamia], of vines, figs and pomegranates [absent in the Mari sources], a land of olive trees and honey." The "Tale of Sinuhe," an Egyptian story from the 20th century B.C.E., that is, some 200 years prior to the Mari documents,[16] also depicts Canaan as such a fertile land.

Notes

1. For a list of the Mari volumes, see A. Malamat, *Mari and the Early Israelite Experience* (Oxford, 1989), p. 124; to which should now be added J.-M. Durand et al., *ARMT* 26, 1–2.

2. For a summary of the texts mentioning Hazor, see note 1.

3. *ARMT* 6, 23: 23. For the various suggestions proposed for the illegible place-name, see Malamat, *Mari* (see note 1), p. 62.

4. Cf., for example, M. Rowlands, M. Larsen, K. Kristiansen (eds.), *Centre and Periphery in the Ancient World* (Cambridge, 1987) and the introduction there by M. Rowlands, "Theoretical Perspectives." For the ancient Near East, see the chapters by L. Marfoe, M.T. Larsen and C. Zagganini.

5. See K.A. Yenner and H. Ozbal, "Tin in the Turkish Taurus Mountains," *Antiquity* 61 (1987): 220–226.

6. Published by G. Dossin, *RA* 64 (1970): 97–106, and cf. A. Malamat, *IEJ* 21 (1971): 31–38 and P. Villard, *ARMT* 23, 528ff.

7. Cf. Malamat, (see note 6).

8. The absence of any bronze artifacts at Hazor in MB II is noteworthy; see the excavation reports, most recently A. Ben-Tor (ed.), *Hazor III–IV. Text* (Jerusalem, 1989).

9. Cf., for example, *ARMT* 7, 238. For the most recent references to these foodstuffs dispatched from the West, channeled here through the city of Emar, see J.-M. Durand, *MARI* 6 (1990): 72ff. For earlier documentation, see, for example, H. Limet, "Les relations entre Mari et la côte Mediterranéene sous la règne de Zimri-Lim," in *Studia Phoenicia* 3 (Leuven, 1989), pp. 13–20, and for previous literature, see note 1.

10. See Limet, "Les relations" (see note 9), pp. 13ff; A. Malamat in *Reflets des deux fleuves (Mélange A. Finet) (Leuven, 1989)*, pp. 117ff.

11. A. Malamat, *JJS* 53 (1982): 71–79; and adjustments as well as additional insights, idem, *BA* 46 (1983): 169–174.

12. Thus, our translation for *kunukku* in line 22 of the document, which means not only "seal," but also "sealed document," referring here, most likely, to a "bill of sale."

13. On the reverse of the letter is a damaged part of about twelve lines. In Malamat, *Mari* (see note 1), p. 66, we suggest that Zimri-Lim demanded help from Yarim-Lim in obtaining the release of a Mari caravan detained by Hazor. A collation of the original tablet (T-H 72–16, to which we had no access) yielded a different but satisfactory reading of the lacuna; see Durand, *MARI* (see note 9), pp. 63ff, who believes lacuna relate to the Mari messenger of whom the king of Aleppo wishes to get hold.

14. On Byblos, see G. Dossin (1939): 111 and idem, *RA* 64 (see note 6).

15. Regarding *Amurru* horses, cf. the Alalaḥ texts, which are slightly later than Mari. See D.J. Wiseman, *The Alalah Tablets* (London, 1953), no. 269, 1.2 49, and cf. B. Landsberger, *JCS* 8 (1954): 56a (n. 103).

16. For a translation of the story of Sinuhe and the relevant passage there, see M. Lichtheim, *Ancient Egyptian Literature* I (Berkeley, 1973), pp. 226ff.

Metallurgical Production and Power Politics on Bronze Age Cyprus

A. Bernard Knapp

From the vantage point of Cambridge University, one sees widespread optimism about recovering "mind" (what *Annales* historians call *mentalité*) from archaeological data (Renfrew 1982a); however, the retrieval of mental precepts — "cognitive archaeology" — from the material record is a formidable undertaking. As the study of Anglo-American archaeology increasingly breaks down into various *-isms* (e.g. structuralism, contextualism, post-processualism), and as cognitive archaeology increasingly gains respect within the discipline, perhaps it is worthwhile to reaffirm some of the basic materialist principles upon which archaeology is founded.

The remnants of production, consumption, and exchange form a significant part of the archaeological record of complex societies, however many transforms, middle range loops, or mental constructs are imposed on them. Fundamental to Marxist-based archaeology, a materialist approach is in fact fundamental to the entire field of archaeology (Trigger 1989: 338–341). Similarly ideology, production, and power may be Marxist-inspired concepts, but their rich application in archaeology today has little to do with doctrinaire Marxism, within or without archaeology. To focus on such politico-ideological aspects of the material record, furthermore, permits archaeologists to assess in part the human, behavioral aspects of the material record, and to consider, albeit more in a theoretical than an applied manner, the maintenance of power relationships in society.

This paper examines the development, maintenance, and legitimization of power relationships in Bronze Age Cyprus. Such relationships were predicated on control over the production and distribution of Cyprus's most important material resource — copper. Wide-ranging and detailed consideration of several key factors (demographic, economic, socio-political) represented in the material record of both Prehistoric Bronze Age (PreBA: ca. 2500/2400–1700 B.C.E.) and Protohistoric Bronze Age (ProBA: ca. 1700–1100 B.C.E.) Cyprus indicates that increased social differenti-

71

ation, developed economic integration, and concentrated political power stemmed directly from elite control over copper production and exchange (Knapp 1990, 1992). The trajectory of politico-economic change from the PreBA to the ProBA, between about 1700 and 1400 B.C.E., reveals the deepest discontinuity to be seen in the material record of prehistoric Cyprus. Intensification of production and politico-economic innovations — clearly evident in a diverse and extensive archaeological database — represent the transformation of an isolated village-based culture into an international, urban-oriented, complex society. By the 14th century B.C.E., centralized control (from the site of Enkomi) over copper production and exchange may have faltered, since there is evidence of control by local political hierarchies, a situation which fragmented further by the end of the 12th century B.C.E.

In what follows, I attempt to incorporate — in very general terms — the Cypriot Bronze Age archaeological evidence within a theoretical, behavioralist framework that focuses on politico-economic forces at work in the transformation of Bronze Age Cypriot society.

Production and Power on Bronze Age Cyprus

> Although ideology and military might are potent forces..., the maintenance of power relationships would seem to involve economic control over people's everyday lives. (Earle 1989: 86)

In a series of recent papers, I have discussed the emergence of distinctive new subsistence and productive strategies within the PreBA (about 2500/2400–1700 B.C.E.); Sherratt's concept of the secondary products revolution provided the framework for discussion of settlement patterns and the subsistence base (Sherratt 1981; Knapp 1990, 1992). The emergence of copper production and the development of bronze metallurgy was evaluated within a politico-economic framework that also sought to take account of social factors at work in processes of production and legitimization of sociopolitical power during the first stage of the subsequent ProBA (about 1700–1500/1400 B.C.E.), was presented in terms of expanding urban organization, the intensification of copper production and exchange, developing commodity exchange, and the elaboration of ritual (Knapp 1986a, 1986b, 1988). Increased external demand for Cypriot copper within the Aegean and eastern Mediterranean, the associated need to organize formally the internal and external administration of the copper trade, and the closely related strategic (market) location of Cyprus combined to heighten social complexity and concentrate political power on the island. Ongoing work seeks to reassess the material base in terms of the economic, political, and ideological aspects of power, production, and exchange.

Because the development, maintenance, and legitimization of power relationships are predicated on control over basic subsistence and mineral resources, politico-economic strategies must take account of environmental and demographic constraints that may have an impact on the generation, organization, distribution, and consumption of surplus production (production beyond subsistence — PBS; see Renfrew 1982b: 266–268); such strategies must also manipulate effectively the ideological factors that delimit and define sociopolitical action. These constraints, which may also be regarded as potentials, are both natural and cultural, and therefore continually modified by human intervention (Earle 1989: 87), human need, and human decision-making.

In order to create and maintain a durable sociopolitical order, several strategies may be involved. Subsumed implicitly by Earle (1989: 85) under three power categories, these strategies may be defined more explicitly from a materialist, developmental perspective:

1) *establishment of power* — economic control over subsistence and wealth;
2) *stabilization of power* — military/civil control over people and resources;
3) *legitimization of power* — political/ideological control over the forces and relations of production.

Assessment of these changing modes of power helps to contextualize the material and behavioral factors involved in the emergence, development and decline of sociopolitical complexity on Bronze Age Cyprus.

Establishment of Power

The sociopolitical system of Bronze Age Cyprus crystallized during the latter part of the 3rd millennium B.C.E. in the wake of a new subsistence package, the development of extractive copper metallurgy, and incipient demand for Cypriot copper from an interregional, eastern Mediterranean system (Knapp 1990). The island ecosystem was altered irrevocably by human interference, as new metal tools (axe, plow) and the introduction of cattle altered the infrastructure of subsistence production: larger tracts of cultivable land, increasingly specialized animal husbandry, facilities for the bulk storage of comestibles, and more people to manage the entire system, promoted an efficient agro-pastoral economy, and ensured the provision of PBS for non-producing (elite) members of society. Such a system, termed a "staple finance" system by D'Altry and Earle (1985: 188), may have supported *supralocal* as well as local administrative activities.

Whereas settlement expansion and population increase did not break down earlier (regional) demographic patterns, the concentration of sites at the interface between agricultural and mineral zones, and an incipient site hierarchy, must be associated in part with the exploitation of copper resources. The conspicuous metal wealth of burials in north coast cemeteries (whose occupants may have dwelt in still-unidentified coastal centers), and the more utilitarian copper tools and scraps typical of industrial or agricultural villages nearer the copper sources (e.g., Alambra *Mouttes*, Ambelikou *Aletri*), represent not only distinctive attitudes towards metals but also social differentiation. For the actual producers of copper, the value of metal — as commodity — rested on its exchange value; for the consumers and distributors of copper, the value of metal — as status item — lay in its potential for monopolizing power, prestige, and external exchange (D. Frankel — personal communication; Knapp 1990).

The development of extractive copper metallurgy involved complex organization in both the production and distribution spheres, and necessitated the adoption of several innovations: technological skills, the assignment of time and manpower, and the reorganization of society in a manner that allowed producers, metalsmiths, and traders to interact, cooperatively or competitively (Cole 1981: 96–98). The establishment of the metal industry — and the attempt to control access to copper resources and metal goods — triggered the development toward a more stratified social order and the growth of power differentials.

The mineral and agricultural wealth of the island also provided the potential for politico-economic intensification. The dramatic changes that took place during the PreBA in both the subsistence and metallurgical sectors of the economy undermined existing power strategies and necessitated new modes of social interaction. Although a domestic (or lineage) mode of production may have persisted in the manufacture of non-specialist goods such as ceramics (Frankel 1988: 31, 50), some segment of the population had to manage the requirements of specialized production, the subsistence needs of the new specialists, external exchange, and the transfer of information (van der Leeuw 1986: 42) within an interregional system. Emergent elites which controlled the production of both staples and metals provided the material base and politico-economic capacity to establish and manipulate external contacts, and to exploit external demand. By the beginning of the 2nd millennium B.C.E., emergent power groups in the northern region of the island assumed control over productive resources (copper/metals, agricultural/pastoral products, import/export trade), accumulated greater wealth, and intensified socio-economic divisions within Cypriot society.

Stabilization of Power

The extension and stabilization of power is usually based on some sort of military, civil, or juridical authority (the material correlates of the last are difficult to isolate), and involves the establishment of control over the internal and external production and distribution of wealth. If elite groups were able to control access to ores as well as the output of dependent smiths or artisans (Rowlands 1971; Welbourn 1981), they would have not only solidified their power base, but also succeeded in excluding other sectors of society from the metallurgical products that became symbolic of elite membership (Morris 1989: 506–507). The predominance of metal grave goods in the Lapithos and Vounous tomb groups of the PreBA (Knapp 1990: 159–160), and in the Enkomi tomb groups of the ProBA (Keswani 1989a), almost certainly reflects this exclusivity principle.

Although competition for dominance over copper production and exchange intensified during the first phase of the ProBA (17th–15th centuries B.C.E.) (Knapp 1986a: 38; Knapp 1979: 28–54), the urban center at Enkomi established its pre-eminence early (Muhly et al. 1988: 294–295; Muhly 1989: 299–301). Yet by the time of the urban expansion of the 13th century B.C.E. (ProBA 2--Negbi 1986;

South 1987), a broad range of evidence from various sites demonstrates that regional or local elites effectively exploited various mineral, material, and symbolic resources (Keswani 1989a) and controlled their production or distribution (Knapp 1989). It is uncertain whether Enkomi promoted this "trickle-down" effect, or rather had to suffer it.

The newly-built, densely-populated, urban coastal centers (especially Enkomi *Ayios Iakovos*, Morphou *Toumba tou Skourou*, and Hala Sultan Tekke *Vyzakia*) dominated the island's involvement in interregional exchange, both in the export of refined copper ingots and mass-produced ceramics, and in the import of exotic, prestige goods (metal, mineral, ceramic). Elite manipulation of exotic wealth may have helped to attract and control the indigenous labor force. Distinctive images on metals, pottery, and other minor arts would have linked the dependent population in mining or agricultural villages to the dominant elites in industrial-commercial entrepots on or near the coast. Production in the coastal centers increasingly relied on raw material or agricultural products from the hinterland: local interference had to be checked and the integrity of the island system had to be maintained (Knapp 1988: 151).

During the PreBA, the exploitation of copper and the use of metals *represented* social differentiation; by the ProBA, control over copper production, transport, and distribution had *created* politico-economic distinctions (Shennan 1986: 117; Knapp 1990: 159). The domination and regulation of copper production provided the basis for unequal (or "polyadic") exchange (Smith 1976: 323–324) within the island, and for more extensive contacts and equivalent (prestige-goods) exchange beyond the island. Such a system, termed a "wealth finance" system by D'Altroy and Earle (1985: 188), supplemented the (ongoing?) staple finance system of the PreBA, supported all of the more centralized administrative activities of the emergent state polity, and underwrote the intensified long-distance exchange in copper and other metals, and in exotic goods.

The natural circumscription of the island of Cyprus, and the scarcity of land and resources (the result of more extensive plow agriculture, and increased exploitation of copper), may have facilitated the concentration of productive resources — and the concomitant centralization of authority — in the hands of an emergent elite. Physical manifestations of power (weaponry, fortifications; monumental public or ceremonial architecture; high-status burials) contributed to the integration of subsistence and specialist production factors (the economic base of power) as Cyprus's emergent politico-economic authority extended its scope of power (Haas 1982; Knapp 1986a: 49). The maturation of the political economy resulted from the interplay of trade, external demand, the accumulation and reinvestment of wealth, and the division of labor into specialist production activities. Participation in an interregional trade network provided opportunity for further investment, and elite manipulation of trade became the basis for further sociostructural change.

Legitimization of Power
The stabilization and maintenance of political control over the forces and relations

of production necessitates ideological legitimization (Claessen and van de Velde 1985: 254). If the metals wealth of the north coast signified emergent status distinctions during the PreBA, the power insignia adopted by Cypriot elites during the ProBA — bronze statuettes and stands, miniature ingots, representations of ingots on ceramics, stands and seals — indicate a real discontinuity in politico-economic reality, and suggest a redefinition of social relationships based on the exploitation of natural and symbolic resources (Knapp 1988: 156). These paraphernalia of power at once symbolize and focus attention on the legitimization of power differentials and the economic aspirations of the elite.

Whereas emergent state elites may seek to anchor and enhance their authority by dominating access to exotic goods associated with external ideologies (Earle 1989: 85), the paraphernalia of power adopted by Cypriote elites were predominantly local in inspiration and form (even if represented occasionally on "foreign" objects: e.g., the copper oxhide ingot portrayed on "Mycenaean" ceramics or Asiatic cylinder seals — discussion in Knapp 1988: 145–146). However, this is not to deny that, particularly during the 14th–12th centuries B.C.E., entrepreneurial activity associated with copper production and exchange stimulated the multidirectional movement of metals (tin, gold, silver), luxury items (ivory, precious or semi-precious stones), comestibles, and ceramics in an interregional, eastern Mediterranean exchange system. On Cyprus itself, the manipulation and use of such wealth objects — as indicators of limited access to other networks of power — would have helped to proclaim a distinct social identity and to maintain a high level of international contact (Schortman 1989: 59). But the legitimization of dominion within the island was symbolized otherwise.

Power relationships with ProBA Cyprus were legitimized with direct reference to the economic basis of society. Having established control of the wealth in metals on the island, the emergent state elite adopted new material indices and built new ceremonial structures — both intricately linked to copper production and exchange — in order to draw the population into the changing politico-economic system, and to sanction its own centralized authority. While the external economic environment helped to catapult demand for Cypriot copper within an interregional system, the internal politico-economic environment — the "structural preconditions of hierarchy" (Earle 1989: 86) — dictated the development and utilization of symbols that linked managers and producers, maintained intra-island integrity, and served to legitimize the sociopolitical status and power of a non-ascriptive elite directly tied to the production, transport and exchange of copper.

The Cypriot archaeological record of the mid–2nd millennium B.C.E. provides ample evidence for increased social differentiation, developed economic regulation, and concentrated politico-economic power (Knapp 1988: 142–143, Table 1). Such heightened social complexity often necessitates greater external input in the form of utilitarian goods to supply a growing population, and of prestige goods to meet the status-differentiation needs of an elite (Schortman 1989: 60). Despite the masses of Cypriot pottery in the Levant (e.g., Gittlen 1981; Artzy 1985), Cyprus remained "indifferent" to the palatial organizations typical of western Asia (Muhly 1985: 43).

Similarly, apart from the distinctive Mycenaean and Minoan pottery so widespread on ProBA 2 Cyprus, Aegean influences are non-existent (Muhly 1985: 43), and indeed, there is now reason to think that — on metallurgical grounds — we must discount a close association between Cyprus and Crete during the 15th–14th centuries B.C.E. (Knapp 1991; Knapp and Cherry 1991). Although Cyprus's pivotal location between Orient and Occident ensured some impact from foreign sources, the ideological legitimization of elite authority on Cyprus was not linked to an external ideology, no matter how tightly Cypriot and foreign elites were bound in the economic sphere.

Even if economic factors served to strengthen bonds amongst Cypriot, Levantine, and Aegean polities during the mid-late 2nd millennium B.C.E., it remains unlikely that the basic identification of such links will help to establish the ethnic identity of the Cypriot elite. Without a detailed, comparative, inter-site analysis of prestige-goods production and consumption in all ProBA contexts (mortuary aspects now available in Keswani 1989b: 706–718, Tables 6.3 to 6.13), it remains difficult to speak definitively even about supralocal ethnic associations. Nonetheless, the establishment of distinctive material or behavioral indices that may symbolize "salient identities" — one of the most important means by which elites differentiate themselves from non-elites (Schortman 1989) — should be a top research priority for the study of the Cypriot Bronze Age. Only through such a program of research, combined with the evidence of onomastica (Knapp 1979: 257–265), can insight be gained into ethnicity on Bronze Age Cyprus, and into Enkomi's apparent superordinance (16th through 14th centuries B.C.E.) vis-a-vis local political hierarchies (particularly in the 13th–12th centuries B.C.E.).

Competitive, interpolity dynamics ensure that centralizing tendencies will often be offset by localizing ones (Adams 1978; Earle 1989: 87). The power relationships, economic ties, and ideological insignia that helped to integrate the Cypriot polity were altered irrevocably in the face of a system-wide collapse at the end of the Late Bronze Age. Heightened investment in ideological energy helped to offset socioeconomic stress, but could not prevent alterations to the ideological basis of Cypriot society. Cypriot elites no longer had easy access to imported resources or prestige goods that had helped to legitimize their regime (Knapp 1988: 154). Whereas the revitalization of industrial, commercial, and political power on early Iron Age Cyprus is not in doubt, new regional polities seem to have displaced centralized authority and adopted new or revamped ideological insignia, in some cases suggestive of Aegean or Levantine origins.

Conclusion

The study of Cypriot Bronze Age prehistory — in large measure — has eschewed theoretical approaches to production and exchange, and instead seeks to reconstruct cultural groups through intensive study of architecture, pottery, minor arts and technology (less often through study of certain, obvious facets of the economy). The social fabric, politico-economic base, and ideological basis of power on Bronze or Iron Age Cyprus are rarely considered (cf. Frankel 1988; Rupp 1988; Keswani 1989b: 506–613; Knapp 1988). But it must be reiterated that the explanation of the past involves the use of both detailed, particularistic arguments (i.e., the usual classificatory, chronological, and comparative tools of the trade), and broader, generalization principles (e.g., state formation; the establishment and maintenance of power in society).

At the risk of preaching to the converted, or testing the tolerance of those who practice applied archaeology rather more often than they do the theoretical variety, I should like to suggest that — despite the material record's recalcitrance in providing instantly useful production figures or meaningful social relationships — archaeologists in general have an obligation to explore methodologies associated with locational analysis, taphonomy, ethnoarchaeology, social and ideological theory, and political and economic anthropology. With particular reference to Cyprus, the ongoing strengths of Cypriot archaeological research (the orderly collection, comparative analysis, and prompt publication of data) should be complemented by the adoption of theoretical frameworks geared to help explain the past through generalization.

References

R.M. Adams, 1978. "Strategies of Maximization, Stability, and Resilience in Mesopotamian Society, Settlement and Agriculture," *Proceedings of the American Philosophical Society* 122,5: 329–335.

M. Artzy, 1985. "Supply and Demand: A Study of Second Millennium Cypriote Pottery in the Levant," in A.B. Knapp and T. Stech (eds.), *Prehistoric Production and Exchange: The Aegean and East Mediterranean.* (UCLA Institute of Archaeology, Monograph 25), pp. 93–99. Los Angeles.

H.J.M. Claessen and P. Van De Velde, 1985. "Sociopolitical Evolution as Complex Interaction," in H.J.M. Claessen, P. Van De Velde and M.E. Smith (eds.), *Development and Decline: The Evolution of Socio-Political Organization*, pp. 246–263. South Hadley, MA.

J.M. Coles, 1981. "Metallurgy and Bronze Age Society," in N. Lorenz (ed.), *Studien zur Bronzezeit*, pp. 95–108. Mainz.

T.N. D'Altroy and T.K. Earle, 1985. Staple Finance, Wealth Finance, and Storage in the Inka Political Economy," *Current Anthropology* 25: 187–206.

T. Earle, 1989. "The Evolution of Chiefdoms," *Current Anthropology* 30: 84–88.

D. Frankel, 1988. "Pottery Production in Prehistoric Bronze Age Cyprus: Assessing the Problem," *Journal of Mediterranean Archaeology* 1,2: 27–55.

B.M. Gittlen, 1981. "The Cultural and Chronological Implications of the Cypro-Palestinian Trade during the Late Bronze Age," *BASOR* 241: 49–59.

J. Haas, 1982. *The Evolution of the Prehistoric State.* New York.

P.S. Keswani, 1989a. "Dimensions of Social Hierarchy in Late Bronze Age Cyprus: An Analysis of the Mortuary Data from Enkomi," *Journal of Mediterranean Archaeology* 2: 49–86.

——— , 1989b. "Mortuary Ritual and Social Hierarchy in Bronze Age Cyprus." (Ph.D. diss., University of Michigan, Ann Arbor).

A.B. Knapp, 1979. "A Re-Examination of the Interpretation of Cypriote Material Culture in the MC III–LC I Period in the Light of Textual Evidence." (Ph.D. diss., University of California, Berkeley).

——— , 1986a. "Production, Exchange and Socio-Political Complexity on Bronze Age Cyprus," *Oxford Journal of Archaeology* 5: 35–60.

——— , 1986b. *Copper Production and Divine Protection: Archaeology, Ideology and Social Complexity on Bronze Age Cyprus* (Studies in Mediterranean Archaeology, Pocketbook 42). Göteborg.

——— , 1988. "Ideology, Archaeology and Polity," *Man* 23: 133–163.

——— , — — , 1989. "Copper Production and Mediterranean Trade: The View from Cyprus," *Opuscula Atheniensia* 18: 109–116.

——— , 1990. "Production, Location and Integration in Bronze Age Cyprus," *Current Anthropology* 31: 147–176.

——— , 1991. "Trade Patterns in the Eastern Mediterranean: Archaeometry and Bronze Age Society," in *Biblical Archaeology Today*. (Proceedings of the Second International Congress on Biblical Archaeology). Jerusalem.

——— , 1992. "Emergence, Development and Decline on Bronze Age Cyprus," in C. Mathers and S. Stoddart (eds.), *Development and Decline in the Mediterranean Bronze Age*. Cambridge.

A.B. Knapp and J.F. Cherry, 1990. "Archaeological Science, Statistics and Cultural Solutions: Trade Patterns in the Bronze Age Eastern Mediterranean," in E. Pernicka and G.A. Wagner (eds.), *Archaeometry* 90: 183–198. Basel.

I. Morris, 1989. "Circulation, Deposition and the Formation of the Greek Iron Age," *Man* 24: 502–519.

J.D. Muhly, 1985. "The Late Bronze Age in Cyprus: A 25 Year Retrospect," in V. Karageorghis (ed.), *Archaeology in Cyprus 1960–1985*, pp. 20–46. Nicosia.

——— , 1989. "The Organization of the Copper Industry in Late Bronze Age Cyprus," in E.J. Peltenburg (ed.), *Early Society in Cyprus*, pp. 298–314. Edinburgh.

J.D. Muhly, R. Maddin and T. Stech, 1988. "Cyprus, Crete and Sardinia: Copper Oxhide Ingots and the Metals Trade," *Report of the Department of Antiquities, Cyprus*: 281–298.

O. Negbi, 1986. "The Climax of Urban Development in Bronze Age Cyprus," *Report of the Department of Antiquities, Cyprus*: 97–121.

A.C. Renfrew, 1982a. "Towards an Archaeology of Mind," (Inaugural lecture as Disney Professor, Cambridge University). Cambridge.

——— , 1982b. "Polity and Power: Interaction, Intensification and Exploitation," in C. Renfrew and M. Wagstaff (eds.), *An Island Polity: The Archaeology of Exploitation on Melos*, pp. 264–290. Cambridge.

M.J. Rowlands, 1971. "The Archaeological Interpretation of Prehistoric Metalworking," *World Archaeology* 3: 210–224.

D.W. Rupp, 1988. "The 'Royal Tombs' at Salamis, Cyprus: Ideological Messages of Power and Authority," *Journal of Mediterranean Archaeology* 1,1: 111–139.

E.M. Schortman, 1989. "Interregional Interactions in Prehistory: The Need for a New Perspective," *American Antiquity* 54: 52–65.

S.J. Shennan, 1986. "Central Europe in the Third Millennium B.C.: An Evolutionary Trajectory for the Beginning of the European Bronze Age," *Journal of Anthropological Archaeology* 5: 115–146.

A.G. Sherratt, 1981. "Plough and Pastoralism: Aspects of the Secondary Products in Revolution," in I. Hodder, G. Issac, and N. Hammond (eds.), *Patterns of the Past: Studies in Honour of David Clarke*, pp. 261–305. Cambridge.

C.A. Smith, 1976. "Exchange Systems and the Spatial Distribution of Elites: The Organization of Stratification in Agrarian Societies," in C.A. Smith (ed.), *Regional Analysis* Vol. I: *Economic Systems*, pp. 309–374. New York.

A. South, 1987. "Contacts and Contrasts in Late Bronze Age Cyprus: The Vasilikos Valley and the West," in D.W. Rupp (ed.), *Western Cyprus: Connections* (Studies in Mediterranean Archaeology 77), pp. 83–95. Göteborg.

B.G. Trigger, 1989. *A History of Archaeological Thought*. Cambridge.

S.E. Van Der Leeuw, 1986. "On Settling Down and Becoming a 'Big-Man', " in M.A. Van Bakel, R.R. Hagensteijn and P. Van de Velde (eds.), *Private Politics: A Multi-Disciplinary Approach to "Big-Man" Systems* (Human Society I), pp. 33–47. Leiden.

D.A. Welbourn, 1981. "The Role of Blacksmiths in a Tribal Society," *Archaeological Review from Cambridge* 1: 30–40.

SESSION III
POWER

JAK YAKAR, Session Chairman, *Tel Aviv University*

ISAAC GILEAD, *Ben-Gurion University of the Negev*
Sociopolitical Organization in the Northern Negev
at the End of the Chalcolithic Period
WILLIAM G. DEVER, *University of Arizona*
The Rise of Complexity in the Land of Israel
in the Early Second Millennium B.C.E.
ISRAEL FINKELSTEIN, *Bar-Ilan University*
The Sociopolitical Organization of the Central Hill Country
in the Second Millennium B.C.E.
ITAMAR SINGER, *Tel Aviv University*
The Political Organization of Philistia in Iron Age I
SHLOMO BUNIMOVITZ, *Tel Aviv and Bar-Ilan Universities*
The Changing Shape of Power in Bronze Age Canaan

Sociopolitical Organization in the Northern Negev at the End of the Chalcolithic Period

Isaac Gilead

The origins of the Early Bronze Age cultures, and the emergence of urbanism in particular, are a focal point in the protohistoric research of Israel. The Chalcolithic period is an obvious starting point for discussing this topic. The main issue considered here is the influence of Chalcolithic social traditions on succeeding Early Bronze Age societies.

Until the late 1960s it was generally accepted that there was a cultural gap between the Ghassulian and the Early Bronze Age I (hereafter EB I) cultures.[1] Although some scholars listed similarities in a number of ceramic traits between Ghassulian and EB I assemblages, most admitted — sometimes in strong terms — the existence of a clear break.[2] K. Kenyon, for one, thought that the Chalcolithic groups "...directly contributed surprisingly little to the ultimate civilization of Palestine."[3]

More recently, an alternative hypothesis suggests that a greater degree of continuity between the Ghassulian and the EB I can be traced in the shapes and techniques of artifacts, settlement patterns,[4] and even in the entire matrix of the material culture.[5] According to this hypothesis, the origin of Early Bronze urbanism can be discerned in the preceding period, since there is evidence of local evolution from the Neolithic to the Early Bronze Age.[6] Some of those supporting the latter interpretation even condemn the former as being either "Hegelian"[7] or "diffusionist."[8]

Southern Israel, and especially the northern Negev (Fig. 1),[9] provides the richest data-base relevant to this question. This is attested by the numerous and rich Chalcolithic sites along Naḥal (Wadi) Beersheba, Naḥal Patish, Naḥal Gerar and Naḥal ha-Besor, and the Early Bronze Age urban settlements of ʿErani and Arad — along with the many smaller sites of this period. The relatively high quality of the data from southern Israel, and the need to first study the details of phenomena on a regional basis, are sufficient reason for concentrating on the archaeology of this region.

In 1981 I summarized the Chalcolithic period in the southern Shephelah and argued for continuity between the two periods under discussion.[10] The revision I advocated resulted from six years of study in the framework of two projects[11] focussing on Chalcolithic[12] and Early Bronze Age remains:[13]

1. The studies of sites and assemblages indicate that a cultural variability existed in the northern Negev during the Chalcolithic period. This variability, which could also have been temporal, demonstrates that different modes of sociopolitical organization prevailed in a broadly uniform cultural entity — the Ghassulian.

2. The ʿErani excavations (jointly with A. Kempinski) clearly indicated that there is no Chalcolithic stratum at the base of the EB I sequence. Also important is the finding that the cultural assemblages of the latter are neither related to nor influenced by the former.

3. Numerous carbon–14 dates from Chalcolithic and Early Bronze Age sites in the Negev have accumulated in recent years. These dates, coupled with the variability of the cultural assemblages, provide further evidence indicative of continuity between the two cultures.

The Cultural Entities and the History of the Chalcolithic Period in the Northern Negev

The main sites of the Chalcolithic period in the northern Negev are concentrated along the major drainage systems of this area. They can be divided into the Beersheba and Besor-Gerar clusters, representing two different aspects of one broad cultural entity best referred to as the Ghassulian.[14] The full details are beyond the scope of this paper, and will only be summarized here.

The sites of the Beersheba cluster are concentrated mainly along Naḥal Beersheba and are best represented by Abu Matar, Bir es-Safadi,[15] Ḥorvat Beter,[16] and Shiqmim.[17] They are characterized by the presence of stone architecture and underground structures, by copper and ivory industries and by the absence or relative rarity of cornets, sickle blades and microliths. The animals common in the faunal remains are sheep, goats, and cattle.

The sites of the Besor-Gerar cluster are concentrated mainly along Naḥal ha-Besor and Naḥal Gerar and are best represented by Macdonald's sites E and O[18] and by Gerar[19] and Qatif (Y2).[20] The architecture here, where preserved, consists of brickwork. There are no copper or ivory artifacts and the quantification of cornets, microliths and sickle blades ranges from common to abundant. The violin-shaped figurines found here are virtually unknown at the Beersheba sites. Worth mentioning is also the importance of domesticated pigs at many of the sites in this cluster.[21]

Although it has been suggested that the nature of the Besor sites, and thus Gerar too, indicates that they were pastoral camps[22] this seems no longer tenable. For example, the frequency of sickle blades in the flint assemblages of these sites is two to seven(!) times higher than at the Beersheba sites, which are commonly regarded as agricultural communities. Moreover, the presence of domesticated pigs in most of the faunal assemblages of the Besor-Gerar sites further supports a sedentary agricultural determination.[23] The subsistence economy of the inhabitants in the two clusters was thus basically similar: mixed farming based on cultivation of cereals and herding.

Unfortunately, since the two clusters seem to occupy two essentially different regions, they have never been found in one stratigraphic sequence and their relative dates cannot be established. Moreover, there are radiometric dates (see detailed discussion below) only for the Beersheba cluster sites. One possibility is that the Besor-Gerar sites are either earlier and/or contemporary with the Beersheba sites. If this is the case, the radiometric evidence described below indicates that these entities had ceased to exist many centuries prior to the first EB I settlements in the area, and clearly implies discontinuity between the Chalcolithic and the EB I. However, the possibility that the Besor-Gerar sites were later than the Beersheba sites cannot be excluded, and we will examine this alternative to show that even in such a case, there was discontinuity between the two periods.

The history of the Chalcolithic period in the northern Negev can thus be sketched in the following manner.[24] The local Late Neolithic-Chalcolithic is represented by the assemblages from Qatif (Y3),[25] P14, and materials from sites D and M.[26] They are followed by the main assemblages of sites D, and M and those from A and B. This sequence is based mainly on techno-typological grounds.[27]

Most of the large and numerous sites of the Chalcolithic period in the northern Negev are of later date than the above-mentioned sites and are best represented by the Beersheba and Besor-Gerar clusters. The lack of carbon–14 dating for the second cluster implies that either the Chalcolithic settlement there terminated when both entities disappeared contemporaneously, or when the later Besor-Gerar cluster terminated.

The Early Bronze Age I Entities in the Northern Negev

The stratified EB I sequence at ʿErani demonstrates what is lacking for the Chalcolithic period. ʿErani was excavated during 1956–1961 by S. Yeivin,[28] and his EB sequence from that site was recently reexamined and summarized by B. Brandl.[29] In 1985, 1987 and 1988 Kempinski and Gilead reexcavated their Area DII, immediately adjacent to Yeivin's Area D which was the main source for his sequence.[30]

Yeivin's subdivision of the EB I occupation in Area D into seven sequential strata (XI-V) was not confirmed by us. These strata must have been of a very limited spatial validity, and cannot be regarded as phases in the history of ʿErani during the Early Bronze Age. Yeivin's[31] section and plans indicate that some of the EB I walls were left unchanged, and minor alterations, also encountered by us, are therefore of a very localized significance.

The combined stratigraphy of our excavation and Yeivin's suggest, however, that the Early Bronze Age I at ʿErani may be divided into three major phases. The earliest is our Layer D, where no structures have been uncovered to date. The pottery assemblage of Layer D is different from the assemblages above, most importantly in the presence of a group of brown-red burnished vessels (mainly jars and bowls) in an Egyptian style. A few even resemble "black-topped" vessels. White-washed jars with red bands are also common. Burnish is very common on the open vessels in the ʿErani Early Bronze Age I sequence. For convenience, in the following discussion this phase will be referred to as early EB I.

The following phase within the ʿErani EB I sequence — middle EB I (Layer C) — is the most important phase uncovered in the course of our excavations, and probably in Yeivin's as well. It consists mainly of large and massive structures and courts. The most common vessels (40–52 percent) in the pottery assemblage are large pithoi with plastic decoration, and jars, most of which feature ledge handles and white wash, sometimes with red bands. The presence of Egyptian vessels seems to be less pronounced than previously. These vessels were made of fine yellow-brown silt, rich in organic remains. Red slip and burnish are common in this group. Many pieces of this group were made of local raw materials, as indicated by the petrographic analysis conducted by Y. Goren. While vessel shapes suggest an Egyptian influence, most were not Egyptian imports.

The remains of the later ʿErani EB I phase were not encountered in our excavations. They are, however, well known from Layer V of Yeivin's excavations[32] and within the ʿErani sequence they represent the latest EB I phase, late EB I in my sequence. The pottery assemblages of this phase are characterized by the typical vessels of the 1st Dynasty. The Narmer *serekh* also originated in the deposits of this phase. Among the flint artifacts, the typical Egyptian(?) bitruncated blades, which make up an important element of the ʿErani collection studied by S. Rosen,[33] are also missing from our collection. Such assemblages were not found in our excavations and it is likely that the strata relating to Narmer are missing from our sequence. This is most probably due to our excavations having been carried out in the lower part of the terrace, below the higher deposits that were excavated by Yeivin.

The EB I sequence at ʿErani consists of fully developed Early Bronze Age pottery and flint assemblages. The influence of Chalcolithic shapes is at best marginal. Moreover, Egyptian influence[34] in morphology and technology is apparent from the earliest stages of the EB I occupation, and is basically unknown in the Chalcolithic assemblages. Although a few intrusive Chalcolithic pottery fragments, mainly cornets and V-shaped bowls, are encountered through the section, their origin is unclear and it is obvious that they are not related to the development of the EB I settlement.

The nature of the earliest settlement (early EB I) at ʿErani is as yet unknown. The middle and late EB I urban center was settled by inhabitants with ceramic traditions similar to those of the first settlers.

The sequence of ʿErani is the best available, but it is not the only EB I site in southern Israel. At the other sites, only parts of this sequence are found. Macdonald's[35] Site H,[36] ʿEn Besor,[37] and Nizzanim and Taur Ikhbeineh,[38] for example, are probably sites of the early EB I, as substantiated by a carbon–14 date from the latter.[39] More sites are of the late EB I, i.e., Yeivin's Layer V at 'Erani, broadly contemporary with the early First Egyptian Dynasty: Arad IV,[40] Small Tell Malḥata,[41] 'En Besor III,[42] Tel Ḥalif terrace,[43] Tel Ma'aḥaz,[44] and Afridar (Ashkelon).[45] These sites reflect Egyptian activities in southern Israel, probably trade,[46] and are contemporary with the western Sinai stations.[47] It is noteworthy that the EB I sites tend to cluster in the northern and western parts of southern Israel, and even further north,[48] but never in the Naḥal Beershcba region.

Radiometric Chronology of the Chalcolithic-Early Bronze Age Entities

During the last four decades, a relatively large number of carbon–14 dates have been accumulated from Chalcolithic and EB I sites in southern Israel.[49] With the recent advent of high-precision calibration, the dates from southern Israel can be correlated with those from Egypt.[50]

In this section, the cultural entities described above will be discussed in terms of their absolute ages, when available. To do so, it is preferable to rely more on series of dates from the same site, or cluster of sites, than on isolated dates. This is why the arguments below are based primarily on the series of dates from the Beersheba sites and from 'Erani, although other dates are mentioned when necessary.

To compare the dates, all of them were calibrated to B.C.E. in calendar years, using the Stuiver and Reimer[51] computer program for radiocarbon age calibration.[52] For

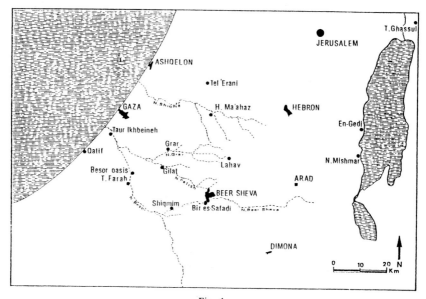

Fig. 1

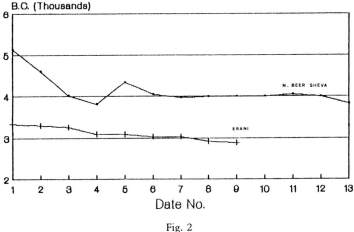

Fig. 2

Fig. 2 I have used the calibrated age. The one-sigma range with other details are presented in Table I, and the probable sequence of cultural entities in Table II. When the Libby date intercepts the calibration curve more than once, I have used the youngest date for the Chalcolithic period series and the oldest for the EB I series.

The Chalcolithic dates from Bir es-Safadi, Ḥorvat Beter and Shiqmim are presented in Fig. 2, in an attempt to reject as few dates as possible. Only one date from Ḥorvat Beter III (C–919), calibrated to 6187 B.C.E., is not included here.

The best approximation suggests that the range of dates for the Naḥal Beersheba sites is from the last third of the 5th millennium B.C.E. to the 40th century B.C.E. The two earlier dates from the upper village of Shiqmim are an exception. The dates from Tuleilat el-Ghassul and the Golan sites fall comfortably within this time span. The radiometric evidence from the Naḥal Beersheba sites therefore suggests that this part of the northern Negev was occupied until about 4,000–3,900 B.C.E. or earlier.[53] It would appear significant that three different sites give broadly similar dates, early in the Chalcolithic period.

The second series of nine dates to consider originates from the EB I-II sequence of ʿErani. Generally, the range conforms with a long time span covering all or most of EB I and the early part of EB II: the last third of the 4th millennium to the 30th century B.C.E. F.A. Hassan and S.W. Robinson's[54] suggestion that the first monarchs of Dynasty I date radiometrically to the 31st century B.C.E. agrees well with the earliest occupation of ʿErani, contemporary with Hassan's[55] Terminal Predynastic (3,300–3,100 B.C.E.).

It is obvious that there is a considerable gap — about 400–500 years — between the occupation of the Naḥal Beersheba sites and the earliest settlements of the EB I at ʿErani and elsewhere in southern Israel. There is no series of other radiometric dates from the other Negev Chalcolithic sites, mainly because there is no charcoal in the Besor-Gerar sites.[56] One reasonable possibility is that the Chalcolithic settlement of the northern Negev did not terminate after the desertion of the Naḥal Beersheba sites. In such a case, it is probable that sites of the Besor-Gerar cluster are of the first half of the 4th millennium B.C.E., thus bridging the hiatus between the Beersheba sites and ʿErani and other EB I settlements.[57]

The only series of carbon–14 dates that seems to fall in the time span between the Beersheba cluster and ʿErani is the one from the Judean Desert sites, mainly those from the Cave of the Treasure. Of the four dates from Naḥal Mishmar, three are in the second quarter of the 4th millennium — 300–200 years later than the Beersheba cluster. Although the scatter of dates is large, it is reasonable to assume that the Cave

Table I: Carbon–14 Dates from Chalcolithic and Early Bronze Age Sites in Southern Israel

Site	Uncalibrated	Calibrated	Range	Material	Laboratory
Chalcolithic Dates					
Naḥal Beersheba Series					
1. Shiqmim, upper village	6150 ± 180	5139	5309–4856	charcoal	RT–649D
2. Shiqmim, upper village	5750 ± 180	4601	4837–4370	charcoal	RT–649B
3. Shiqmim, lower village	5250 ± 140	4010	0–3828	charcoal	RT–554A
4. Shiqmim, lower village	5050 ± 490	3816	4360–3340	charcoal	
5. Safadi, low phase	5420 ± 110	4333	4674–3820	burned wood	M–864A
6. Safadi, middle phase	5270 ± 350	4043	4454–3726	burned wood	M–864B
7. Safadi, upper phase	5120 ± 350	3969	4350–3531	burned wood	M–864C
8. Safadi, Locus 721	5170 ± 110	3991	4216–3818	?	Ly–3904
9. Safadi, Locus 528	5190 ± 100	3996	4218–3824	?	Ly–3905
10. Safadi, Locus 309	5190 ± 100	3996	4218–3824	?	Ly–3906
11. H. Beter, Level III	5280 ± 150	4044	4340–3970	charcoal	W–254 12.H.
12. Beter	5180 ± 70	3994	4039–3828	charcoal	Pta–4212a
13. H. Beter	5100 ± 130	3826	4035–3725	charcoal	Pta–4312b
Naḥal Mishmar Series					
1. Naḥal Mishmar	5390 ± 150	4243	4360–4007	mat (inner part)	BM–140
2. Naḥal Mishmar	4880 ± 250	3693	3970–3370	mat (outer edge)	W–1341
3. Naḥal Mishmar	4780 ± 100	3535	3690–3380	mat (outer edge)	I–285
4. Naḥal Mishmar	4760 ± 120	3527	3690–3370	wood	I–353
5. Naḥal Mishmar, Cave 2	4725 ± 230	3389	3777–3108	Cloth	I–1819
Early Bronze Age Dates					
Tel ʿErani Series					
1. Area DII, Layer C	4520 ± 60	3331	3352–3089	charcoal	Pta–4579
2. Area D, Stratum II	4500 ± 130	3307	3370–2928	charred grain	BM–387
3. Area N Below wall	4470 ± 140	3263	3360–2920	charcoal	BM–392
4. Area N Below wall	4450 ± 140	3096	3360–2920	charred grain	BM–393
5. Area D, Stratum IV	4430 ± 140	3091	3350–2910	Olive stone	BM–391
6. Area D, Stratum IV	4410 ± 250	3037	3493–2701	charred grain	W–916
7. Area D, Stratum IV	4400 ± 130	3034	3300–2910	charred grain	BM–389
8. Area D, Stratum IV	4340 ± 130	2922	3264–2748	charred grain	BM–388
9. Area D, Stratum II	4200 ± 130	2880	2920–2590	charcoal	BM–390

Table II: Chronology of the Chalcolithic and EB I Sequence in Southern Israel

Years B.C.E.	Period	Cultural entity	Sites
2500			
	EB II		Arad III
3000			
		Late EB I	ʿErani V, Arad IV*, ʿEn-Besor
	EB I	Middle EB I	ʿErani C*,
3500		Early EB I	Site H, Taur Ikhbeineh* ʿErani D
		Besor-Gerar	
	Late Chalcolithic	cluster	Gerar, sites E, O?
4000		Beersheba	Safadi*, Beter*
		cluster	
	Early/Middle Chalcolithic		Matar, Shiqmim*
			Sites A, B, D, M
4500			
	Early Chalcolithic/		
	Late Neolithic	Qatifian	P14, Qatif-Y3*
5000			
5500			
	Late Neolithic		Nizzanim*

* Radiometrically dated site

of the Treasure is of a relatively late date in the Chalcolithic sequence of southern Israel. Moorey[58] suggested that the copper hoard of the cave was produced at the Beersheba sites, but the role of the Judean Desert sites in the history of the northern Negev is as yet unknown.

Chalcolithic-EB I Sociopolitical Developments

All the Chalcolithic settlements of the northern Negev show the same common cultural traits and the typical artifact types which constitute the fossil indices of that time span. The cultural assemblages share, for example, a similar flint and pottery technology and typology. In addition, the basic subsistence economy and mode of life are similar: agricultural villages and hamlets where dry farming and herding was practiced.[59] A few artifacts and raw materials point to contacts with Egypt and the northern provinces, but the intensity of such contacts and their influence on the local culture seem to be very marginal.[60] The sociopolitical implications of the cultural assemblages cannot be easily deciphered. Some tend to indicate the existence of hereditary chiefs in a well-structured, redistributive, society;[61] others tend to emphasize the egalitarian aspects of Chalcolithic society.[62] It is important in this context to avoid generalization. Since there were clusters of sites with different attributes, probably belonging to different time spans, it is possible that there were different patterns of sociopolitical organization at different times and in different places throughout the Chalcolithic period.

The Negev evidence seems to indicate that the material culture is a product of a society organized in a similar way to the one F. Hole[63] suggests for Susa: "The evidence best conforms with an aggregate society composed of numerous small semiautonomous units... demographically coincident with the multiplicity of villages."[64] The dominant element of the Chalcolithic village is the domestic unit, the household cluster. Unfortunately, the architectural organization of the Chalcolithic villages in the northern Negev is poorly known. The layout of the upper village at Tuleilat el-Ghassul, the best available, clearly indicates that a village consisted of houschold clusters, very similar to each other, where no hierarchical relations between the units can be discerned. This suggests that the elementary unit of the social order was the head of the household, either male or female. The assembly of the household heads was probably the central political organ of such a village.[65] There is no evidence that local leaders amassed wealth or owned symbolic objects that signified social rank. The same applies to the northern Negev too.

On a more detailed level, the different Chalcolithic entities of the northern Negev vary — sometimes considerably — in terms of settlement distribution, architecture, crafts, and economy. The differences outlined above between the Beersheba and the Besor-Gerar clusters exemplify this. This variability may reflect different patterns of socioeconomic integration caused by environmental or demographic changes. The more diversified material culture of the Beersheba cluster probably represents such a response, limited in time (the last third of the 5th millennium B.C.E.) and space (the Naḥal Beersheba basin). The fact that typical attributes of this cluster (e.g., copper, ivory, stone architecture) hardly spread to other sites farther to the north and west in the Negev, further illustrates the rather limited spatio-temporal role played by the Naḥal Beersheba sites in the later history of the Chalcolithic period.

Turning to the earliest EB I settlements, such as ʿErani D, Site H, or Taur Ikhbeineh, they do not seem to be similar either to the Naḥal Beersheba sites nor to those of the Besor-Gerar. Although there are a few similar pottery[66] and flint[67] forms, these industries are entirely different from the Chalcolithic industries in terms of technology and typology. The relatively low diversity of material culture is similar to that of the Besor-Gerar sites, the possible local late Chalcolithic predecessors of the period.

That the flint and pottery assemblages of ʿErani C, with its complex architecture, are similar to the earlier EB I assemblages is obvious, and a continuity between the EB I phases is unquestionable. The evidence from southern Israel thus strongly supports the idea that, during a period of about 100–200 years, a local population, rural in nature and with a relatively low level of sociopolitical integration, either developed or changed into a society with an urban component. This is first evinced in the EB I of ʿErani C, and later, at Arad III during the EB II.

The presence of the EB I predecessors of the ʿErani town dwellers in southern Israel for about a century prior to the transition to urbanism considerably reduces and practically eliminates the role of the late Chalcolithic settlement of the Negev in the urbanization process. The possible indirect continuity of a few artifact types, atavists in a new set of assemblages, cannot be regarded as the trigger for the urbanization process. If, indeed, the northern Negev was settled by late Chalcolithic communities of the Besor-Gerar tradition, there is nothing in their low social complexity to explain the urbanization which emerges hundreds of years later.

As a continuum of sociopolitical complexity from the Chalcolithic-EB I cannot be maintained, the possibility of a local development from Chalcolithic origins to local pristine states becomes quite remote. Other explanations that take events beyond the southern Levant in general, and the northern Negev in particular, into account should be considered. The Chalcolithic communities in the southern Levant seem to have existed in relative isolation. Although there is evidence for long-distance trade, it was a minor element in the material culture of most of the sites. Styles or techniques of different cultures were not adopted by the Chalcolithic crafts-men. The long-distance influences of the Halafian[68] or Ubaid[69] ceramic traditions that spread over huge parts of the Near East, hardly penetrated the southern Levant[70] and are virtually unknown in central and southern Israel. Nor did Egyptian traditions influence the local craftsmen.

This relative isolation of the Ghassulian ended with the inception of the EB I, best evinced in southern Israel. The quantity of Egyptian or Egyptian style vessels and tools increases significantly at the EB I sites. Beginning with the early EB I in south-ern Israel, the ceramic assemblages represent "...an unusual mixture of Egyptian and local techniques, forms and types."[71] In the ʿErani C sample from the main building, the Egyptian or Egyptian-like ware comprises 21 percent of all sherds.[72] At ʿErani D they become even more common.[73] This suggests that the Egyptian presence was most pronounced in the early EB I and that it diminished later. It seems to reflect a decisive event rather than a slow, cumulative process. The Egyptian presence in northern Sinai,[74] as well as the similar assemblages in eastern Sinai,[75] further indicate that Egyptian penetration was an important event in the EB I history of southern Israel. Both local and Egyptian evidence suggest that this penetration began prior to the 1st Egyptian Dynasty.[76]

The evidence concerning contacts with Egyptians is not based solely on the pres-ence of Egyptian elements in southern Israel. Canaanean imports found in Egypt[77] indicate that the contact was bi-directional. Long-distance trade seems to have had a marked effect on the development of the Egyptian state[78] and there is no reason to suppose that such contacts did not affect the social organization of the communities in southern Israel. The nature of the ongoing Egyptian influence in southern Israel throughout the entire EB I is, as yet, unclear. Did it involve trade,[79] occupation,[80] colonization,[81] or all of the above? Whatever the mechanism, the Egyptian presence in southern Israel must have affected local life styles. It is a reasonable assumption that the end of local isolation and the impact of a large, developing state in Egypt triggered the sociopolitical changes discerned mainly in the middle and late EB I. This implies that the first towns or provincial city-states in southern Israel are secon-dary, rather than pristine states that evolved locally and independently.[82] Chalcolithic modes of sociopolitical integration, already extinct for centuries, could not have played any significant role in these new developments. The Early Bronze Age I of southern Israel signifies either an intrusion of EB I groups or a dramatic, non-evolutionary, modification of Late Chalcolithic modes of life. The EB towns in southern Israel emerged as a response to rapid sociopolitical change in the Near East during the last third of the 4th millennium B.C.E.[83]

I am aware that the scheme of the Chalcolithic-EB transition described above relates in its details only to the southern part of Israel, mainly the northern Negev. However, in most other parts of the southern Levant there is no substantial evidence to suggest that Chalcolithic sociopolitical traditions were precursors to the evolution to urbanism. The Chalcolithic settlements of the coastal plain are few, poorly known, and as yet undated. It seems that most of the Chalcolithic settlements in the central coastal plain were small and of short duration and that the population was very sparse.[84] In his study of settlement distribution in the Lod Valley, R. Gophna noted a post-Chalcolithic occupational hiatus and a change in settlement pattern of the middle EB I settlements.[85] The relations of the burial caves[86] to the settlements is virtually unknown. The only dates from such contexts are those from the Naḥal Qanah Cave. The average range of the two Chalcolithic samples is 4228–3819 B.C.E.[87] — early in the Chalcolithic period and within the range of dates from the Naḥal Beersheba sites.

The quality and the quantity of evidence from northern Israel is also poor. There are hardly any Chalcolithic sites in Galilee[88] to enable discussion of transition to EB I. The two late 5th millennium dates of the Golan Chalcolithic[89] are also early.[90] The structures reflect a social organization based on extended families,[91] not hierarchically organized. The too few EB I sites of the Hula Basin[92] further argue for Chalcolithic-EB I discontinuity. In the only stratified site of this region, Tel Teʾo, domestic units of the Chalcolithic period and the EB I show fundamental changes in architecture and cultural assemblages.[93]

Evidence from Transjordan, and especially from Bab edh-Dhraʿ, was used prior to the 1970s to suggest that the EB I was the result of penetration of newcomers from outside the Levant.[94] More recently, R.T. Schaub[95] and J.W. Hanbury-Tenison[96] advocated the recognition of continuity between the Ghassulian and EB I cultures.[97] Since the intensive research in Transjordan is not yet synthesized and there are too few carbon–14 dates, assessments regarding the Chalcolithic-EB transition there remain tentative.

Conclusions

In recent years, Chalcolithic settlement of the northern Negev has been regarded as having consisted of broadly contemporary sites, featuring the same sociopolitical organization. Although many sites are still undated, it seems that such overall broad contemporaneity and organizational similarity cannot be taken for granted. The clusters of sites with different cultural assemblages suggest that settlement here was not uniform throughout the entire Chalcolithic period.

The series of radiometric dates for the large sites along Naḥal Beersheba tend to indicate that their occupation did not continue long after the turn of the 5th millennium B.C.E. The earliest EB I occupation began after 3,500 B.C.E. In northern Negev terms, it seems most appropriate to refer to the first half of the 4th millennium B.C.E. as late Chalcolithic, as distinct from the early (or early-middle) Chalcolithic (prior to the 40th century B.C.E.).

As no northern Negev sites that can be dated to this late Chalcolithic period are known, it would appear that either the region was not settled during that time span or, more probably, that settlement consisted of the sites of the Besor-Gerar cluster. The material culture of these sites was less diversified than that of earlier Chalcolithic sites. They were clearly rural farming communities of low social complexity. It is as yet unknown whether the first EB I settlers were late Chalcolithic groups with transformed cultural assemblages, or newcomers. Whatever the case, there were no social institutions in the local culture to enhance the development of either social complexity or urbanism among the EB I settlers of the area. For about one or two centuries, the EB I settlers preserved their material culture and the rural character of their settlement. An important trait of their cultural assemblages is the relatively high frequency of Egyptian-type vessels. Later, probably in the 33th–32th century B.C.E., their descendants, bearers of the same cultural traditions with Egyptian elements still intact, inhabited what would appear to be the first urban center in Israel.

Foreign influence reached southern Israel, after many centuries of Chalcolithic isolation, from the Terminal Predynastic of Egypt. Pronounced changes in demography and social organization took place in Egypt and culminated in the establishment of the Egyptian state. The Egyptian-type elements in the EB I of southern Israel suggest that the events in Egypt had a direct impact on the local inhabitants. It cannot be mere coincidence that the first towns in southern Israel developed at a time when strong states emerged in Egypt and Mesopotamia. The first urban centers in southern Israel were thus not pristine towns that developed in isolation out of an evolving late Chalcolithic social system. They were, rather, secondary in nature, and constitute a local reorientation of provincial farming communities adapting to the new geopolitical realities of the Near East.

Notes

1. For summaries of research prior to 1970 see: G.E. Wright, "The Archaeology of Palestine from the Neolithic Through the Middle Bronze Age," *JAOS* 91 (1971): 276–295; P.W. Lapp, "Palestine in the Early Bronze Age," in J.A. Sanders (ed.), *Near Eastern Archaeology in the Twentieth Century: Essays in Honor of Nelson Glueck* (New York, 1970), pp. 101–131. For more recent treatments see: J.W. Hanbury-Tenison, *The Late Chalcolithic to Early Bronze Age I in Palestine and Transjordan*, BAR No. 311 (Oxford, 1986); articles in the first session of P. de Miroschedji, *L'urbanisation de la Palestine à l'âge du bronze ancien, bilan et perspectives des recherches actuelles*, BAR No. 527 i,ii (Oxford, 1989) (hereafter *L'urbanisation*).

2. For a summary of the Ghassulian abandonment see: C. Elliott, "The Ghassulian Culture in Palestine: Origins, Influences and Abandonment," *Levant* 10 (1978): 37–54.

3. K.M. Kenyon, *Archaeology in the Holy Land*, 4th edition (London, 1979), p. 64. The same view is shared by J. Perrot, "Préhistoire palestinienne," in *Supplément au Dictionnaire de la Bible* (Paris, 1968), pp. 286–446 (especially p. 349); and R. de Vaux, "Palestine During the Neolithic and Chalcolithic Periods," *Cambridge Ancient History* I, pp. 498–538. For additional recent interpretations of discontinuity between the Chalcolithic and the Early Bronze Age see: E. Braun, "The Transition from the Chalcolithic to the Early Bronze Age in Northern Israel and Jordan: Is There a Missing Link?" in *L'urbanisation* (see note 1): pp. 7–27; E. Eisenberg, "The Chalcolithic and Early Bronze Age I Occupations at Tel Teʾo," in *L'urbanisation* (see note 1): pp. 29–40; A. Ben-Tor, "Byblos and the Early Bronze Age I of Palestine," in *L'urbanisation* (see note 1): pp. 41–52.

4. R. Amiran, "Pottery from the Chalcolithic Site near Tell Delhamiya and Some Notes on the Character of the Chalcolithic- Early Bronze Age I Transition," *EI* 13 (1977): 48–56 (Hebrew); idem, "The Transition from the Chalcolithic to the Early Bronze Age," in *Biblical Archaeology Today* I (Jerusalem, 1985), pp. 108–112.

5. Hanbury-Tenison (see note 1).

6. T.E. Levy, "Social Archaeology and the Chalcolithic Period: Explaining Social Organizational Change During the 4th Millennium in Israel," *Michmanim* 3 (1986): 5–20, and especially pp. 6–7.

7. J. Hanbury-Tenison, "Hegel in Prehistory," *Antiquity* 60 (1986): 108–114.

8. Levy (see note 6), pp. 6–7.

9. The term "northern Negev" applies in this paper to the area between Qatif in the west to Arad/Lahav in the east, and from Qiryat Gat in the north to the Beersheba Valley in the south (see Fig. 1).

10. I. Gilead, "The Southern Shefelah During the Chalcolithic Period," in E. Stern and D. Urman (eds.), *Man and Environment in the Southern Shefelah* (Ramat Gan, 1988), pp. 66–73. The paper was published in 1988, after I had the chance to revise my opinion.

11. One project was my excavation from 1981–1987 of the Chalcolithic sites at Naḥal Gerar and Naḥal Besor, with comparative studies of cultural assemblages from the northern Negev, mainly of pottery and flint. The second project, from 1985, concentrated on excavating the earliest strata at ʿErani with A. Kempinski.

12. I. Gilead, "Grar: a Chalcolithic Site in Nahal Grar, Northern Negev, Israel," *Journal of Field Archaeology* 16 (1989): 377–393; I. Gilead and D. Alon, "Excavations of Protohistoric Sites in Nahal ha-Besor and the Late Neolithic of the Northern Negev and Sinai," *Mitekufat Haeven* 21 (1988): 109–137; I. Gilead, "The Transition Neolithic-Chalcolithic in the Northern Negev and Sinai," *Levant* 22 (1990).

13. A. Kempinski and I. Gilead, "Tel ʿErani," *Excavations and Surveys* 4 (1985): 29–30; idem, "Tel ʿErani, 1987," (Notes and News), *IEJ* 38 (1988): 88–90.

14. Gilead (above note 12: first item).

15. J. Perrot, "Excavations at Tell Abu Matar Near Beersheba," *IEJ* 5 (1955): 17–40, 73–84, 167–189; idem, "Structure d'habitat, mode de la vie et environnement des villages souterrains des pasteurs de Béersheva dans le sud d'Israël, au IVe millénaire avant l'ère chrétienne," *Paléorient* 10 (1984): 75–92; I. Eldar and Y. Baumgarten, "Neve Noy, a Chalcolithic Site of the Beer Sheba Culture," *BA* 48 (1985): 134–139.

16. M. Dothan, "Excavations at Horvat Beter (Beersheba)," *ʿAtiqot* 2 (1959): 1–42.

17. T.E. Levy (ed.), *Shiqmim I, Studies Concerning Chalcolithic Societies in the Northern Negev Desert, Israel (1982–1984)*, BAR 356, i,ii (Oxford, 1987).

18. E. Macdonald, "Prehistoric Fara" *Beth Pelet* II, (London, 1932).

19. Gilead (above note 12, 1st item).

20. E. Oren, "Sites on the Khan Younes Coast," *Ḥadashot Arkheologiyot* 84–85 (1980): 51–53 (Hebrew).

21. Additional sites that cannot yet be incorporated in the current analysis are locations in the eastern Negev, between Arad and Lahav: R. Amiran, *Early Arad, the Chalcolithic Settlement and Early Bronze Age City* (Jerusalem, 1978), pp. 4–9; Y. Govrin, "Horvat Hor: a Dwelling Cave from the

Chalcolithic Period in the Northern Negev," *Mitekufat Haeven* 19 (1987): 119*–127*. For sites in the Lahav area such as Abu-Ḥof see: D. Alon, "The Spatial Distribution of Chalcolithic Settlements in the Southern Shefelah," in E. Stern and D. Urman (eds.), *Man and Environment in the Southern Shefelah* (Ramat Gan, 1988), pp. 74–78 (Hebrew). These sites, most of them unpublished, are characterized by caves and pits and a low level of cultural diversity. They are clearly different from the Nahal Beersheba sites and more similar to the Besor-Gerar sites.

22. Kenyon (see note 2), p. 59; T.E. Levy, "The Emergence of Specialized Pastoralism in the Southern Levant," *World Archaeology* 15 (1983): 15–36.

23. I. Gilead, "Farmers and Herders in Southern Israel during the Chalcolithic Period," in O. Bar-Yosef and A. Khazanov (eds.), *Pastoralism in the Levant* (in press); idem, "The Economic Basis of the Chalcolithic Settlement in the Northern Negev," *Michmanim* 3 (1986): 17–30 (Hebrew).

24. After Gilead and Alon (see note 12), Table 4.

25. C. Epstein, "A Pottery Neolithic Site near Tel Qatif," *IEJ* 34 (1984): 209–219.

26. Gilead and Alon (see note 12).

27. Gilead and Alon (see note 12); R. Gophna, "The Settlement of the North-Western Negev During the Chalcolithic Period (the Fourth Millennium B.C.)," in A. Shmueli and Y. Gradus (eds.), *The Land of the Negev* Part 1 (Tel Aviv, 1979), pp. 203–208.

28. S. Yeivin, *First Preliminary Report on the Excavations at Tel "Gat" (Tel Sheikh Akhmad el-Areyny). Seasons 1956–1958* (Jerusalem, 1961); idem, "El ʿAreini, Tel Esh Sheikh Ahmed (Tel ʿErani)," *EAEHL*, Vol. 1, 89–97.

29. B. Brandl, "Observations on the Early Bronze Age Strata of Tel ʿErani," in *L'urbanisation* (see note 1): pp. 357–387.

30. Kempinski and Gilead (see note 13).

31. Yeivin (see note 28).

32. S. Yeivin, "Early Contacts Between Canaan and Egypt," *IEJ* 10 (1960): 193–203.

33. S. Rosen, "A Preliminary Note on the Egyptian Component of the Chipped Stone Assemblages from Tel ʿErani," *IEJ* 38 (1988): 105–116.

34. See also: J.M. Weinstein, "The Significance of Tel Areini for Egyptian-Palestinian Relations in the Beginning of the Bronze Age," *BASOR* 256 (1984): 61–69.

35. Macdonald (see note 18).

36. R. Gophna, "The Early Bronze I Settlement at ʿEn Besor Oasis," *IEJ* 40 (1990): 1–11.

37. Gophna (Above, note 36).

38. R. Amiran, "Taur Ikhbeineh," *ʿAtiqot*, English Series, 11 (1976): 105–106; E. Oren, R. Gophna, and Y. Yekutieli, "Taur Ikhbeine-Nahal Gaza," *Ḥadashot Arkheologiyot* 90 (1987): 53–54 (Hebrew).

39. E. Oren and Y. Yekutiely, personal communication.

40. R. Amiran, *Early Arad, the Chalcolithic settlement and Early Bronze Age City* (Jerusalem, 1978).

41. R. Amiran, O. Ilan, and C. Arnon, "Excavations at Small Tel Malhata: Three Narmer Serekhs," *The Israel Museum Journal* 2 (1983): 75–83.

42. R. Gophna, "Excavations at ʿEn Besor," *ʿAtiqot*, English Series, 11 (1976): 1–9; idem, "Excavations at ʿEn Besor, 1976," *ʿAtiqot*, English Series, 14 (1980): 9–16; S.M. Mittmann, "Frühägyptische Siegelinschriften und ein SRH-Emblem des Horus 'H' aus dem nordlichen Negev," *EI* 15 (1981), pp. 1*–9*.

43. R. Gophna, "Egyptian First Dynasty Pottery from Tel Halif Terrace," *Museum Haaretz Bulletin* 14 (1972): 47–52.

44. A. Schulman and R. Gophna, "An Archaic Egyptian Serekh from Tel Maʾaḥaz," *IEJ* 31 (1981): 165–167.

45. R. Gophna, "Afridar," (Notes and News), *IEJ* 18 (1968): 256.

46. A. Ben-Tor, "The Relations Between Egypt and the Land of Canaan During the Third Millennium B.C.," *Journal of Jewish Studies* 33 (1982): 3–17; idem, "New Light on the Relations Between Egypt and Southern Palestine During the Early Bronze Age," *EI* 20 (1989), pp. 31–36 (Hebrew); R. Gophna, "Egyptian Trading Posts at Southern Canaan at the Dawn of the Archaic Period," in A.F.

Rainey (ed.), *Egypt, Israel, Sinai: Archaeological and Historical Relationships in the Biblical Period* (Tel Aviv, 1987), pp. 12–22.

47. E.D. Oren, "The Overland Route Between Egypt and Canaan in the Early Bronze Age (Preliminary Report)," *IEJ* 23 (1973): 198–205; idem, "Early Bronze Age Settlement in North Sinai: a Model for Egypto-Canaanite Interconnections," in *L'urbanisation* (see note 1), pp. 389–405.

48. Azor and Tel ʿErani feature the largest concentration of Egyptian artifacts, and it has been suggested that an element of the population of the former originated in Egypt, see: A. Ben-Tor, "Two Burial Caves of the Proto-Urban Period at Azor, 1971," in *Qedem* 1 (Jerusalem, 1975), p. 29.

49. J.M. Weinstein, "Radiocarbon Dating in the Southern Levant," *Radiocarbon* 26 (1984): 297–366; I. Gilead, "The Chalcolithic Period in the Levant," *Journal of World Prehistory* 2 (1988): 397–443, Table I, Fig. 2; J.A. Callaway and J.M. Weinstein, "Radiocarbon Dating of Palestine in the Early Bronze Age," *BASOR* 225 (1977): 1–16; H.T. Waterbolk, "Working with Radiocarbon Dates in Southwestern Asia," in A. Aurenche, J. Evin and F. Hours, *Chronologies in the Near East, Relative and Absolute Chronology 16,000–4,000 B.C.*, BAR No. 379 (Oxford, 1987), pp.39–59, mainly Graph 6.

50. F.A. Hassan, and S.W. Robinson, "High-Precision Radiocarbon Chronometry of Ancient Egypt and Comparisons with Nubia, Palestine and Mesopotamia," *Antiquity* 61 (1987): 119–135.

51. M. Stuiver and P.J. Reimer, "A Computer Program for Radiocarbon Age Calibration," *Radiocarbon* 28 (1986): 122–130.

52. The calculations were carried out by method A, without sample age spans.

53. This suggestion generally conforms with the dating of the Beersheba sites as presented by J. Mellaart, "Egyptian and Near Eastern Chronology: a Dilemma?" *Antiquity* 53 (1979): 6–18. For his (too) early dating of the EB I see J. Weinstein, "Palestinian Radiocarbon Dating: a Reply to James Mellaart," *Antiquity* 54 (1980): 21–24.

54. Hassan and Robinson (see note 50).

55. F.A. Hassan, "The Predynastic of Egypt," *Journal of World Prehistory* 2 (1988): 135–185.

56. Samples of bone from Gerar and Qatif were submitted in 1986 to J. Vogel for dating, but the collagen content of the samples was too poor to yield good results.

57. However, see the discussion above on the possibility that the Besor-Gerar sites are earlier than the Beersheba sites.

58. P.R.S. Moorey, "The Chalcolithic Hoard from Naḥal Mishmar, Israel, in Context," *World Archaeology* 20 (1988): 171–189.

59. Gilead (see note 23).

60. Gilead (see note 49).

61. Levy (see note 6).

62. Gilead (above note 49); J. Perrot and D. Ladiray, *Tombes à ossuaires de la région côtière palestinienne au IVe millénaire avant l'ère chrétienne* (Paris, 1980).

63. F. Hole, "Symbols of Religion and Social Organization at Susa," in T.C. Young, P.L.E. Smith and P. Mortensen, *The Hilly Flanks: Essays on the Prehistory of Southwestern Asia* (Chicago, 1983), pp. 315–331.

64. Hole (see note 63), p. 327.

65. For a model of social evolution without chiefdoms see: C.K. Maisels, "Models of Social Evolution: Trajectories from the Neolithic to the State," *Man* 22 (1987): 331–359.

66. Amiran (see note 4).

67. S. Rosen, "The Analysis of Early Bronze Age Chipped Stone Industries: A Summary Statement," in *L'urbanisation* (see note 1), pp. 199–222, especially pp. 216–218.

68. P.J. Watson, "The Halafian Culture: a Review and Synthesis" in T.C. Young, P.L.E. Smith and P. Mortensen, *The Hilly Flanks: Essays on the Prehistory of Southwestern Asia* (Chicago, 1983), pp. 231–249.

69. G. Algaze, "The Uruk Expansion: Cross Cultural Exchange in Early Mesopotamian Civilization," *Current Anthropology* 30: (1989): 571–608.

70. For the rare exceptions, see R. Gophna and S. Sadeh, "Excavations at Tel Tsaf: an Early Chalcolithic

Site in the Jordan Valley," *Tel Aviv* 15–16 (1988–1989): 3–36; R. Frankel and R. Gophna, "Chalcolithic Pottery from a Cave in Western Galilee," *Tel Aviv* 7 (1980): 65–69.

71. Gophna (see note 36), p. 7, in describing the assemblage of site H.

72. Y. Yekutieli, personal communication.

73. Ben-Tor (see note 46, first item, p. 4) suggests that Egyptian pottery may constitute as much as 90 percent of the entire assemblage in sites where it is dominant.

74. Oren (see note 47).

75. O. Bar-Yosef, A, Belfer, A. Goren, and P. Smith, "The *Nawamis* near ʿEin Ḥuderah (Eastern Sinai)," *IEJ* 27 (1977): 65–88; O. Bar-Yosef, A. Belfer-Cohen, A. Goren, I. Hershkovitz, O. Ilan, H.K. Mienis, and B. Sass, "*Nawamis* and Habitations Sites near Gebel Gunna, Southern Sinai," *IEJ* 36 (1986): 121–165.

76. A.R. Schulman, "At the Fringe: the Historiography and Historicity of the Relations of Egypt and Canaan in the Early Bronze Age I," in *L'urbanisation* (see note 1), pp. 433–453.

77. For a recent survey see K. Kroeper, "Palestinian Ceramic Imports in Pre- and Protohistoric Egypt," in *L'urbanisation* (see note 1), pp. 407–422; S. Tutundzic, "Relations Between Late Predynastic Egypt and Palestine: Some Elements and Phenomena," in *L'urbanisation* (see note 1), pp. 423–432.

78. B. Trigger, "The Rise of Civilization in Egypt," *Cambridge History of Africa* Vol. 1, pp. 478–547.

79. Gophna (see note 46); Ben-Tor (see note 46, first item), p. 10.

80. Y. Yadin, "The Earliest Record of Egypt's Military Penetration into Asia?" *IEJ* 5 (1955): 1–16; Oren (see note 47: second item), p. 404; Schulman (see note 76), p. 449.

81. Rosen (see note 33).

82. D.L. Esse, "Secondary State Formation and Collapse in Early Bronze Age Palestine," in *L'urbanisation* (see note 1), pp. 81–96, mainly p. 91; S. Rosen, (in this volume).

83. A. Kempinski, *The Rise of an Urban Culture: The Urbanization of Palestine in the Early Bronze Age, 3000–2150 B.C.* (Jerusalem, 1978).

84. R. Gophna, S. Lifschitz and S. Lev-Yadun, "Man's Impact on the Natural Vegetation of the Central Coastal Plain of Israel During The Chalcolithic Period and the Bronze Age," *Tel Aviv* 13–14 (1986–1987): 71–84, mainly p. 79.

85. R. Gophna, "From Village to Town in the Lod Valley: A Case Study," in *L'urbanisation* (see note 1), pp. 97–107, particularly pp. 104–105.

86. Perrot and Ladiray (see note 62); E.L. Sukenik, "A Chalcolithic Necropolis at Hadera," *JPOS* 17 (1937): 15–30; R. Gophna and S. Lifschitz, "A Chalcolithic Burial Cave at Palmahim," ʿ*Atiqot*, English Series, 14 (1980): 1–8.

87. A. Gopher, T. Tsuk, S. Shalev and R. Gophna, "Earliest Gold Artifacts in the Southern Levant," *Current Anthropology* (in press).

88. For exceptions see: Frankel and Gophna (above note 70); I. Gilead, "Chalcolithic Sites in the Beit Netofa Valley, Lower Galilee, Israel," *Paléorient* 15 (1989): 263–267. The pottery assemblages of these sites suggest that they belong relatively early in the Chalcolithic period.

89. C. Epstein, "A New Aspect of Chalcolithic Culture," *BASOR* 229 (1978): 27–45.; idem, "The Chalcolithic Culture in the Golan," *Ariel* 50–51 (1987): 49–55 (Hebrew).

90. Gilead (see note 49), Table I.

91. Epstein (see note 89, second item), p. 52.

92. R. Greenberg, "The Settlement of the Hula Basin During the Early Bronze Age II-III." MA diss. (Hebrew University of Jerusalem, 1987), p. 10–11 (Hebrew).

93. Eisenberg (see note 2), p. 38–39.

94. Lapp (above note 1).

95. R.T. Schaub, "The Origins of the Early Bronze Age Walled Town Culture in Jordan," in A. Hadidi (ed.), *Studies in the History and Archaeology of Jordan* I (Amman, 1982), pp. 67–75.

96. Hanbury-Tenison (see note 1).

97. See also S.W. Helms, "Jawa, Tel Um Hammad and the EB I/Late Chalcolithic Landscape," *Levant* 19 (1987): 49–81.

The Rise of Complexity in the Land of Israel in the Early Second Millennium B.C.E.

William G. Dever

The wording of the topic is just as it was assigned to me, but I would have chosen it in any case. Increasing social "complexity" is probably the most useful description of the phenomenon we confront in the shift from the EB IV to the beginning of the Middle Bronze Age in the Land of Israel around 2,000 B.C.E. In looking briefly at this topic before a select audience such as this, I shall assume knowledge of the basic data and of previous scholarly discussions. What I intend to do here is to define the fundamental issues more sharply, then employ a General Systems Theory model to suggest ways of analyzing and measuring the process of rising complexity.[1]

On Defining the Terms of the Analysis

Previous analyses of the MB I (Albright's MB IIA, ca. 2000–1800 B.C.E.) have sought to characterize the period's uniqueness in terms of ceramic and metallic typologies, urban renascence, trade and the Syrian connection, "Amorite" newcomers and even the notion of an Egyptian empire in Asia.[2] But no analysis thus far has focused on social complexity as an organizing principle. That does not seem so surprising when we consider the fact that the term "complexity" itself remains ill-defined.

By recent consensus in the fields of archaeology, anthropology and social theory, vague and moralistic concepts like "civilization" have been replaced by the notion of "complexity." This term is not only more precise and neutral but it also allows us to focus on, and to begin to quantify, the single most basic and significant variant in cultural evolution. This variant is not "urbanism" or the development of a "state" level of organization, but rather social stratification, with its implications for every aspect of culture and history (see below). Israel archaeologists, however, a generation behind in social and anthropological theory, have clung to outworn and fuzzy notions of "the rise of civilization," never bothering to define the concept, of course. As a single example, I cite Aharon Kempinski's 1978 *The Rise of an Urban Society: The Urbanization of Palestine in the Early Bronze Age, 3000–2150 B.C.* This approach should have died with V. Gordon Childe.[3]

The above treatment at least has a model, if an outdated one. Most treatments have none. Let us begin to remedy this sad deficiency by clarifying several concepts which must serve as basic categories when we come to assess social change.

1) "Urbanization." Clearly this term is superior to "civilization," even though they both denote the process by which a society becomes "citified," as it were. But how are we to specify this process? Despite the fact that we all use the terms "urban/ urbanization," and the concept is particularly apropos for the MB I in the Land of Israel, what precisely do we mean by them? I cannot find a working definition in the literature (unless we accept rather simple-minded descriptions such as "large," "walled," etc.)

One model of urbanization developed in the general field of archaeology in the last few years derives from human and economic geography, especially from an approach called Central Place Theory. First pioneered in Europe for dealing with agricultural valleys, this model sought to analyze sites according to size. It usually assumed a three-tiered hierarchy; in a typical network there would be hamlets and villages, a fair number of towns, and relatively few large, centrally located market towns that dominate the economy. Where the settlement landscape could be plotted this way (sometimes in near-perfect mathematical "Thiessen polygons"), one could be assured that one was dealing with an urban configuration.

Central Place Theory, or even the simpler "rank-size" models, have enjoyed only limited use in archaeology, however, because of the difficulties of transferring the basic assumptions to other than modern European economies. On the other hand, Dr. Wade Kotter has applied the model to Middle Bronze Age sites in the Land of Israel in a 1986 University of Arizona dissertation, with somewhat promising results.[4] Whatever the limitations, such analyses are at least systematic; they can be tested against the data and they suggest ways of evaluating urbanism in ancient Israel in a cross-cultural and comparative manner.

Another Arizona student, S. Falconer, in his 1987 dissertation, "Heartland of Villages: Reconsidering Urbanism in the Southern Levant" (modelled after Adams' *Heartland of Cities* [1981]), has suggested a simple and useful formula for defining a population agglomeration as a "city"; a settlement is a city whenever it grows to the point where it is no longer economically self-sufficient. In the ancient Near East, this means when it can no longer feed itself. At that point it becomes dependent on the surpluses of the countryside and must therefore dominate the means of agricultural production and distribution.

Falconer attempts to quantify this process of urbanization by taking Mesopotamian case-studies. Having worked out the extent of available land surrounding a typical large Mesopotamian site, and then having calculated its annual yield in total calories for food intake, he arrives at a maximum figure of about 3,400–8,500 individuals before a population agglomerate becomes dependent on the hinterland. Thus a city would average about 34 hectares (85 acres) in size. This is the "threshold" beyond which a settlement can properly be termed a city. While Falconer does not elaborate, the factors that govern the process of urbanization in his model would include not only absolute size but also size in relation to resources, the emergence of a managerial class, and sufficient centralization of power to coerce goods and services from the countryside.[5]

Obviously, by Falconer's criteria, no ancient Bronze Age or Iron Age site in the Land of Israel could be considered a city, not even Hazor at 180 acres and an estimated 20,000 people. However, it should be equally obvious that Israel's semi-arid climate, mountainous terrain and generally poor soil cannot be compared with the flat, rich alluvial plains of the Tigris-Euphrates Valley. Israel's unique landscape and lower productivity mean that a population agglomerate will exhaust the carrying capacity of the typical location with many fewer people, so that Falconer's model must be scaled down to suit Israel's unique landscape. Thus I would suggest that when an ancient Israel site reached about 6–8 hectares (15–20 acres), and 1,500–2,000 people, it may be considered a city. By that criterion, MB I Israel could boast several true urban centers: Dan, Acco, Kabri, Megiddo, Gezer, Aphek, several Sharon Plain sites, Ashkelon and Tell el-ʿAjjul.

Whether or not we adopt either of the above models (or any other) in attempting to define urbanism, we should always keep in mind that the phenomenon of urbanization is neither an inevitable nor necessarily beneficial stage of cultural evolution. It is certainly not a prerequisite for the development of social complexity, much less for the attainment of a state-level of political organization. This is borne out by the fact that urbanization has never taken place in many parts of the world, although some of these so-called "primitive" societies are exceedingly complex. Moreover, others, like the Ming Dynasty in China or the Old Kingdom in Egypt, created a true state on the basis of an almost entirely rural society. Finally, a number of recent studies, such as the work edited by my colleagues Norman Yoffee and George Cowgill, *The Collapse of Ancient States and Civilizations* (1988), suggest that urbanization itself is often something of an anomaly.[6] Under certain conditions, such as those in ancient Israel, I would argue that urbanization is, in fact, an artificial form of socio-political organization, one that is inherently unstable and subject to periodic collapse.

Any long-term settlement history of the Land of Israel, using a model like the *longue durée* of Braudel and the *Annales* school of historians, or the recent work of Coote and Whitelam, *The Emergence of Israel in Historical Perspective* (1988), will reveal dramatically the recurring cycles of urbanism and ruralism, centralization and decentralization, advance and abatement.[7] One has only to look at the country — from the Bronze Age through the Israelite monarchy and even into modern times — to bear out the truth of the observation that urbanization always tends to be fragile and impermanent. In that sense, the phenomenon to be explained in this paper is not the collapse of the Middle Bronze Age around 1500 B.C.E. We should rather seek to explain its rise in the first place — especially after the first, disastrous experiment in urban living in the Early Bronze Age which preceded it, an experiment which ended with the abandonment of every urban site in the country in the final centuries before the MB I period.

In one sense, Falconer's intuition on the "heartland of villages" is correct; even though ancient Israel may be considered a prime example of Rowton's "dimorphic society," the village-pastoral morpheme is better suited to the natural conditions of this region and has tended to predominate throughout history at the expense of the urban morpheme. Leon Marfoe has made the same point with regard to parts of southern Syria in antiquity and even for modern Lebanon.[8]

2) *"Complexity."* A second term we must define further is "complexity." Obviously, all societies are complex to some degree, since no truly "egalitarian" social system, ancient or modern, has ever been encountered. But for the purposes of our discussion we understand complexity to denote basically the phenomenon of stratification, that is, the process by which groups within a society become differentiated, elite classes.

Ultimately, of course, the distinction of "elite" is based upon class or inherited status. To that extent, the complex society may seem to resemble earlier stages of social evolution such as the so-called "tribal" or "chiefdom" levels, which are lineage groups or kinship-based societies that confer privilege by birth rather than achievement. But complexity differs not only in the fact that only relatively few members of society inherit privilege, but also in the origins of this privilege. In a complex society, elite classes may not be born as such, but may become so through craft specialization, entrepreneurship, the accumulation of capital, the wielding of power in a variety of ways, or through other means. Thus, there emerges a minority ruling class which enjoys differential access to goods and services and in turn manipulates the majority of the less privileged in order to maintain itself. Social institutions like kingship and priesthood serve to legitimize its special role and function.

Such an elite group, once established, may persevere not only through ideology but frequently through coercion, since the society at large may resist this funnelling of resources to the privileged few. As long as an approximate equilibrium can be maintained, peace and prosperity are the apparent result, although at an enormous price. When the balance shifts, however, as it inevitably does, the elite classes may be displaced, social institutions may fragment, urban centers may become depopulated and the economy may revert to a lower (that is, simpler) level of integration and production. In ancient Israel, this simpler level means ruralism and pastoralism in place of industry and trade. Thus, there ensues what we call "collapse," even if temporary, or the reversal of the process that produced "complexity." Finally, it must be noted that, according to our current understanding, upheavals and even radical socio-cultural changes are not likely to be satisfactorily explained by positing invasions of new peoples, catastrophic natural disasters, or even the diffusion of new ideas. Rather, such change may be explained by indigenous developments which lead to a shift in the competing demands of elements within the local society.

3) *"State."* A third term, "state," should be defined, if for no other reason than for

the sake of our discipline. I would argue, however, that this category is completely irrelevant to a discussion of the Middle Bronze Age, or even the Late Bronze Age in the Land of Israel. Even a brief perusal of the archaeological and anthropological literature reveals a remarkable consensus on what we mean by "state." A "state" level of organization refers to a society in which power and decision making are completely centralized in a single place, in a single set of social institutions, and in the hands of a single administrative body.

Normally this centralization process is the result of an autochthonous process of social evolution, in which case we denote a "pristine" or primary state, in contrast to an imposed or "secondary" state. Both Egypt and parts of Mesopotamia would be examples of pristine states in the ancient world (along with the Indus Valley civilization, Ming Dynasty China, Peru, and the Maya, the only such examples recognized by social theorists).[9] It is evident, I think, that ancient Israel, despite strong tendencies toward urbanization, did not achieve statehood in the Bronze Age but only in the Iron Age, with the Israelite United Monarchy of the 10th century B.C.E. (And not until 1948 would a fully viable independent state emerge again on the soil of the Land of Israel.)

4) "City-State." A final definition is appropriate, namely that of "city-state," a term much abused in our discipline. One has the impression that the use of "city-state" by archaeologists means little more than "beyond urban" or "not-quite-state." Yet we can easily be more precise. A city-state is simply a large, centrally located urban site that has come to autonomy by monopolizing its hinterland as far as the border of the influence of its nearest urban rival; in short, what economic geographers call a "central place" (above). It is a state written small, a state in miniature, possessing the centralized authority needed to command essential resources but on a regional rather than national scale. City-states are thus one stage short of state-level development and seem to be the form ideally suited to marginal areas like the Land of Israel.

The numerous regional centers of the Land of Israel in the Bronze Age (especially those of the Late Bronze Age, where the Amarna letters add textual documentation to the rich data from the archaeological record) are excellent examples of ancient city-states. The city-state seems to be an authentic institution of the Land of Israel, one that, as we shall see, re-emerges dramatically in the MB I period. (See, above, however, Falconer's emphasis on villages and Marfoe's "ruralism.")

A General Systems Theory Approach to Assessing Complexity in the First Phase of the Middle Bronze Age

In turning from definition to description (if not explanation), let me suggest that the growth of complexity in the MB I period in the Land of Israel may be best understood and compared with the preceding EB IV by analyzing the period in terms of the General Systems Theory (GST). This model is borrowed, of course, from the biological sciences; it applies the basic notion of "the organized state" in living organisms to

the study of human culture and society. Although not always spelled out so specifically, the concept is often implicit in "holistic" or "systemic" approaches to culture-
history which are gradually making an impact on archaeology.[10] The basic
assumption is that society, like nature, is composed of numerous interacting sub-
systems. When these sub-systems maintain a proper balance, stability (or
"homeostasis") is the result. Changes in any sub-system can occur, however, through
a variety of causes, and these tend to affect the whole, either negatively or positively
("deviation amplifying mechanisms"). Thus, because of a series of mutual outputs and
inputs of information and energy ("feedback loops") social systems, like organisms,
are not static but are dynamic; subject constantly to a variety of internal and external
forces which promote either growth or decay (the "complexity"-"collapse" syn-
drome noted above).

While there are obvious limitations to the use of biological models in analyzing
social systems, the attractions of the General Systems Theory are such that in recent
years it has become one of the most widely adopted models for the study of anthropology and archaeology. Although it has rarely been used in our branch of archaeology,
at least explicitly, I have applied the General Systems Theory to seek explanations
for the end of the Early Bronze Age and to the Late Bronze/Iron I transition; and
I will use it here to assess socio-cultural changes between the EB IV and MB I periods.

The principle sub-systems found in MB I provide both the ideal categories of analysis and the means to move beyond generalities to specifics. Let us look in turn at: 1)
settlement types and distribution patterns, 2) ecological setting, technology and subsistence, 3) social structure and demography, 4) political organization, 5) ideology
and art, and 6) international relations. In each case our assignment is to measure only
social complexity, and in particular the rise of elite classes, not the overall characteristics of the period; these have been amply discussed elsewhere by myself and others.
We shall also need to keep in mind the essential nature of the preceding EB IV period,
in order to have some basis for comparison.

1) **Settlement types and patterns.** Here the data are abundant and clear: in comparison with EB IV, MB I witnesses a dramatic shift in the type and distribution of settlement. Predominantly pastoral EB IV encampments, rural sites and small villages,
scattered in the hinterland and even in semi-arid steppe zones, are mostly abandoned,
then rapidly replaced by re-occupied EB II–III tell sites in central Israel. In addition,
many sites established *de novo* soon grow into larger settlements, while hundreds of
new villages spring up throughout the countryside.

Although the general trend is beyond dispute, precise statistics are hard to come
by. Broshi and Gophna have attempted a pioneering settlement-history and demographic analysis of the Land of Israel in the Middle Bronze Age, suggesting the following:[11]

EB II–III		MB I		MB II–III	
Sites	Area (ha.)	Sites	Area (ha.)	Sites	Area (ha.)
260	600	130	555.1	337	660.3

In any case, recent settlement-history studies show beyond doubt that the demographic growth, the nucleation of population, and the three-tiered hierarchy of settlements which above all characterize our definition of "urbanism," are all manifest in MB I; some features, I would argue, from a rather early phase of the period. In that sense, MB I, like EB I, could well be characterized as the "Proto-Urban" phase of the Middle Bronze Age.

No

With respect to "complexity," it would appear that it too was present almost from the beginning, since complexity is both a necessary component of and an outgrowth of urbanism. Specifically, we must presume that cities (and soon city-states) could not have developed without the emergence of an elite class. Such a class had to be capable of centralized planning and administration and funding of collective activities: food production, building projects, commerce and trade and relations with both neighboring cities and more distant regions and states.

Such a complex society is not difficult to envision in the MB I, for it had forerunners in 3rd millennium B.C.E. Syria and Israel, as shown by studies of numerous EB II–III sites. What we see, then, in MB I is simply the re-emergence, after a long break in EB IV, of an older type of city-state social system that had prevailed for some six or seven hundred years during an earlier period. In MB I, however, I would argue that the level of complexity was higher and more intensified, as the following will show.

2) **Ecological setting, technology and subsistence.** These sub-categories, all having to do with the economy, cannot easily be separated. At first glance, the natural setting would seem to be the same as that of EB IV. There are, however, those who posit environmental deterioration, and even climatic change, as explanations for the "dark age" in EB IV. If we accept that view, we can see the urban renascence in MB I as due to an amelioration of natural conditions.

But, in any case, the study of "ecology" embraces not only environmental conditions per se, but both culturally and technologically derived mechanisms for exploiting that environment (i.e., subsistence). And these clearly have changed from EB IV to MB I. In particular, we can see that the much less specialized mixed economy of EB IV, combining pastoralism and dry farming, was eclipsed in MB I. It was replaced by a multi-faceted economy comprised of intensified high-yield agriculture, industry (especially true tin-bronze metallurgy and wheel-made mass-produced ceramics) and trade, some of it long-distance.

Canaanite jar

Again, not only is the new economy clear evidence of urbanism, but also of growing social complexity. We cannot possibly imagine that an "egalitarian" or non-stratified society, without centralized management, could have produced either the quantity or the quality of the goods and services that we see reflected in the archaeological record of MB I. For example, an economy based on intensified agriculture requires skillful organization of both city and countryside so as to produce surpluses of food that can be stored and redistributed. Mass production of metals and pottery requires not only sophisticated and specialized technology, but enforced standardization and the capital to develop markets. Long-distance trade, such as that needed to procure tin for the manufacture of bronze, requires an exceptionally high degree of centralized planning. The presence of all these activities in MB I strongly suggests an elite managerial class.

3) **Social structure.** Skeptics sometime say that "archaeologists do not dig up social systems." Of course not; but they do bring to light material remains which are products of social organization, some features of which we can indeed extrapolate. In the MB I period I would isolate, as evidence for social stratification, two particular phenomena: (a) craft specialization, and (b) the emergence of a ruling class.

a) In the first instance, developments in several areas — ceramic production, — *metal* bronzeworking and the replication of imported luxury items — yield clues. The *skeuomorphs* introduction of true tin-bronze, which with rare exceptions, began suddenly in the Land of Israel in MB I, constituted a true technological revolution. It required not only imported tin (above), but a vastly more sophisticated process of controlled amalgamation, smelting, casting, tempering and cold-hammering.

The typical MB I bronze types — duck-bill axes, notched chisel-axes, veined daggers, socketed spears and elaborate toggle-pins — are a far cry from the simple copper implements of EB IV. They cannot any longer have been produced by itinerant metalsmiths, or even by a simple cottage industry. They are certainly the work of highly skilled specialists, possibly organized in craft guilds and probably occupying a coveted niche in society because of the demand for their products. (Elsewhere I have suggested that the preponderance of weapons in the bronze repertoire of MB I may be evidence that some city-states maintained a standing army, or at least a militia).[12]

The same observations may be made for ceramic production. The MB I fast-wheel-made, beautifully decorated pottery has, despite the objections of some, virtually nothing to do with the relatively crude pottery of EB IV. It is another world, not only much more advanced but closely aligned with the cosmopolitan ceramic style of Syria. The fast potter's wheels, the improved kilns and firing techniques and vastly superior decorative designs all point to craft specialization, and, I would say, to the first true mass-produced and widely traded pottery in the history of the Land of Israel.

Finally, highly trained artists and craftsmen first learned in MB I how to imitate imported luxury goods, such as Egyptian alabasters (in local calcite) and, particularly, scarab seals, first attested in this period and soon to become common.

In all of the above (and possibly in other) cases, we have evidence for at least one class of specialists who were no longer hunters or farmers or the like. They now commanded sufficient leisure, skill and access to markets to enable them to make a livelihood by pursuing an art or a craft. It is likely, furthermore, that a new elite class emerged from these entrepreneurs and their accumulated capital, an elite which could maintain its status and even pass it on to its heirs because its skills were necessary for the preservation of the new social order.

b) An even more important elite class was made up of those who ruled the new MB I city-states; but we shall treat them separately, since they represent both a social and a political elite.

4) **Political organization.** An MB I ruling class might not have been recognized

solely from the archaeological record, but the presence of local "princes" in ancient Israel is abundantly clear from the Egyptian Execration Texts. Identifiable MB I sites in the Land of Israel include 'Iyyon, Laish, Qadesh, Hazor, Achshaph (Tell Keisan?), Acco, Shechem, Reḥov, Pella, Jerusalem and Ashkelon. It is significant that these princes, all with Amorite or Canaanite-style names, and associated with specific city-states and major regions in both Syria and the Land of Israel, were sufficiently promi-nent that they and their activities were intimately known to the far-off court of the Egyptian 12th Dynasty.

Surely these "princes" were an elite class, the product of a highly segregated social system. Their emergence must be dated before the end of MB I, not later than about 1850–1800 B.C.E., to judge from the Brussels texts. Whether or not we accept Albright's attempt (based on the earlier Berlin texts) to distinguish an earlier EB IV/MB I "tribal" political organization, with several rulers named for each site, it is nonetheless clear that by the time of the later Brussels texts we are dealing not only with single rulers who were elite "princes" but also with highly integrated central-ized city-states, powerful enough to be the subject of 12th Dynasty Egyptian interna-tional intelligence.

At this point we might note not only textual but artifactual evidence of ruling elite classes. The well-documented MB I "palace" at Tel Aphek, a splendidly constructed building comparable to anything in MB I Syria, as well as several rich tombs, certainly reflect a wealthy and privileged class. (As archaeologists in other branches have always recognized, burials are especially significant for distinguishing elite classes, not only in the evidence of luxury grave goods but also in signs of differential treat-ment of certain of the dead.)

A final (though not necessarily crucial) aspect of a city-state level of political orga-nization in MB I is the existence of massive city wall systems at many sites. This is evidence not only of inter-urban rivalry, but also of the ability of local rulers to com-mand impressive resources in men and material, as well as the engineering and organi-zational skill necessary to construct such defenses.

5) **Ideology, art, religion.** Ideology, including aspects of art and religion, is even more difficult than social structure to specify archaeologically, but again we have hints in MB I. We have already noted the evidence for specialized art in our discussion of alabaster and scarabs, but that is partly derivative from Egypt. Thus far we have little indigenous Canaanite art in this first phase of MB I. Temples, however, are attested: at Nahariya, Megiddo and Tell el-Hayyat 5.[13]

From this admittedly meager data, we might nevertheless suggest that the typically West Semitic (or by now specifically "Canaanite") fertility cults, which are so well attested in later MB II–III and the Late Bronze Age, were already well established by MB I. If so, we may then posit another elite class: priests, or, at least, specialized religious functionaries of some sort. It is likely that these religious officials served to legitimatize, and in turn were subsidized by, the local princes whom we have just discussed. This situation would have been similar to that of 3rd–2nd millennium B.C.E. Egypt and Mesopotamia. There we have much more specific evidence, both textual and artifactual, for the alliance between palace and temple which together dominated the society and the economy (although in the Land of Israel, of course, on a smaller scale).

6) **International relations.** The Land of Israel's chief contacts with the wider world in MB I were with Syria on the one hand and Egypt on the other. Connections with Syria are clearly seen in material culture: architecture, tomb types, ceramics and metallurgy, as I and others have documented elsewhere. As indicated above, craft specialization allied to an international trading network is undoubtedly attested.[14]

The case is somewhat different with Egypt. Numerous Egyptian 12th Dynasty artifacts are known from Syria and the Land of Israel (as discussed, for example, by Posener, Weinstein, and others).[15] Here the question is whether these objects, plus the Egyptian interest so transparently clear in the Execration Texts, indicate merely trade, or rather an attempt at establishing an Egyptian "empire" in Asia. Whether we take the maximalist or minimalist view on this issue (and I prefer the latter), the point is the same: the Land of Israel, an obscure cultural backwater in the Levant in EB IV, has come out of its total isolation and into international visibility by the MB I period. And that is clear witness to the emergence of a society which has moved far beyond pastoral nomadism and ruralism and into urban complexity. If, as I have maintained, Canaanite urbanists expanded into the Egyptian Delta and founded the later Hyksos capital of Avaris as early as MB I, then we have dramatic evidence for the rapid cultural development of this first phase of the Middle Bronze Age.[16]

A final point concerns Cyprus. If my argument in 1976 (now supported independently by several other scholars) was correct,[17] then the first Cypriot imports — specifically Cypriot WP IV–VI "Line Pendant" pottery — appear in MB I. That is significant because it documents not only overland trade but also seafaring trade, which requires even more centralized management. Once again, we see that characteristics of the fully developed MB II–III period appear already in MB I, further testimony to the cultural dynamism of this first formative phase of the Middle Bronze Age.

Conclusion

Throughout this paper I have argued that the MB I period is properly characterized by what social theorists call "complexity," with all its implications. The argument is, of course, partly speculative, for we lack some of the data needed to corroborate it in full. We lack, in particular, the textual data for the Land of Israel which is available for Syria, even though I would argue that in the Middle Bronze Age the Land of Israel (for once) may have outstripped Syria in the development of urban complexity. The archaeological data, on the other hand, are relatively abundant, and when fully exploited with an appropriate model, yield surprisingly good results.

That leads me to a final point. The notion of "complexity" is, after all, only a model. In our discipline there seems to be a great deal of unnecessary confusion, not to mention skepticism, about the use of social science "models" in archaeology. Yet a model is simply a heuristic device, an aid in the interpretation and understanding of the basic evidence. It is, if you wish, a hypothesis to be tested against the evidence; to be replaced, if necessary, by one that is more useful as new evidence becomes available. A model is simply a way of framing appropriate questions. And without doing that explicitly, I would argue that we can never hope to convert so-called archaeological "facts" into true and meaningful data, data that can elucidate the complex cultural process that took place in the ancient Land of Israel.

Notes

1. For the rationale of the terminology and chronology used in the following, and on the MB I period generally, see W.G. Dever, "The Beginning of the Middle Bronze Age in Syria-Palestine," in F.M. Cross, W.E. Lemke and P.D. Miller (eds.), *Magnalia Dei: The Mighty Acts of God. Essays on the Bible and Archaeology in Memory of G. Ernest Wright* (Garden City NY, 1976), pp. 3–38; idem, "Palestine in the Middle Bronze Age: The Zenith of the Urbanite Canaanite Era," *BA* 50 (1987): 149–176. For an orientation to the use of General Systems Theory in the archaeology of Syria and the Land of Israel, see W.G. Dever, "The Collapse of Urban Early Bronze Age in Palestine: Toward a Systems Analysis" in P. de Miroschedji (ed.), *L'urbanisation de la Palestine à l'âge du bronze ancien* (BAR International Series) (Oxford, 1989), pp. 225–246.
2. For general surveys of MB I, see my works cited in note 1, above, and P. Gerstenblith, *The Levant at the Beginning of the Middle Bronze Age* (Winona Lake IN, 1983); J.N. Tubb, "The MB IIA Period in Palestine: Its Relationship with Syria and its Origin," *Levant* 15 (1983): 49–62.
3. See A. Kempinski, *Syrien und Palästina in der letzten Phase der Mittlebronze IIB Zeit (1050–1470 v. Chr.)* (Wiesbaden, 1983). See my review in *JAOS* 110 (1990): 345–347.
4. See W. Kotter, "Spatial Analysis of the Urban Development of Palestine During the Middle Bronze Age." (Ph.D. diss., University of Arizona, 1986).
5. See Stephen E. Falconer, "Heartland of Villages: Reconsidering Early Urbanism in the Southern Levant." (Ph.D. diss., University of Arizona, 1987).
6. See N. Yoffee and G.L. Cowgill (eds.), *The Collapse of Ancient States and Civilizations* (Tucson, 1988); J.A. Tainter, *The Collapse of Complex Societies* (Cambridge, 1989). Both these works have full references to earlier literature, a critique of various theories and abundant case-studies. That the ancient Land of Israel nowhere appears is a sad witness to the parochial nature of our discipline; neither Israelis nor Americans have succeeded in "mainstreaming" Land of Israel and "Biblical" archaeology.
7. See R.B. Coote and K.W. Whitelam, *The Emergence of Israel in Historical Perspective* (Sheffield, 1987); for the application of Braudel's *la longue durée* to our branch of archaeology, see W.G. Dever, "Impact of the 'New Archaeology'," in J.F. Drinkard, G.M. Mattingly and J.M. Miller (eds.), *Benchmarks in Time and Culture. An Introduction to Palestinian Archaeology* (Atlanta, 1988), pp. 337–352.
8. L. Marfoe, "The Integrative Transformation: Patterns of Socio-Political Organization in Southern Syria," *BASOR* 243 (1979): 1–42.
9. See E.R. Service, *Origins of the State and Civilization: The Process of Cultural Evolution* (New York, 1975), p. 5.
10. See Dever, "Collapse of the Urban Early Bronze Age" (see note 1), pp. 235–239.
11. M. Broshi and R. Gophna, "Middle Bronze Age Palestine. Its Settlement and Population" *BASOR* 261 (1986): 73–90; add now Kotter, *Spatial Analysis* (see note 4).
12. Dever, "Middle Bronze Age" (see note 1), pp. 160–161; add E. Oren, "A Middle Bronze Age I Warrior Tomb at Beth-shan, *ZDPV* 89 (1971): 109–139.

13. For the Nahariya temple, see provisionally M. Dothan, "Sanctuaries along the Coast of Canaan in the MB Period: Nahariyeh," in A. Biran (ed.), *Temples and High Places in Biblical Times* (Jerusalem, 1981), pp. 74–81. The Megiddo Stratum XV megaron temples may well have been built in EB III, as several scholars maintain, but I suspect that the "sacred area" continued in use in MB I (XIV); see Y. Aharoni, "Megiddo," *Encyclopedia of Archaeological Excavations in the Holy Land*, Vol. III, pp. 837–841. For the Tell el-Hayyat temples, see S.E. Falconer and B. Magness-Gardiner, "Bronze Age Village Life in the Jordan Valley: Archaeological Investigations at Tell el-Hayyat and Tell Abu en-Niʾaj," *National Geographic Research* 5 (1989): 335–347.

14. See Dever, "Beginning of the Middle Bronze Age" (see note 1), pp. 10–16 and full references there; and Gerstenblith, *The Levant* (see note 2), pp. 38–100.

15. For a convenient listing of 12th Dynasty artifacts found in Syria and the Land of Israel, see G. Posener, "Syria and Palestine c. 2160–1780 B.C.: Relations with Egypt," *CAH* 3 Vol. I, Part 2; and see J. Weinstein "Egyptian Relations With Palestine in the Middle Kingdom," *BASOR* 217 (1975): 1–16.

16. For Tell ed-Dabʾa, see principally M. Bietak, *Avaris and Piramesse: Archaeological Exploration in the Eastern Nile Delta* (Proceedings of the British Academy, Vol. 65) (London, 1979); idem, "Problems of Middle Bronze Age Chronology: New Evidence from Egypt," *AJA* 88 (1984): 421–485. For my critique, see W.G. Dever, "Relations between Syria-Palestine and Egypt in the 'Hyksos' Period," in J.N. Tubb (ed.), *Palestine in the Bronze and Iron Age: Essays in Honor of Olga Tufnell* (London, 1985), pp. 69–87; idem, "Tell ed-Dabʾa and Levantine Middle Bronze Chronology: A Rejoinder to Manfred Bietak," forthcoming in *BASOR* (1991).

17. See Dever, "Beginning of the Middle Bronze Age" (see note 1), pp. 14, 34, 35. A similarly early date for Cypriot imports was subsequently advanced by D.L. Salz, "The Chronology of the Middle Cypriot Period," *Report of the Department of Antiquities in Cyprus 1977* (1977): 51–70; see also P. Johnson, "The Middle Cypriot Pottery Found in Palestine," *Opuscula Atheniensia* 14,6 (1982): 49–72.

The Sociopolitical Organization of the Central Hill Country in the Second Millennium B.C.E.

Israel Finkelstein

Two main human ecosystems — highland and lowland — can be distinguished around the Mediterranean and in the Middle East. They differ in almost every physical aspect — geomorphology, topography, hydrology, climate and vegetation — and hence also in their economic potential. Consequently, they developed different settlement and demographic patterns, socioeconomic frameworks and political formations.[1] In recent years, this observation about the highland-lowland dichotomy has found its way into research concerning the ancient Near East,[2] including Canaan-Israel.[3]

Recent archaeological investigations in the central hill country of Israel depict an interesting asymmetry in highland and lowland settlement patterns and material culture in the Middle Bronze and Late Bronze Ages. In light of this research, this article deals with demographic patterns and sociopolitical formations in the highlands of Canaan during the 2nd millennium B.C.E. The results seem to have far-reaching implications for the study of the territorial and sociopolitical roots of the Israelite monarchies.

Geographical Background

The Lowlands
The lowlands constitute the most fertile part of the Land of Israel. They were intensively cultivated, and their subsistence economy was generally dominated by dry-farming. The lowlands were densely settled and were characterized by continuity of sedentary occupation, even in periods of decay. The population was concentrated in urban centers, surrounded by smaller rural communities. The major towns were the centers of city-states — the typical political system of the lowlands in the 3rd–2nd

110

millennia B.C.E. Most parts of the lowlands were not available for pastoralism, since intensive cultivation was a better economic strategy. Coastal ports and proximity to international trade routes contributed to the prosperity of these regions. Military campaigns of neighboring powers, social strife, and epidemics were secular disadvantages for the inhabitants of the lowlands.

The Highlands

Large parts of the highlands of Canaan can be described as ecological frontier zones. Limitations to sedentary activity stem from harsh topography, difficult rock formations and dense cover of natural vegetation.[4] In contrast to the continuity of occupation in the lowlands, the frontier areas (both highlands and steppe) were characterized by oscillations in sedentary activity. Waves of settlement were punctuated by intervals of decline during which very few sedentary sites existed. Even during periods of prosperity, the number of fortified centers in the highlands was relatively limited, and most sites were no more than small rural communities. But there were some clear advantages for inhabitants of the highlands, mainly relative social and economic freedom.[5]

The subsistence base differed in the various ecological niches of the highlands. In the central hill country, animal husbandry and dry farming predominated in the eastern flank of the central range; horticulture in the heart of the hilly regions, especially in their western part; and mixed economy in the intermontane valleys and in flat areas of the central range. The expansion of horticulture opened the way to the development of specialized economy, which required a certain degree of sociopolitical organization.

The hilly regions, never densely populated, were always receptive to population surplus from the lowlands. Hence, the ecological frontier zones were the last to be populated in every wave of settlement and the first to suffer in times of settlement crisis. At the same time, the special environmental conditions made them ideal refuges for marginal elements of society.

The environmental and ecological conditions, and the fact that the frontier zones of the highlands were never densely populated nor cultivated (especially in the 3rd–2nd millennia B.C.E.; large parts of the highlands were very thinly populated even in periods of settlement expansion) made them ideal for pastoral activity. They were especially convenient for summer herding of pastoral groups which practiced "enclosed nomadism."[6] The hill country offered niches of green pasture in the dry season; the proximity to the steppe areas played an important role in this routine, as the pastoralists could utilize the grazing areas of the latter in the winter. Another possible mode of pastoral transhumance was summer in the hilly regions and winter in the Negev.[7] The eastern flank of the hilly regions was convenient for sedentarization of pastoral groups. They could continue to practice husbandry in the desert fringe while dry-farming in the eastern part of the central range. As a result of all these factors, the highlands were inhabited by pastoralists throughout the 3rd–2nd millennia B.C.E., in varying degrees, depending upon the fate of the sedentary communities.[8]

The central hill country can be divided into four subunits, which are briefly described here. The biblical names are used for the sake of convenience only.

1) Manasseh — the area north of Shechem. This is the most convenient part of the hill country for habitation, mainly because of the large and fertile intermontane valleys and the abundance of water sources. In the western part of the region the terrain is rocky and less conducive to cultivation.[9]

2) Ephraim — the area between Shechem and Ramallah. The morphology here is more diverse: in the northern part of its central range there are small intermontane valleys, which were the focus of habitation in the area in antiquity. The southern part of the central range, which is the continuation of the plateau of Benjamin, is also advantageous for human exploitation. The western half of the region, which is characterized by rugged and rocky terrain, was an ecological frontier-zone in antiquity. However, terracing the slopes can make it useful for horticulture.

3) Benjamin — between Ramallah and Jerusalem. This region can also be divided into three sections: the central range plateau, which is amenable for habitation; the desert fringe, also favorable for human activity; and the western slopes — the continuation of the rugged area of western Ephraim.

4) Judah — the area south of Jerusalem. This region has desert fringe areas on both east and south. The central range is relatively flat and its western flank rugged and steep. Recent surveys indicate that this part of the hill country was only sparsely inhabited by sedentary populations until Iron II. This was apparently due to the following factors: a. The difficult rock formations made the area inhospitable for agricultural activity; b. The extensive marginal lands on both east and south made pastoralism a better economic strategy. The recent human landscape is therefore a result of intensive farming in the last three millennia.

From the point of view of land-use (in antiquity), the central hill country can therefore be divided into two parts: a northern one, which offered relatively large areas for sedentary agriculture (Manasseh, Ephraim and Benjamin), and a southern one, which was more conducive to pastoralism (Judah).

The Archaeological Data

The review of the archaeological data is divided into two sections, dealing respectively with the results of excavations and surveys. This chapter is based on the results of the excavations at Shiloh[10] and of the Land of Ephraim Survey,[11] on previous excavations in the area, and on the regional surveys in Manasseh,[12] Benjamin[13] and Judah.[14] The information will be summarized briefly, since most of it has already been published elsewhere.[15]

Excavations

Two pivotal sites — Shiloh and Shechem — supply valuable data on the layout of Middle Bronze Age fortified centers in the central hill country.

Shiloh

The earliest settlement at Shiloh dates to MB IIB. The only evidence for its existence comes from pottery retrieved from earthen fills layed in the next phase of occupation at the site. The extensive building and filling activity during MB IIC removed all traces of the early settlement, hence it is impossible to reconstruct its nature or extent. We assume that it was small and unfortified.

In MB IIC there was a drastic change in the nature of the site. Imposing stone- and earthworks, which included a massive stone-wall 3–5 m. wide and a huge supporting glacis, were constructed[16], encompassing an area of about 4.2 acres. Data on the layout of the site was derived from its northern sector, which was not disturbed by later occupations.[17] Adjacent to the fortification there was a row of sunken storerooms; they were bounded on their inner side by a wall that also served as a support for earthen fills deposited towards the summit of the mound. These fills were layed in order to smooth the slope of the tell. In other places inside the fortification, earth and stone fills were layed. They served to level the "pockets" created between the sloping bedrock and the fortification. In fact, most of the stone fortification was buried in the fills which were layed on both its sides, leaving unclear how much of it was exposed. The fills were stabilized by walls incorporated into them. There are some clues for the existence of a cult place on the top of the mound. MB IIC Shiloh was therefore a relatively small site, with heavy fortifications and fills, but with no evidence for living quarters. Of course, it is possible that the residential area was located on the southern slope; however, in the squares excavated in this section of the mound, an extremely limited amount of Middle Bronze Age pottery was found.

There is a sharp contrast in Shiloh between the great effort invested in the construction of the fortifications and earthen fills and the small size of the site. If we use the generally accepted density coefficient for calculating population size, that is, about 6 persons per acre,[18] we find that the entire site, even if filled with residential units, would have accommodated only about 400 inhabitants. When we consider that most of the area lacked such dwellings, we arrive at a much lower figure. In other words, at the end of the Middle Bronze Age there were probably not more than a few dozen male adults living in Shiloh, and it is highly improbable that such a small population had undertaken such a large engineering project. Moreover, Shiloh did not have an extensive system of satellite villages — only nine Middle Bronze Age sites are known within a radius of about 6 kms., with an average size of about .75 acres. Moreover, some of these may already have been abandoned when Shiloh's fortifications were being constructed (see below). The solution to the manpower problem should therefore be sought in a larger area with both sedentary and pastoral populations.

Shiloh was destroyed at the end of the Middle Bronze Age. In the Late Bronze Age there was no settlement at the site. Activity was limited to the northeastern sector of the site, where a dump associated with a cult place was found. Hundreds of vessels, which had been brought to the site as offerings, were uncovered in a vast pit, together with large quantities of bones. Some of the vessels were found filled with bones and ashes. Most of the material belongs to LB I. It seems, therefore, that the ruined Middle

Bronze Age cult site was visited by people living in its vicinity. Since almost no Late Bronze Age sites were found in the survey in the surrounding area, it is reasonable to assume that most of these people were pastoralists who did not leave much in the way of remains. The composition of the animal remains from the dig supports this assumption.[19] The phenomenon of cult places not related to sedentary sites, or built outside urban centers, is known in other parts of Late Bronze Age Canaan. It most probably reflects the intensive pastoral segment in the population of the period.[20]

Shechem

The results of the excavations at Shiloh focused attention on nearby Shechem — the most important Middle Bronze-Late Bronze Age site in the central hill country. The Drew-McCormick expedition unearthed remains from the Middle Bronze, Late Bronze and Iron Ages in the northern section of the tell.[21] However, much of the history of Shechem in the 2nd millennium B.C.E. remained vague. Two main features of 2nd millennium Shechem were uncovered: the fortifications and the *temenoi*. The following occupational phases were described by the excavators:[22]

MB IIA Shechem was an unfortified settlement; the only remains of this period are Temenos Phases 1a and 1b. At the start of MB IIB the site was fortified by Wall D; the Courtyard Temple of Temenos 2 also belongs to this period. In the next MB IIB phase a massive earthen fill (the "embankment"), made of local chalk and marl, was thrown outside and against Wall D. The embankment was 38 m. at its base. Wall C formed a battered stone footing for the embankment slope. The excavators argued that the embankment must have risen to a height of 15 m., and that it was crowned by a defense wall. The Courtyard Temple of Temenos 3 belongs to this phase. The embankment continued to serve as Shechem's main fortification in the two succeeding phases of MB IIB (Temenos Phases 4–5). In the beginning of MB IIC, "cyclopean" Wall A was added. Except for the uppermost courses, this wall was never free-standing: at the same stage, the top of the embankment was leveled and the displaced fill was dumped behind Wall A, in order to create a "defensible plateau" inside the site. The Northwest Gate and the massive Migdal Temple were built at the same time. The latter was constructed on a fill which covered the Courtyard Temple. At the closing phase of MB IIC, Wall B and the East Gate were added.

Since the excavators investigated only the northern section of the site, and as the southern part is covered by the modern village of Balaṭah, it is difficult to estimate the size of Middle Bronze Age Shechem. Wright reconstructed a round site of about 10 acres,[23] while the minimal possibility is ca. 7.5 acres.

Upon rechecking the stratigraphic and architectural evidence from Tell Balaṭah, Lederman reached the conclusion that all elements of the fortifications and the Migdal Temple were built in one phase. According to his interpretation, Wall A served as the exterior defense line of the site, while an earthen fill was constructed inside its perimeter to create a raised platform for the Migdal Temple; Wall C served as a supporting "foot" for this fill.[24]

Recently, Ussishkin has thoroughly investigated the issue of the Shechem fortifications (D. Ussishkin, "Notes on the Fortifications of the Middle Bronze II Period at Jericho and Shechem," forthcoming). His main conclusion is that the cyclopean wall is a stone revetment which was erected in order to support constructional fills rather then as a proper city wall. Ussishkin pointed out that the cyclopean wall was supported by a glacis-fill on its outer side as well. His conclusion is that

> Wall A in the northern side of the site, the Northwest Gate, the *huwwar* fill ... in front of them, ... the East Gate ... Wall B, Wall A in the eastern side of the site ... and the glacis in the eastern section between Walls A and B — are all parts of one monumental fortification system.

Thus, there is a great similarity in the layout of Middle Bronze Age Shiloh and Shechem. At both sites, a small unfortified MB IIA–B settlement was buried under later fills. In MB IIC both sites were encircled by huge stone walls, which retained earthen fills. In order to counterbalance the pressure of these fills, a supporting glacis was layed outside the fortification. The inner fills were stabilized by retaining walls. The main structures, including cult places, were built on top of the fills, in the northern section of both sites. There is no evidence for Middle Bronze Age residential quarters at either site. The few dissimilarities between the two sites probably stem from the different topographical conditions of a tell in the plain as opposed to one on a steep hill: the fills at Shechem were intended to create a podium, whereas at Shiloh a natural podium existed, and all that was needed was to smooth the surface of the slope by covering it with white earth.

Middle Bronze Age Shiloh and Shechem must have both been strikingly impressive from the outside: enormous outer earthen fills; gigantic revetments (although it seems that most were buried in the fills); immense inner earthen fills creating a platform at Shechem and a smooth white slope at Shiloh; and a major building complex standing at the highest point of each site.

According to the excavators, Middle Bronze Age Shechem was destroyed in the course of an Egyptian campaign.[25] However, there is no clue whatsoever to the identity of the aggressor, and the two "violent conflagrations" observed at the site may very well represent internal strife or struggles with neighboring sites. In LB I the site may have been abandoned. In the later stages of the Late Bronze Age, the fortifications and Migdal Temple were reused. There is no evidence for a Late Bronze Age residential quarter. The site was destroyed again at the turn of the 14th century B.C.E.[26]

Other Sites
Finds at other Middle Bronze-Late Bronze Age sites in the central hill country and its vicinity may hint at a somewhat similar layout:

At Middle Bronze Age Hebron the large stone fortification is similar in its dimensions and construction methods to the wall of Shiloh. The size of the site at this period is not clear, but according to the plan published by Hammond,[27] it is doubtful if it exceeded 3.7 acres (contra Ofer[28] who argued that the size of Middle Bronze Age

Hebron was 6 to 7.4 acres). In one place, a glacis was traced adjacent to the wall. In another place, within the site, a light earthen fill was found. The cuneiform tablet recently discovered at the site[29] may hint that there was a cult place at Hebron in the Middle Bronze Age.[30] The site was not occupied in the Late Bronze Age.

Bethel was an unfortified, loosely-spread settlement in MB IIB.[31] In MB IIC the site was surrounded by a strong stone wall. The shape of the Bethel fortification resembles that of Shiloh, but for reasons probably connected with the area's rock formations, it is built of smaller stones. In one place the excavators discerned an earth and stone glacis.[32] The excavators assumed that a shrine stood at the northwestern side of the mound.[33] The area of MB IIC Bethel was apparently similar to that of Shiloh. Bethel was abandoned in LB I and was reoccupied by a small village in LB II.

The area of Middle Bronze Age Beth-Zur was between 2 and 3.7 acres. In MB IIC it was surrounded by a wall 2.5 m. thick, built of large boulders. A tower in the wall, similar to the one unearthed in the northern sector of Shiloh, was 6 m. thick.[34]

Middle Bronze Age Jerusalem was fortified by a strong stone wall, within which some fills were found.[35] In the Late Bronze Age, stepped terraces were built on the slopes and supporting walls and fills were constructed at the top of the site. They probably created a podium for the major buildings of the site; Kenyon suggested that this was the biblical *millo.*[36]

Summary

The layout of Middle Bronze Age Shiloh and Shechem (probably also Bethel, Hebron and Beth-Zur, and possibly also Jerusalem) was utterly different from that of the lowland sites. In the highlands, huge fortifications served as revetments for fills at sites which were apparently lacking residential units. In the lowlands, the sites were much larger in area and, most important, had significant residential areas.[37] Consequently, if we accept the definition of the main lowland fortifications as city walls and of the sites as fortified cities, we need a different definition for the hill country sites. The best way to describe their special features would apparently be "highland strongholds." The different layout most probably reflects a distinct sociopolitical organization: there is a consensus on the definition of the 2nd millennium lowland sites as city-states; the political formations of the highlands will be discussed below.

Surveys — The Settlement Patterns

Adhering to the view that settlement and demographic transformations should be investigated in a *longue durée* perspective,[38] I wish to discuss settlement patterns in the central hill country from the Intermediate to the Late Bronze Age, with special emphasis on the Middle Bronze Age. This topic has been treated elsewhere,[39] Therefore, only a short account will be presented here.

The Intermediate Bronze Age

Zertal[40] has recorded 34 Intermediate Bronze Age sites in his Manasseh survey. Only one of these appears to be a cemetery. There is a concentration of sites in the northeastern and eastern parts of the region, not related to perennial water sources and first inhabited during this period. Eighty-five percent of the sites are located east of the Nablus-Jenin line.

In Ephraim, sites are also concentrated in the eastern part of the region,[41] but settlement activity here was much weaker than in northern Samaria. Another important difference between Ephraim and Manasseh is the significant share of burial grounds in the total number of sites in Ephraim. Seven settlement sites and 11 shaft-tomb cemeteries have been recorded in Ephraim. The largest cemetery, with hundreds of tombs concentrated in several groups, is found in the area around ʿEin Samiya. Some of the cemeteries also yielded Middle Bronze Age sherds (see below).

Four settlement sites and 20 shaft-tomb burial grounds have been recorded in the hill country of Benjamin.[42] All four settlement sites are located in the eastern flank of the region. Fifteen of the cemeteries are located in the desert fringe, four of them are large burial grounds. Only few cemeteries were found near settlement sites.

Five sites and 10 cemeteries are known in Judah.[43] Emeq Rephaim and Manahat are neighboring vast rural sites in a wadi-valley southwest of Jerusalem. Two strata with spread-out structures dating to the Intermediate Bronze Age and MB IIB were uncovered. The houses of the later phase, while superimposed upon those of the earlier phase, exhibit distinct plans.[44] Three Judean hill country cemeteries have been excavated: Khirbet el-Kirmil — the second largest cemetery in the country — where some 850 shaft-tombs were counted,[45] Efrat,[46] and Khirbet Kufin.[47] In all three there was evidence for reuse of tombs in the Middle Bronze Age.

To sum up, in the Intermediate Bronze Age 49 sites and 42 burial grounds (including the two huge cemeteries of ʿEin Samiya and Khirbet el-Kirmil) are known in the central hill country. Sixty-seven percent of the sites (but only one cemetery) are located in Manasseh, whereas 98 percent of the cemeteries, but only 33 percent of the sites, are found in the area south of Shechem.

The Middle Bronze Age

The Middle Bronze Age is marked by an unprecedented wave of settlement in the hill country: 248 settlement sites have been recorded, compared to 123 in the Early Bronze and 49 in the Intermediate Bronze Age.

The Manasseh survey has yielded 120 Middle Bronze Age sites. Sixty-six are small sites (.25–1.25 acres in size), 19 are medium-size sites (1.5–2.5 acres), 25 are large sites (3.7–8.6 acres), six very large sites (9.9–19.8 acres; in this category we find the well known sites of Shechem, Dothan and Tell el-Farʿah), and four are cemeteries not related to any settlement site. Fifteen of the sites were defined as tells or fortified sites.[48] There is now a shift back to the western part of the area: Sixty-five percent of the sites are located west of the Nablus-Jenin line, compared to 15 percent in the Intermediate Bronze and 58 percent in the Early Bronze Age.

The Land of Ephraim survey revealed 88 Middle Bronze Age sites: 68 small sites (.25–3.7 acres), eight medium-size sites (1–1.5 acres), six large, fortified tells (2.5–3.7 and more acres) and six cemeteries. The sites are distributed in four geographical subregions as follows: 16 (18 percent), including the large tell of Khirbet Marjameh, in the desert fringe; 37 (42 percent), including the large tells of Khirbet ʿUrmeh, Sheikh Abu Zarad, Shiloh and Bethel, in the central range; 30 (34 percent) in the slope area; and five in the foothills. This was the first wave of occupation in the western part of the region, but most of the western sites were small in size. Some of the small sites found throughout the region were possibly seasonal camp-sites. There is a massive concentration of small sites around Bethel, and a smaller concentration around Shiloh. Four of the seven Intermediate Bronze Age settlement sites and at least four of the cemeteries were active in the Middle Bronze Age.[49]

In the area between Ramallah and Jerusalem 42 sites and nine shaft-tomb burial grounds have been recorded.[50] Only one site (Jerusalem) was a large fortified settlement, two are classified as large sites of 3.7–7.4 acres, one was ca. 2.5 acres in size and all the rest were small sites. Sixteen sites are located in the desert fringe, 21 in the central plateau of the region and five in the western slopes. As in Ephraim, this was the first penetration into the western part of the region: 16 of the settlement sites are located west of the Jerusalem-Ramallah road.

Only eight settlement sites and 11 burial grounds have been recorded in the Judean hill country, west and south of Jerusalem.[51] The most important sites are the fortified strongholds of Hebron and Beth-Zur;[52] Manahat and Emeq Rephaim are large sprawling sites; the remaining four sites are small settlements. All three excavated large Intermediate Bronze Age cemeteries of the Judean hills revealed shaft-tombs reused in MB IIA.[53]

To sum up, 248 Middle Bronze Age settlement sites and 30 cemeteries have been recorded so far. In this period the density of occupation declines from north to south: Forty-five percent of the sites and 75 percent of the estimated population lived in the northern part of the region, between Shechem and the Jezreel Valley. On the other hand, the phenomenon of burial grounds not connected to sedentary activity is found mainly south of Shechem.

The pottery retrieved in many of the small Middle Bronze Age sites of Ephraim, including small sites around Shiloh and Bethel, is identical to that found in the earliest occupation of Shiloh, whereas they did not yield some of the types common in MB IIC Shiloh. Adding these facts to data accumulated in other excavations in the vicinity, especially Shechem, Tell el-Farʿah[54] and Bethel, the following reconstruction of the Middle Bronze Age settlement process in the entire central hill country can be suggested: In the beginning of MB IIA there is almost no evidence for sedentary occupation.[55] The wave of settlement in the region began at a slightly later stage, in the 19th–18th centuries B.C.E. In that phase the sites were small and unfortified. In MB IIC some of the small sites were abandoned and few major settlements were fortified.

The Late Bronze Age

In the Late Bronze Age there was a severe settlement crisis in the hill country.

Thirty-one Late Bronze Age sites have been found in Manasseh.[56] This number includes four cemeteries and five LB I sites; it may further decrease with a different pottery classification, since Zertal identifies Late Bronze Age sites according to local pottery which, in some cases, may be ascribed to Iron I (note his dating of the "Bull Site" to the Late Bronze Age).[57] This means that during LB II there were no more than 20 settlement sites in Manasseh, compared to 116 during the Middle Bronze Age.

A mere five Late Bronze Age sites — the main Middle Bronze Age tells — are known in Ephraim, but some of them may have shrunk in size ('Urmeh and Sheikh Abu Zarad). At Shiloh there was a small cult site only. Bethel was abandoned in LB I, to be reoccupied in LB II.

In Benjamin and Judah there are only two major sites — Jerusalem and Khirbet Rabud,[58] two additional small sites and five cemeteries not related to sedentary activity.[59]

All together, about 30 LB II settlement sites and 10 cemeteries have been recorded in the central hill country. Two-thirds of the sites and the majority of the population were found north of Shechem.

Historical and Archaeological Synthesis

The Intermediate Bronze Age

In the Intermediate Bronze Age the hill country population was composed of rural groups living in small villages and of a large component of pastoralists. The evidence for the latter is indicated by several factors: First, it is the most reasonable explanation for the sudden "disappearance" of the relatively large Early Bronze Age sedentary population.[60] The concentration of sites in the eastern part of the area also hints at a more pastoral-oriented society. Finally, the huge cemetery sites, such as 'Ein Samiya and Khirbet el-Kirmil, do not have any significant sedentary population in their vicinity; furthermore, they are located in the more "pastoral" niches of the hill country, thus, the only way to understand them is to assume that they served pastoral groups covering vast areas.

The Intermediate Bronze Age people practiced a dry-farming/animal-husbandry subsistence, with no large scale orchard activity. This is evident from the distribution of the sites: most of them are located on the eastern flank of the hill country, while the classic horticulture niches on the western slopes were not occupied. The limited distribution of sites and the absence of specialized economy are among the reasons for the apparent lack of complex sociopolitical organization.

In all periods during the 3rd–2nd millennia B.C.E. there is a clear decline in permanent settlements (number of sites and/or their size) from north to south. The reason for this demographic distribution should be sought in the ecological background described above: northern Samaria is more conducive to sedentary occupation due to the moderate topography and the wide intermontane valleys. Less so, but still hospitable, are the small intermontane valleys of the Ephraimite hill country and the plateau of Benjamin. On the other hand, the frontier areas south of Shechem, especially the Judean hills, were convenient for pastoral activity, as attested by the large number of cemeteries not related to permanent occupation. Thus, in the Intermediate Bronze Age there seems to be a clear change in the socioeconomic structure as one moves from north to south: in northern Samaria, there was a relatively large rural population, concentrated in the eastern part of the area and practising dry farming and animal husbandry. Exclusive pastoralism in this region was relatively limited. This may be the reason for the absence of large shaft-tomb cemeteries. In the area between Shechem and Jerusalem the demographic distribution was different: there was some sedentary activity in the east, but the share of the pastoral groups in the population was very significant, as is shown by the large ʿEin Samiya and eastern Benjamin cemeteries. The Judean hills were inhabited almost exclusively by pastoral groups. There was, therefore, a change from a basically agrarian economy in the north to a basically pastoral economy in the south, with an intermediate area in the middle. This pattern, already evident in the Early Bronze Age, continued to dominate in the highlands until the beginning of the 1st millennium B.C.E.

The Middle Bronze Age

The transition from the Intermediate Bronze Age to the Middle Bronze Age in the central hill country is characterized by both continuity and change. The latter is marked by a new wave of settlement, by the shift back to a more balanced east/west distribution in Manasseh, and by penetration into the western slopes in Ephraim and Benjamin, an area which was completely devoid of any sedentism in the previous period. The expansion into the western parts of the hill country indicates that horticulture was practiced in part of the area. The Middle Bronze Age sites were established by the local population, with a possible influx of groups from the densely settled lowlands. Some of them were probably seasonal camps of pastoral groups. The continuity between the two periods is evidenced by the fact that many of the Intermediate Bronze Age sites in Manasseh were also occupied in the Middle Bronze Age. But even more important is the evidence from the burial grounds: as noted above, some of the shaft-tombs in many of the Intermediate Bronze cemeteries were reused in the early phase of the Middle Bronze Age.

Two historical sources — the Khu-Sebek Stele and the Execration Texts — shed some light on the sociopolitical system in the central hill country during the new wave of settlement which took place in the 19th–18th centuries B.C.E.

The Khu-Sebek Stele describes a military campaign to the region in the 19th century B.C.E. The reference to the "land" of Shechem and the mention of Shechem as a parallel to Retenu possibly hint that it was the center of a large territorial entity.[61] Only two central hill country sites — Shechem and Jerusalem — are mentioned in the Execration Texts,[62] apparently indicating that the entire area was divided between two large political bodies — a northern one centered in Shechem and a southern one centered in Jerusalem. The results of the surveys point out that both had dimorphic structure, but that the northern one was more sedentary and the southern one more pastoral. The division of the area between the Jezreel and the Beersheba valleys into two political bodies would last for many centuries to come. Unfortunately, we know very little about Shechem and Jerusalem of that period. Shechem was apparently a small unfortified settlement; the huge stone and earthen fortifications of the later period make it impossible to trace the nature of the early settlement. The precise date of Jerusalem's Middle Bronze Age fortifications has not yet been established.

In MB IIC a new development took place in the central hill country: many of the small sites were abandoned and in some of the main sites heavy building activities were undertaken, the most important being Tell el-Far'ah, Shechem, Shiloh, Bethel, Beth-Zur and Hebron. This change in the settlement pattern can be explained in two different ways: 1. There was a process of agglomeration, that is, the population of the small sites concentrated in fortified centers. 2. A political or sociodemographic crisis drove part of the population to establish fortified centers, while other segments of the society experienced a process of nomadization. Two archaeological clues support the second explanation: a. It seems that the Middle Bronze Age fortified strongholds were without residential quarters; b. The society of the following period — the Late Bronze Age — is indeed characterized by a large non-sedentary component. One way or another, it is clear that in MB IIC, too, the population consisted of both sedentary and pastoral components, with more sedentary communities in the north and more pastoral groups in the south.

The role of the northern elements, which penetrated the hill country in the Middle Bronze Age[63] in the processes described above, is not clear. Mazar[64] argued that they brought feudal-like systems with them.

The fortified centers of Shechem, Shiloh, Bethel, Jerusalem, Beth-Zur, Hebron (and possibly some other places, such as Khirbet Urmeh and Sheikh Abu-Zarad), were government strongholds for chiefs who ruled over large territories with mixed sedentary and pastoral groups. These strongholds were different than the conventional settlements of the lowlands: They served as the seats of the chiefs, with storage facilities and central cult places, but with almost no residential quarters. The impressive stone-and earthworks, which were undertaken by the population of large territories, demonstrated the power of the chief and the legitimacy of his rule.[65]

Tell el-Far'ah is different from the above mentioned sites: it was a larger settlement, with residential quarters.[66] Its features resemble the lowland towns more than the highland strongholds. The reason should be sought in environmental factors: Tell el-Far'ah is located in the fertile, densely settled land of northern Samaria.

It is extremely difficult to reconstruct the exact mechanisms which led to the emergence of large political entities in the highlands of Canaan in the Middle Bronze Age, but some of the components seem to be traceable. This was the first period in which the central hill country had a significant population. As a result, some groups expanded into inhospitable regions which were conducive only to horticulture. This, in turn, led to the development of specialized agriculture, which required balancing institutions to control the intra-regional flow of commodities.[67] Also, the isolated and inaccessible hill country lay beyond the Egyptian sphere of interest in the lowlands.[68]

Were all the fortified strongholds centers of independent highland entities? The fact that historical sources of both MB IIB and the Late Bronze Age mention only two main political bodies in the central hill country hints at another possibility: There were several chiefs, each ruling from a fortified stronghold, but they were organized under two main political entities: a northern one with Shechem as its center, including the chiefs of Shiloh and Bethel, and a southern one, with Jerusalem as its center, including the territory of Hebron.[69] Shechem and Jerusalem were therefore *primii inter pares* among the Middle Bronze Age highland strongholds.

The Late Bronze Age

A severe crisis took place in the Late Bronze Age, when almost all MB IIC sites, including the majority of the central strongholds, were abandoned, or shrank in size.

The upheaval in MB IIC/LB I transition brought about a change in the political structure of the hill country: the small Middle Bronze Age strongholds were destroyed or abandoned, and only the two main centers — Shechem and Jerusalem — survived. The reasons for this turmoil should, in my opinion, be sought in local political and sociodemographic troubles, rather than in a destructive Egyptian campaign.[70] Most of the inhabitants of the Middle Bronze Age sites withdrew to pastoralism,[71] that is, the demographic balance tilted towards the nomadic elements, which were larger now than in the previous period. This process is apparently attested in the Amarna tablets, which indicate the existence of large non-urban and non-sedentary groups in the region — the Apiru and the Shosu-Sutu. The marginal elements, including nomads, were the backbone of the political and military power of the hill country entities.[72] The exceptional strength of Shechem should be understood in the light of the special composition of its population: Shechem was the only hill country center with a relatively strong and dense rural and urban "countryside" (especially in northern Samaria), which gave it economic strength, and with a large number of non-sedentary groups (mainly south of Shechem), which gave it military vigor. The combination of a large territory with a relatively large population and with good economic potential, protected in the south and west by dense woodland, made the kingdom of Lab'ayu the most powerful entity in Late Bronze Age Canaan. Lab'ayu, then, was a typical highland chief, ruling over a vast territory inhabited by mixed sedentary and pastoral population and governing this area from a fortified stronghold with no residential quarters. His political manoeuvers should apparently be seen as an attempt to unite large parts of the country, especially in the highlands, under one leadership. The same seems to go for 'Abdu-Heba of Jerusalem.

The only central hill country political entities mentioned in the Amarna period are Shechem and Jerusalem.[73] Hebron was not inhabited in the Late Bronze Age,[74] which rules out the possibility that it was the seat of Shuwardata.[75] Na'aman's suggestion[76] that Bethel and Debir were independent city-states cannot be accepted for both textual and archaeological reasons: textually, one cannot ignore the simple fact that they are not mentioned in the tablets; archaeologically, there is no evidence that Bethel or Debir were important centers in the Late Bronze Age.

The territory of Shechem extended to the Jezreel valley in the north and to the coastal plain in the west. The political involvement of Shechem with Gezer[77] seems to indicate that it governed the former territory of Bethel. In light of the large territories dominated by the house of Lab'ayu, it is not surprising that *EA* 289 refers to the "Land of Shechem." The Shechem entity included about 25 sedentary sites, most of them north of Shechem, and large areas inhabited primarily by pastoralists, mainly south of Shechem.

If we accept the identification of Bit Ninurta with Beth Horon,[78] then Jerusalem dominated the plateau of Gibeon. The concern of Jerusalem with the events in Keila, seems to indicate that the territory of Jerusalem included the entire Judean hill region;[79] it probably extended to the Beersheba Basin in the south and to the slopes to the Shephelah in the west.[80] The southern entity included only very few sedentary sites, but was inhabited by a large number of pastoral groups.[81]

Dimorphic Chiefdoms

The question remains concerning how to describe the peculiar sociopolitical system of 2nd millennium B.C.E. Shechem and Jerusalem. Alt was the first to distinguish between lowland city-states and highland territorial formations.[82] Kempinski referred to the Middle Bronze Age central hill country "state of Shechem",[83] and suggested that it was the most important city in Retenu[84] while at the same time describing it as a city-state.[85] Na'aman viewed Late Bronze Age Shechem more as a territorial state than as a city-state.[86]

This turns the discussion to Rowton's seminal works on the dimorphic society of the ancient Near East, and especially on the phenomenon of a city in a nomadic environment.[87] In Western Asia, nomads were active either in pastoral enclaves in sedentary lands or on their fringe. The combination of city-state, tribe and nomadism is typical of mountainous and steppe regions. Rowton described four possible sociopolitical systems in these areas: feudal chiefdom, tribal chiefdom, dimorphic chiefdom and dimorphic state. In the feudal chiefdom there is no nomadic component; in the tribal chiefdom there is no non-tribal component. Dimorphic chiefdom is a political system based on a government urban center in a tribal territory; it is generally connected to areas of enclosed nomadism. The population of a dimorphic chiefdom is therefore composed of both sedentary and nomadic groups. The difference between dimorphic chiefdom and dimorphic state is that the former is autonomous, while the latter is sovereign. Dimorphic chiefdoms can be parts of larger political entities. When central states deteriorate, the pastoral enclaves grow in size, and a dimorphic chiefdom can then redevelop into a real state. Destruction of a dimorphic chiefdom may cause political turmoil and may even lead to nomadization of the population.[88]

Rowton presented examples of dimorphic chiefdoms in Iran and Turkey in the

Middle Ages and in recent generations. The ruling dynasties of these entities built forts from which they governed their territories. The dimorphic chiefdom of Sadhandjan in southern Kurdistan "combined clans living in tents with strongholds serving as treasuries and refuges in time of danger."[89] Another interesting example of dimorphic chiefdoms in the mountainous sections of western Asia in recent generations is the Kalat Khanate of Pakistan.[90] The population there comprised all components of the dimorphic society, from villagers to nomads. Rowton[91] applied these political structures to Mari and its vicinity in the early 2nd millennium B.C.E.[92]

The sociopolitical formations in the central hill country in the 2nd millennium B.C.E. fit Rowton's description of dimorphic chiefdoms. Indeed, some of their characteristics, especially the government strongholds, also match the definitions of feudal chiefdoms; but their large pastoral component rules out such interpretation. (Except, maybe, for Middle Bronze Age sites in sedentary northern Samaria, such as Tell el-Far'ah). In using the term dimorphic chiefdom, I refer to mountain enclaves with both sedentary and pastoral elements, governed from central strongholds. In fact, if we look at the details of Rowton's discussion of dimorphic entities, it is possible to describe Middle Bronze Age Shechem as a dimorphic state encompassing few dimorphic chiefdoms.

The Iron Age

The demographic, economic and sociopolitical patterns of the hill country changed drastically in the beginning of the Iron Age. However, there are also several lines of continuity from the Bronze Age. Therefore, although the political formations and the settlement patterns of the Iron Age are beyond the scope of this article, these points of continuity will be mentioned briefly and will be treated in detail in another place.

From the end of the 13th century through the 11th century B.C.E. a new wave of settlement spread through the hill country of Canaan. About 300 sites have been revealed in surveys so far.[93] The origins of most of these settlers, which later consolidated as the Israelite national entity, are to be sought in the pastoral groups of Late Bronze Age society; but sedentary Late Bronze Age elements were also incorporated into the newly emerging force. Archaeologically speaking, part of the hill country was now inhabited for the first time, but in northern Samaria there was significant demographic/settlement continuity from the previous period.[94]

In this period as well, there is a clear difference in settlement patterns between the two classical regions of the central hill country: the northern area was densely populated, while the southern part was very sparsely inhabited. The 2nd millennium phenomenon of a mostly sedentary north vs. a mostly pastoral south continues well into the 1st millennium B.C.E. (In fact, this is also reflected in the Bible, especially in the treatment of the Judean hills and steppe elements). The two subregions were occupied by different tribal groups — the House of Joseph in the north and Judah and its associate elements in the south.[95] The boundary between these groups corresponded to that dividing the two 2nd millennium units: the House of Joseph occupied the former territory of Shechem,[96] while Judah and its fellow tribal units occupied the former territory of Jerusalem.[97] However, in the centers of these territories — Shechem and Jerusalem — Canaanite life continued for a considerable period of time.

The phenomenon of local chiefs ruling over dimorphic territories in the hill country is still evident in Iron I. David in Hebron may be taken as one example, but the case in point is, again, Shechem.

The reference to Shechem in Judges 9 gives an extremely interesting description of an Iron I autochthonic hill country center, which sheds light on the system of government in the highlands of Canaan in the 2nd millennium B.C.E.[98] Reviv argued that the political system in Shechem (as well as in Hebron) was different from the conventional one in the city-states of Canaan; especially important, in his opinion, is the fact that the ruler of the town is called *nesi ha-arez* rather than a king.[99] The term *nasi* is possibly derived from tribal terminology.[100] Turning to the layout of the site, which did not change significantly from previous periods, it seems that Migdal-Shechem was the name of the entire stronghold,[101] and that the fortress-temple was called *beth-millo*, since it was erected on a large earthen fill.[102]

At the end of the 11th century B.C.E., as a result of external pressures and internal processes, the hill country groups united to establish one highland state. This was facilitated, in part, by the political vacuum prevailing in Palestine.

In the 10th century B.C.E., Jerusalem — the capital of the United Monarchy — was apparently still a typical hill country stronghold; most of its area was occupied by the citadel of Zion, the *millo* (the terracing system on the slopes) and the Temple. Jerusalem spread to become a typical, densely populated, Iron Age city only in a much later phase of Iron II.[103]

There are several explanations for the selection of Jerusalem as David's capital: Alt argued that it was the exploit of an individual — David;[104] Mazar claimed that it was due to Jerusalem's strategic location;[105] Other scholars have emphasized the neutrality of Jerusalem, located between the territories of Judah and Benjamin.[106] Beyond these arguments, it is clear that the importance of Jerusalem in the Iron Age also stemmed from its long history as the political center of the southern part of the central hill country.[107]

The traditional tensions between north and south surfaced time and again before the consolidation of the Monarchy (the struggle between Saul and David) and during its initial stages (the attempts of the north to overthrow the yoke of David). These tensions finally led to the break-down of the United Monarchy, that is, to the reversion to the deeply rooted tradition of two hill country entities: the Judean Kingdom, centered in Jerusalem, and the Israelite Kingdom, centered around Shechem (later Samaria). The border between the two followed the traditional boundary between the 2nd millennium entities of Shechem and Jerusalem.

Alt pointed to a major difference in the political features of the two Israelite monarchies — a unified, stable dynastic leadership in Judah vs. a loosely connected, charismatic leadership of diverse origins in Israel.[108] It is now clear that the roots of this contrast lie, in part, in the political conditions of the 2nd millennium, which, in turn, stemmed from environmental differences between the two subregions. The northern part of the central hill country, fragmented by intermontane valleys, had several political centers which struggled for supremacy, whereas the homogeneous mountain-bloc of the south had only two centers — Jerusalem and Hebron. The supremacy of Jerusalem was never threatened because Hebron was too remote and isolated.[109]

Summary

The ecological differences between lowlands and highlands in the 2nd millennium B.C.E. dictated distinct socioeconomic systems, which, in turn, brought about the emergence of different political formations. The typical political entity in the lowlands was the city-state. City-states encompassed urban and rural populations. Their territories were relatively limited and their capitals were densely inhabited. In the hill country, the dimorphic society consisted of rural communities and of relatively large pastoral groups. Their political formations may be defined, in Rowton's terminology, as dimorphic chiefdoms. These entities had large territories with relatively sparse population and their centers were no more than government strongholds for the ruling elite.

There was a significant territorial and political continuity in the highlands throughout the 2nd millennium B.C.E. Shechem and Jerusalem were the centers of the two main political formations; for environmental reasons, the northern entity was more sedentary and larger in area, whereas the southern entity was more pastoral in nature.

Throughout the Levant, early states emerged in highlands or in steppe regions.[110] Similarly, attempts to establish large political entities in Palestine of the 3rd–2nd millennia B.C.E. took place in the hill country.[111] The reason is both geographic and demographic. The area was isolated and far from the interests of the main powers which dominated the lowlands; it was not densely populated and, thus, not fragmented into small political systems; its dimorphic nature gave it an unusual strength; and its specialized economy, mainly the expansion of horticulture, triggered intra-regional trade and consequently stimulated the emergence of balancing institutions.

The Israelite monarchy did not emerge, then, from a political vacuum, but from a long history of attempts to establish a territorial-state in the hill country. The breakdown of the United Monarchy into two separate states — Shechem (later Samaria) and Jerusalem — was also a reflection of the situation in the 2nd millennium. As in the Middle Bronze Age, the northern state was more fragmented, with several competing political centers, while the southern one was much more homogeneous.

The Israelite states completely changed the human landscape of the hill country: demographic growth pushed large groups of the population into frontier zones of the area, and all niches of the region were conquered for intensive agricultural activity. The withdrawal of the pastoral groups into marginal zones brought an end to the traditional dimorphic character of highland society.

Notes

1. F. Braudel, *The Mediterranean and the Mediterranean World in the Age of Philip II* (New York, 1966).
2. See for example, M.B. Rowton, "The Topological Factor of the Hapiru Problem," *Anatolian Studies* 16 (1965): 375–387; idem, "The Physical Environment and the Problem of the Nomads," in J.R. Kupper (ed.), *La civilisation de Mari. XVe Rencontre assyriologique internationale* (Paris, 1967), pp. 109–121; idem, "The Woodlands of Ancient Western Asia," *JNES* 26 (1967): 261–277; L. Marfoe, "The Integrative Transformation: Patterns of Sociopolitical Organization in Southern Syria," *BASOR* 234 (1979): 1–42.
3. R.B. Coote, and K.W. Whitelam, *The Emergence of Early Israel in Historical Perspective* (Sheffield, 1987); I. Finkelstein, "Pastoralism in the Highlands of Canaan in the Third and Second Millennia BCE," in O. Bar Yosef and A. Khazanov (eds.) *Pastoralism in the Levant: Archaeological Materials in Anthropological Perspectives* (forthcoming).
4. D.C. Hopkins, *The Highlands of Canaan* (Sheffield, 1985).
5. Braudel, *The Mediterranean* (see note 1), p. 39.
6. For this term, see M.B. Rowton, "Enclosed Nomadism," *JESHO* 17 (1974): 1–30.
7. See for example, W.G. Dever, "New Vistas on EB IV ("MB I") Horizon in Syria-Palestine," *BASOR* 237 (1980): 35–64, for the Intermediate Bronze Age.
8. Finkelstein, "Pastoralism" (see note 3).
9. A. Zertal, *The Israelite Settlement in the Hill Country of Manasseh* (Haifa, 1988), pp. 26–64 (Hebrew).
10. I. Finkelstein, "Summary and Conclusions: History of Shiloh from Middle Bronze Age II to Iron Age II," in I. Finkelstein (ed.), "Excavations in Shiloh 1981–1984: Preliminary Report," *Tel Aviv* 12 (1985): 159–177.
11. I. Finkelstein, "The Land of Ephraim Survey 1980–1987: Preliminary Report," *Tel Aviv* 15–16 (1988–1989): 117–183.
12. Zertal, *The Israelite Settlement* (see note 9).
13. A. Feldstein and Y. Kamaisky, (forthcoming), Maps 16–13, 16–14 and 17–14, in I. Finkelstein and Y. Magen (eds.), *Archaeological Survey in the Hill Country of Benjamin* (forthcoming) (Hebrew); U. Dinur and N. Feig, (forthcoming), Map 17–13 in I. Finkelstein, and Y. Magen (eds.), *Archaeological Survey in the Hill Country of Benjamin* (forthcoming) (Hebrew).
14. A. Ofer, "The Judaean Hill Country — from Nomadism to a National Monarchy," in N. Na'aman and I. Finkelstein (eds.), *From Nomadism to Monarchy: Archaeological and Historical Aspects of Early Israel* (Jerusalem, 1990), pp. 155–214 (Hebrew).
15. Finkelstein, "Summary" (see note 10); idem, *The Archaeology of the Israelite Settlement* (Jerusalem, 1988); idem, "The Land" (see note 11); idem, "The Central Hill Country in the Intermediate Bronze Age," (forthcoming).
16. Z. Lederman, "The Middle Bronze Age IIC Defence System," in I. Finkelstein (ed.), "Excavations in Shiloh 1981–1984: Preliminary Report," *Tel Aviv* 12 (1985): 140–146.
17. Finkelstein, "Summary" (see note 10), pp. 161–163.
18. M. Broshi and R. Gophna, "The Settlement and Population of Palestine in the Early Bronze Age II–III," *BASOR* 253 (1984): 41–53.
19. S. Hellwing, and M. Sadeh, "Animal Remains," in I. Finkelstein (ed.), "Excavations in Shiloh 1981–1984: Preliminary Report," *Tel Aviv* 12 (1985): 177–180.
20. I. Finkelstein, *The Archaeology of the Israelite Settlement* (Jerusalem, 1988), pp. 341–345.

21. G.E. Wright, *Shechem: The Biography of a Biblical City* (London, 1965); G.E. Wright, "Shechem," *Encyclopedia of Archaeological Excavations in the Holy Land IV* (Jerusalem, 1978), pp. 1083–1094.
22. J.D. Seger, "The Middle Bronze II Fortifications at Shechem and Gezer — A Hyksos Retrospective," *EI* 12 (1975): 34*–45*.
23. Wright, *Shechem* (see note 21), fig. 13.
24. Z. Lederman, "The Building Technique at Shiloh in the Middle Bronze Age II and the "Millo" of Shechem," in *Eleventh Archaeological Conference in Israel: Abstracts of Lectures* (Jerusalem, 1985), p. 38; G.R.H. Wright, *Ancient Building in South Syria and Palestine* (Leiden-Cologne, 1985), p. 44.
25. See for example, Wright, "Shechem" (note 21), p. 1090.
26. L.E. Toombs, "Shechem: Problems of the Early Israelite Era," in F.M. Cross (ed.), *Symposia* (Cambridge, 1979), p. 69–83.
27. P. Hammond, "Chronique archéologique: Hebron," *RB* 75 (1968): 254.
28. Contra A. Ofer, "Excavations at Biblical Hebron," *Qadmoniot* 87–88 (1989): 90 (Hebrew).
29. M. Anbar and N. Na'aman, "An Account Tablet of Sheep from Ancient Hebron," *Tel Aviv* 13–14 (1986–1987): 3–12.
30. Ofer, "Excavations" (see note 28).
31. J.L. Kelso, *The Excavation of Bethel (1934–1960). AASOR* 39, p. 46; According to W.G. Dever, "Archaeological Methods and Results: A Review of Two Recent Publications," *Orientalia* 40 (1972): 459–471, the small MB IIA village was abandoned in the MB IIB, to be reoccupied in the MB IIC.
32. Kelso, *The Excavation* (see note 31), pp. 15–16.
33. Ibid., pp. 13–14; 26–27.
34. O.R. Sellers, et al., *The 1957 Excavations at Beth-Zur. AASOR* 38 (1968): 4–5; O.R. Sellers, *The Citadel of Beth-Zur* (Philadelphia, 1933), p. 26.
35. Y. Shiloh, *Excavations at the City of David I. Qedem* 19 (1984), p. 26.
36. Ibid., p. 26 and Fig. 18; K.M. Kenyon, *Digging Up Jerusalem* (London, 1974), pp. 95–103.
37. A. Kempinski, "Urbanism and City Layout in the Middle Bronze II," in H. Katzenstein, et al. (eds.), *The Architecture of Ancient Israel* (Jerusalem, 1987), pp. 102–106 (Hebrew).
38. F. Braudel, *On History* (London, 1980); already in A. Alt, *Die Landnahme der Israeliten in Palästina* (1925). (translated as: *Essays on Old Testament History and Religion* [Oxford, 1966], pp. 135–169).
39. Finkelstein, *The Archaeology* (see note 20); idem, "The Central Hill" (see note 15).
40. Zertal, *The Israelite Settlement* (see note 9).
41. Finkelstein, "The Land" (see note 11).
42. Feldstein and Kamaiski, (forthcoming) (see note 13); Dinur and Feig, (forthcoming) (see note 13).
43. Ofer, "The Judaean" (see note 14).
44. G. Edelstein and E. Eisenberg, "'Emeq Refaim," *Excavations and Surveys in Israel* 3 (1984): 51–52; G. Edelstein and E. Eisenberg, "'Emeq Refaim," *Excavations and Surveys in Israel* 4 (1985): 54–56; E. Eisenberg "Nahal Refaim," *Hadashot Arkheologiyot* 92 (1988): 43–48 (Hebrew); L. Kolska-Horwitz, "Sedentism in the Early Bronze IV: A Faunal Perspective," *BASOR* 275 (1989): 15–25.
45. W.G. Dever, "A Middle Bronze I Cemetery at Khirbet el-Kirmil," *EI* 12 (1975): 18*–33*.
46. R. Gonen, "A Middle Bronze Age Cemetery at Efrat in the Hebron Mountains," *Qadmoniot* 53–54 (1981): 25–29 (Hebrew).
47. R.H. Smith, *Excavations in the Cemetery at Khirbet Kufin, Palestine* (London, 1962).
48. Zertal, *The Israelite Settlement* (see note 9).
49. For the Sinjil and Dhahr Mirzbaneh cemeteries see W.G. Dever, "Middle Bronze IIA Cemeteries at 'Ain es-Samiyeh and Sinjil," *BASOR* 217 (1975): 23–36.
50. Z. Kallai, "The Land of Benjamin and Mt. Epharaim," in M. Kochavi (ed.), *Judaea Samaria and the Golan: Archaeological Survey 1967–1968* (Jerusalem, 1972): 153–193 (Hebrew); Feldstein and Kamaiski, (forthcoming) (see note 13); Dinur and Feig, (forthcoming) (see note 13).
51. M. Kochavi, "The Land of Judah" in M. Kochavi (ed.), *Judaea Samaria and the Golan: Archaeological Survey 1967–1968* (Jerusalem, 1972), pp. 19–89 (Hebrew); Ofer, "The Judaean" (see note 14).
52. Ofer, "Excavations" (see note 28); Sellers, "The 1957 Excavations" (see note 34).

53. Dever, "A Middle Bronze I" (see note 45), pp. 30–32; Smith, *Excavations* (see note 47); Gonen, "A Middle" (see note 46).

54. J. Mallet, *Tell el-Farah II, 2: le Bronze moyen. Editions recherche sur les civilisations, memoire no. 66* (Paris, 1988).

55. See also, Zertal, *The Israelite Settlement* (note 9), p. 196.

56. Ibid., pp. 201–203.

57. Ibid., p. 114.

58. M. Kochavi, "Khirbet Rabud = Debir," *Tel Aviv* 1 (1974): 2–33.

59. Ofer, "The Judaean" (see note 14).

60. For the central hill country see Finkelstein, "The Central Hill" (note 15); for the entire country see Dever, "New Vistas" (note 7).

61. B. Mazar, *Canaan and Israel: Historical Essays* (Jerusalem, 1974), p. 25 (Hebrew); idem, *The Early Biblical Period* (Jerusalem, 1986); V. Minorsky, "ʿAnnazids," *Encyclopaedia of Islam* (New Edition), Vol. I, (Leiden, 1960), pp. 512–513.

62. See for example, Mazar, *Cannaan* (note 61), p. 46; N. Naʾaman, "Eretz Israel in the Canaanite Period: The Middle and Late Bronze Ages," in I. Ephʿal (ed.), *The History of Eretz Israel Vol. I. Introductions. Early Periods* (Jerusalem, 1982), p. 147 (Hebrew).

63. For the linguistic evidence, see Anbar and Naʾaman, "An Account" (note 29), pp. 10–11; For an archaeological clue, see I. Finkelstein and B. Brandl, "A Group of Metal Objects from Shiloh," *The Israel Museum Journal* 4 (1985): 17–26.

64. Mazar, *The Early* (see note 61), pp. 26–27.

65. On the construction of fortifications as propaganda, see K.W. Whitelam, "The Symbols of Power: Aspects of Royal Propaganda in the United Monarchy," *BA* 49 (1986): 166–173.

66. Mallet, *Tell el-Farah* (see note 54).

67. For the emergence of the Israelite monarchy in the same ecological niche, see I. Finkelstein, "The Emergence of the Monarchy in Israel: The Environmental and Socio-Economic Aspects," *JSOT* 44 (1989): 43–74 and bibliography.

68. J.M. Weinstein, "Egyptian Relations with Palestine in the Middle Kingdom," *BASOR* 241 (1975): map on p. 8.

69. Contra S. Bunimovitz, "Cultural Processes and Socio-Political Change in the Central Hill Country in the Late Bronze-Iron I Transition," in N. Naʾaman and I. Finkelstein (eds.), *From Nomadism to Monarchy: Archaeological and Historical Aspects of Early Israel* (Jerusalem, 1990), pp. 257–283 (Hebrew), who suggests that in the Middle Bronze the central hill country was politically fragmented.

70. Supporting the latter theory are, among others, K.M. Kenyon, *Archaeology in the Holy Land* (London, 1971); J.M. Weinstein, "The Egyptian Empire in Palestine: A Reassessment," *BASOR* 241 (1981): 1–28; opposing it are D.B. Redford, "A Gate Inscription from Karnak and Egyptian Involvement in Western Asia during the Early 18th Dynasty," *JAOS* 99 (1979): 273; W.H. Shea, "The Conquest of Sharuhen and Megiddo Reconsidered," *IEJ* 29 (1979): 3; Bunimovitz, "Cultural Processes" (see note 69).

71. Finkelstein, *The Archaeology* (see note 20), pp. 342–343.

72. Naʾaman, "Eretz Israel" (see note 62), p. 216.

73. Z. Kallai and H. Tadmor, "Bit Ninurta = Beth Horon — On the History of the Kingdom of Jerusalem in the Amarna Period," *EI* 9 (1969): 145 (Hebrew).

74. Ofer, "Excavations" (see note 28).

75. W.F. Albright, "A Case of Lèse-Majesté in Pre-Israelite Lachish, with some Remarks on the Israelite Conquest," *BASOR* 87 (1942): 37.

76. N. Naʾaman, "The Canaanite City-States in the Late Bronze Age and the Inheritances of the Israelite Tribes," *Tarbiz* 55 (1986): 463–488 (Hebrew).

77. *EA* 253, 254; on Shechem in the Amarna tablets see E. F. Campbell, "Shechem in the Amarna Archive," in G.E. Wright, *Shechem: The Biography of a Biblical City* (London, 1965), pp. 191–207;

H. Reviv, "Regarding the History of the Territory of Shekhem in the El-Amarna Period," *Tarbiz* 33 (1964): 1–7 (Hebrew).

78. Kallai and Tadmor, "Bit Ninurta" (see note 73); for a different view see N. Naʾaman, "The Political Disposition and Historical Development of Eretz-Israel According to the Amarna Letters" (Ph.D diss., Tel Aviv University, 1975), pp. 105–108 (Hebrew).

79. Kallai and Tadmor, "Bit Ninurta" (see note 73), pp. 143–146.

80. Contra A. Alt, *Essays on Old Testament History and Religion* (Oxford, 1966), pp. 152–154; and Naʾaman, "Political Disposition" (see note 78), pp. 104–118; Alt argued that Jerusalem had only a small territory and that it was the only town in the hill country which did not try to expand; Naʾaman was of the opinion that the southern Judean hill country was ruled by the city-state of Debir.

81. See Ofer, "The Judaean" (note 14).

82. Alt, *Die Landnahme* (see note 38).

83. A. Kempinski, "The Middle Bronze Age," in *The Archaeology of Ancient Israel in the Biblical Period* (Tel Aviv, 1989) (Hebrew).

84. A. Kempinski, *Syrien und Palästina (Kanaan) in der letzten phase der Mittelbronze IIB-Zeit (1650–1570 v. chr.)* (Wiesbaden, 1983), pp. 117–118.

85. Kempinski, "The Middle" (see note 83), p. 30.

86. Naʾaman, "Eretz Israel" (see note 62), p. 216; idem, "The Canaanite" (see note 76), p. 466.

87. M.B. Rowton, "Urban Autonomy in a Nomadic Environment," *JNES* 32 (1973): 201–215; M.B. Rowton, "Dimorphic Structure and the Tribal Elite," in *Al-Bahit: Festschrift Joseph Henninger. Studia Instituti Anthropos* 28 (St. Augustin bei Bonn, 1976), pp. 219–257.

88. Ibid.

89. Minorsky, "ʿAnnazids" (see note 61).

90. N. Swidler, "The Development of the Kalat Khanate," in W. Irons and N. Dyson-Hudson (eds.), *Perspectives on Nomadism* (Leiden, 1972), pp. 115–121.

91. Rowton, "Urban Autonomy" (see note 87).

92. M. Anbar, *The Amorite Tribes in Mari* (Tel Aviv, 1985) (Hebrew).

93. Finkelstein, *The Archaeology* (see note 20).

94. For the biblical material see, for example, A. Alt, "Die Reise" *PJb* 28 (1932): 18–46; M. Noth, *The History of Israel* (London, 1958), pp. 145, 152–153.

95. M. Noth, *Das System der zwölf Stämme Israels* (Stuttgart, 1930), pp. 107–108; Alt, *Essays* (see note 80), p. 166; G. Buccellati, *Cities and Nations of Ancient Syria* (Rome, 1967) (*Studi semitici* 26), pp. 146–147.

96. Alt, *Essays* (see note 80), p. 168.

97. For the relations between the Late Bronze territorial division and the allotments of the Israelite tribes see Alt, *Essays* (note 80), p. 169; and especially Naʾaman, "The Canaanite" (note 76).

98. For a different view see N. Naʾaman, "Migdal-Shechem and the 'House of El-berith'," *Zion* 51 (1986): 259–280 (Hebrew).

99. H. Reviv, "The Government of Shechem in the El-Amarna Period and in the Days of Abimelech," *IEJ* 16 (1966): 252–257; idem, "Urban Institutions, Personages and Problems of Terminology in Biblical Presentations of Non-Israelite Cities," *EI* 10 (1970): 258–263 (Hebrew); B. Mazar, "The Early Israelite Settlement in the Hill Country," *BASOR* 241 (1981): 278.

100. E. A. Speiser, "Background and Function of the Biblical Nasi," *CBQ* 25 (1963): 111–117.

101. Wright, *Shechem* (see note 21), p. 126, contra scholars who argued that it was located outside the town — Naʾaman, "Migdal" (see note 98), esp. p. 261, n. 9 for bibliography.

102. Wright, *Shechem* (see note 21), p. 126; Lederman, "The Building" (see note 24).

103. M. Broshi, "The Expansion of Jerusalem in the Reigns of Hezekiah and Manasseh," *IEJ* 24 (1974): 21–26.

104. A. Alt, *Kleine Schriften zur Geschichte des Volkes Israel III* (Munich, 1959), pp. 252–255; Alt, *Essays* (see note 80), pp. 217–218.

105. B. Mazar, "Jerusalem before the Reign of David," in M. Avi-Yonah (ed.), *Sepher Yerushalayim* (Jerusalem, 1956), p. 102 (Hebrew).

106. See for example, Noth, *The History* (note 94), p. 190; J. Bright, *A History of Israel* (Philadelphia, 1974), p. 195; Alt, *Essays* (note 80), pp. 217–218.

107. See also H. Reviv, *From Clan to Monarchy* (Jerusalem, 1979), p. 124 (Hebrew).

108. Alt, *Essays* (see note 80), pp. 239–259; see review in Buccellati, *Cities* (note 95).

109. See for example, Bright, *A History* (note 106), p. 195.

110. Alt, "Die Landnahme" (note 38); Buccellati, *Cities* (note 95), p. 92; Marfoe, "The Integrative" (note 2).

111. Possibly also in the southern steppe — see I. Finkelstein, "Arabian Trade and Socio-Political Conditions in the Negev in the Twelfth-Eleventh Centuries B.C.E.," *JNES* 47 (1988): 241–252; idem, "Early Arad: Urbanism of the Nomads," (forthcoming).

The Political Organization of Philistia in Iron Age I[1]

Itamar Singer

The settlement of the Philistines on the southern coast of Canaan in the second quarter of the 12th century B.C.E.[2] had a crucial and lasting impact on the geopolitical structure of the region. For about a century and a half after the Egyptian withdrawal from Canaan, the Philistines became the dominant power in the land,[3] and their expansion was a major factor in the consolidation of the Israelite tribes and the establishment of the Israelite monarchy.[4]

The socio-political organization of the Philistines in the lands of their origin[5] is yet unknown, but the biblical narrative has preserved the original titles of their rulers: *sranim*. The word is probably related to Luwian *Tarwanis*, a title carried by (Neo-) Hittite rulers.[6] In their new land, the Philistines fully adopted the Canaanite system of city-kingdoms. They located their five principalities in cities which had been Canaanite centers,[7] some, if not all, of which also served the Egyptian administration.[8]

The national deity of the Philistines was Dagon, who was worshipped at Gaza, Ashdod and probably other Philistine cities as well.[9] When Samson was captured, he was brought to Gaza "and the lords of the Philistines gathered to offer a great sacrifice to their god Dagon and to rejoice" (Judges 16: 23). This episode has been taken as evidence for the centrality of Dagon's temple at Gaza and for the reconstruction of a Philistine amphictyony centered around it; later, the amphictyonic center moved to Ashdod, as indicated by the story of the capture of the Ark (I Samuel 5).[10] Noth's theory of the Israelite amphictyony, which was for many years the canonical model for premonarchic Israel, no doubt had a major influence on its Philistine counterpart. Since the early 1960s, Noth's theory has undergone a thorough critique and has gradually been abandoned by most scholars.[11] The scholarly dismantling of Noth's Israelite model need not necessarily lead to a similar verdict for other Near Eastern candidates. On the contrary, it has paved the way for a fresh and independent examination of the Sumerian Kengir League [12] and the Philistine Pentapolis.[13]

Although differing in some respects from the classical examples from Greece and Italy, the Philistine league seems to fulfill quite satisfactorily the basic definition of an amphictyony: a loose political and religious alliance worshipping the same deity at a central shrine. Contrary to Noth's emphasis on the number twelve, with the well-known model of the Delphic league, a scrutiny of other, less-known examples shows that the number of affiliated members is not an essential element in the definition.[14] Another objection raised against the candidacy of the Philistine league, namely that Dagon was not even a Philistine god,[15] can also be dismissed now. Contrary to the traditional view, there is no solid evidence of the cult of Dagon in Palestine before the arrival of the Philistines.[16]

Very little is known about the inner structure of the Philistine Pentapolis. The political relationships among its members and the geographical boundaries between the city-kingdoms are largely ignored, because these issues are obviously not within the scope of interest of the biblical author. There is some indication that in the beginning Gaza was the most important Philistine center, later to be replaced by Gath. This common assumption is based primarily on a comparison between the centrality of Gaza in the story of Samson's death, and the role played by Gath in the times of David.

Although such a shift of power from the coastal to the inland centers would be quite plausible, the actual evidence for it is insufficient. The Kingdom of Gath may have received a relatively larger share of attention in the biblical sources because of its geographical position, bordering on Judah, and especially due to its important role in the biography of David. This, for example, may readily explain the fact that Achish is the only Philistine ruler (except Abimelech King of Gerar in Genesis 21 and 26) whose name is given in the Bible.[17]

The same caution should be applied in evaluating the titles by which the Philistine rulers are mentioned. It has been pointed out, that Achish is the first Philistine ruler to be titled "king" (1 Samuel 21: 11; 27: 2), thus departing from the earlier denomination *sranim* or *sarim*. Mazar has suggested that "possibly at the time the monarchy was established in Israel the political life of the Philistines underwent a similar change," which brought about "the creation of Philistia's monarchy, which had its center at Gath of the Philistines close to Israel's border."[18] Later evidence, however, does not seem to confirm the establishment of a pan-Philistine monarchy. The Philistine city-kingdoms continued to operate separately throughout their history, quite often against each other, according to both biblical and Assyrian sources. On closer examination, there is nothing in the description of Achish's actions to suggest that he exerted power over his fellow Philistine rulers. When the Philistine troops were mustered at Aphek before the decisive battle near Mount Gilboa, the Philistine commanders (called variably *sranim* and *sarim*) were opposed to David's participation in the battle, and had their way despite Achish's will (1 Samuel 29). At most, the king of Gath may have had a status of *primus inter pares*. There is indeed a coincidence in the first appearance of the title "king" (*melekh*) in Israel and Philistia, but this may reflect no more than a tendency on the part of the Biblical author to create an analogical development and terminology. Indeed, from the period of David on, the archaic title *sranim* disappears altogether, and the Philistine rulers are designated as kings.[19]

Another set of questions concerns the system by which the Philistines ruled over the Israelite regions conquered by them following the decisive battle of Eben-ezer. Again, the information is vary sparse and indirect, but it nevertheless provides some preliminary notions. It seems that the Philistines basically adopted the Egyptian system of *Stützpunkte*, i.e., several strongholds (*mazzab*, 1 Samuel 14: 1) located at strategic centers, manned by military garrisons commanded by governors (*nezib*, 1 Samuel 10: 5; 13: 3). Two of these strongholds were located at Gibeah of Benjamin, later to become the capital of Saul, and at Bethlehem of Judah (2 Samuel 23: 15). If these two cases are representative of the overall strategy, it would seem that the Philistines had chosen to locate their strongholds in the main Israelite tribal centers. However, we do not have any data on more northerly areas, e.g., from where did the Philistines rule the territory of Ephraim, after destroying the tribal center at Shiloh. In a more general vein, it is difficult to tell how far north the Philistines ruled effectively.

Since, unlike Israel, the Philistine city-kingdoms seem never to have united into a centralized monarchy, the question may be raised: How did they organize their common rule over Israel for a period of at least half a century? Did the Philistine chieftains rule each over a certain part of the Israelite territories, or, as seems more likely, did they combine their armies in a joined task-force. This was certainly the procedure before decisive battles, such as the battle of Ebenezer (1 Samuel 4: 1) and one at Mount Gilboa, when "the Philistines mustered all their troops at Aphek" (1 Samuel 29: 1). Whether in regular times the domination of Israel was also shared jointly by the Philistine rulers is more difficult to establish. The only information in this respect comes again from the Kingdom of Gath.

The episode of David's stay in Ziklag provides some important insights to the organization of the frontier areas of Philistia. The city, which is probably identified with Tell esh-Shariah (Tel Seraʿ) on Naḥal Gerar, marks the southeastern confines of the Kingdom of Gath. With the conclusive identification of Gath at Tel eṣ-Ṣafi (Tel Ẓafit),[20] this may come as a surprise, since Ziklag lays much closer to Gaza, and even to Ashkelon.[21] This seems to indicate that the territorial division of Philistia into city-kingdoms did not have a pattern of latitudinal bands; rather, Gath held the entire eastern frontline from Naḥal Soreq to Naḥal Gerar, whereas the coastal city kingdoms of Gaza, Ashkelon and Ashdod occupied only a relatively narrow strip along the coastal plain.[22] As noted earlier, this geopolitical reality could readily account for Gath's prominence in the Biblical story. Territorial size, however, does not always coincide with military or political dominance, and more evidence is needed to establish the shifts in the relative power and importance of the Philistine city-kingdoms.

Gath's domination over the distant "country town" of Ziklag (1 Samuel 27: 5) raises some intriguing questions concerning the borders of this Philistine kingdom, especially in comparison with earlier periods. Many years ago Alt outlined the basic principles in the study of territorial divisions which persist over long periods of time.[23] These principles have so far been applied mainly in the comparison of the Israelite tribal allotments with the territories of the Canaanite city-kingdoms, established primarily on the basis of the Amarna letters.[24] It stands to reason that a similar correspondence may be expected in the case of the Philistine city-kingdoms, especially in view of the fact that the Philistines adopted the geopolitical patterns of Pharaonic Canaan to an even greater extent than the Israelites did. The main political divisions of southern Palestine in the Amarna Age included the kingdoms of Ashkelon, Lachish, Gath and Gezer.[25] We shall concentrate here on the Kingdom of Gath, which later became Gath of the Philistines.[26] This kingdom bordered on Gezer in the north, Jerusalem in the east, Lachish in the south, and Ashkelon in the west. Although its capital, located at Tell eṣ-Ṣafi, has not yet been thoroughly excavated, even the chance finds from the surface of the mound and the results of Bliss and Macalister's trial excavation testify to the importance of the site in both the Late Canaanite and the Philistine periods.[27]

Two rulers of Gath are attested in the Amarna correspondence: Shuwardata and his successor ʿAbdi-Ashtarti.[28] Eight letters of the former (EA 278–284, 366) and four letters of the latter (EA 63–65, 335) form a relatively large "dossier," which contains various data on Gath's political history in the Amarna age. Other relevant letters originate from his neighbors, particularly from ʿAbdi-Ḥeba of Jerusalem. Our main concern here is to extract those details which may be relevant to establishing Gath's geographical confines.

Shuwardata was first allied with ʿAbdi-Ḥeba (EA 366: 20f), but the two later became fierce enemies. The main reason appears to be a conflict centering on the domination over Qiltu, Biblical Keilah, a border town between the two kingdoms, safely identified as Tell Qila (near the village of Khirbet Qila) on Wadi eṣ-Ṣur.[29] Shuwardata reports that he has seized Keilah, with the prior approval of Egypt (EA 280: 9–15). This emphatic statement shows that Shuwardata's claim to the city had been recognized by Egypt. The need for military intervention in Qiltu may have followed after a rebellion, probably instigated from outside. Indeed, in the following lines, ʿAbdi-Ḥeba is accused of having bribed the men of Qiltu to join his camp (EA 280: 16–24).

The dispute over Keilah created a new alignment of the regional forces. Faced with the threat of ʿAbdi-Ḥeba (aptly described as a new Labʾayu), Shuwardata now allied himself with his northern neighbor, Milkilu of Gezer. The two had rushed troops of Gazru, of Gimtu and of Qiltu, and had seized the territory of Rubute, a town which must have been situated between the realms of Gezer and Jerusalem (EA 290: 5–11). This Gimtu is usually taken to refer to Shuwardata's city, Gath.[30] However, in another letter of ʿAbdi-Ḥeba the takeover of Rubute is attributed to Milkilu and Taku, the ruler of Gintikirmil, i.e. Gath-Carmel (EA 289: 11–13). Naʾaman has concluded that Gimtu in EA 290 must also refer to this northern Gath, so that Shuwardata's city would never explicitly be mentioned in the Amarna correspondence.[31] Although there is some confusion due to the fact that both Gaths participated in the hostilities against Jerusalem, it is nevertheless more plausible to identify Gimtu in *EA* 290 as Shuwardata's city.[32]

Following the capture of Rubute, ʿAbdi-Ḫeba further reports that a city of the land of Jerusalem, Bit-NINURTA, followed the men of Qiltu (290: 14–18). The reading of the ideogram in the name Bit-NINURTA and the identification of this city have long been a matter of intensive debate.[33] Without dwelling upon the complicated issues involved in establishing a meaningful Canaanite syncretism with the Mesopotamian divinity, it may be noted in passing that from a geographical point of view it is reasonable to search for a city situated somewhere between Jerusalem and Qiltu/Keilah. Bethlehem, one of the current identifications,[34] would fit this prerequisite better than Beth-Horon,[35] but this town is still quite distant from Keilah; moreover, there is no evidence as yet for a Late Bronze Age occupation.[36] Another suggested candidate, Beit-ʿAnat,[37] entails similar difficulties. To the long list of candidates we may tentatively add Beth-Zur, identified with Khirbet et-Tubeiqah. The site is ideally located on the same brook (Wadi eṣ-Ṣur), at a short distance of about 10 kms. from Keilah. From various finds discovered during the excavations at the site, it appears that "there was some kind of activity at the site during the Late Bronze period."[38] The connection between the element *Zur* and NINURTA remains to be established.

Returning to Keilah, the town seems to have changed sites several times, due to bribery rather than military occupation *EA* 289: 25–29; 290: 25–29). Although the town seems to have been of vital importance in ʿAbdi-Ḫeba's foreign policy, he does not claim possession of it as he does in the case of Bit-NINURTA. Perhaps the proximity between the two places (if the suggested identification of Bit-NINURTA and Beth-Zur is valid) is the very reason for ʿAbdi-Ḫeba's intervention in Keilah, since this town had apparently incited rebellion inside his own kingdom. As mentioned before, Keilah was subservient to the Kingdom of Gath, but managed even so to manipulate between the rival kingdoms and to turn its geographical situation to its own advantage. In view of this position, it has often been suggested that Keilah may have enjoyed the status of a small independent kingdom tucked between its larger neighbors. However, it is worth noting that only the "men of Qiltu" (*EA* 280: 18; 289: 28; 290: 18) and the "troops of Qiltu" (*EA* 290: 10, 18) are mentioned, and never a ruler of the city (cf. below, on biblical Keilah). We shall return to this important border town of the Kingdom of Gath.

In the later reign of Shuwardata the general tide of uprising [39] swept over the Kingdom of Gath. In *EA* 283: 18–24 he complains that he must defend himself alone against 30 hostile towns, and asks for urgent reinforcements. It is not clear whether all these towns belonged to his own kingdom. Also, the large number may simply have been a figure of speech.

Eventually Shuwardata, like other southern rulers (Simreda of Lachish and Milkilu of Gezer), disappeared from the scene and was succeeded by ʿAbdi-Ashtarti.[40] During his reign the mutinous atmosphere in Gath and its neighbors did not abate. The only information of any geographical value comes from *EA* 335: 17ff, reporting about a mutiny in Lachish and the seizure of the town of Mu-uḫ/ú-ra-aš-ti. The political status of this latter town, whether it belonged to Lachish or to Gath, is not made clear in the text. The name may plausibly be identified with Biblical Moreshet-Gath, birth-place of the prophet Micah (Micah 1: 1).[41] The town is probably located at Tell el-Judeideh (Tel Goded), about 10 kms. southeast of Tell eṣ-Ṣafi.[42] As indicated by the composite place-name, Moreshet was associated with Gath, and it is reasonable to assume that Muʾurašti of EA 335 was a city of Gath situated near the border of Lachish. The border between the two kingdoms may have run along Naḥal Govrin.

Summing up the Amarna evidence, the Kingdom of Gath appears to have covered a relatively large territory extending from Naḥal Soreq in the north to Naḥal Govrin in the south. Its western border is difficult to establish, but is irrelevant to the main thrust of this study. Our attention is focused on the eastern confines of the kingdom, which must have comprised the entire Vale of Elah. In other words, the eastern border of Gath coincides with the eastern border of the Shephelah, and includes the fertile Senonian trough in which lay the city of Keilah. No wonder that this was a region which Jerusalem set its eyes upon. The question to be examined below is whether this geopolitical reality is still in evidence in later periods, when Gath turned into a Philistine kingdom.

I believe that this question may be answered in the affirmative. A clear indication of the eastern confines of Philistine Gath may be found in the episode of David's intervention in Keilah:

> The Philistines were fighting against Keilah and plundering the threshing-floors; and when David heard this, he consulted the Lord and asked whether he should go and attack the Philistines. The Lord answered, "Go attack them, and relieve Keilah." But David's men said to him, "As we are now, we have enough to fear from Judah. How much worse if we challenge the Philistine forces at Keilah!" (1 Samuel 23: 1–3)

Despite the fears of his men, David attacks Keilah, which is described as a "walled town with gates and bars" (23: 7). He inflicts a heavy defeat on the Philistines and carries off their cattle (23: 5). However, when he finds out through divination that the "lords of Keilah,"[43] whom he relieved from the Philistines, will nevertheless surrender him to Saul, he flees from the city with his men.

David's intervention in Keilah is obviously described as the liberation of a Judahite border town from a Philistine attack. However, there are sufficient indications in the text to show that this was not quite the case. First, David's men explicitly consider Keilah as lying outside of Judah.[44] Second, it is rather strange that after the successful routing of what appears to be nothing more than a Philistine raiding party,[45] David's men carry off their cattle, i.e. the cattle of the Philistines.[46] Cattle is not quite what a plundering party would take along to a foray. Some commentators were compelled to render *miqnehem* as "beasts of burden,"[47] which were brought by the Philistines to transport the grain, or simply as "property."[48] Another explanation, which follows the literal meaning of *miqne*, is that the Philistine raiders, who had deliberately chosen the time of harvest, took along their cattle to Keilah to forage on the crops lying exposed on the threshing floors.[49]

All these attempts are unnecessary, if Keilah is conceived as what it really was; a border town of the Kingdom of Gath. Although nominally Keilah was considered in Joshua 14: 44 as a city of Judah, its real status in the episode described above is quite different,[50] and it seems to have persisted from the Amarna age. Obviously, this does not imply that Keilah was a Philistine city. The town may have been inhabited by a mixed population,[51] but the Philistines could still consider it their rightful possession. Rather than an act of plundering beyond the border, their pillaging of the threshing-floors of Keilah may simply have been the collection of tribute from a vassal town. Quite contrary to the impression evoked by the description, it was David's band which conducted a raid on the Philistine frontier. In fact, this raid, conducted from nearby Adulam, bears close similarity to the raids conducted by David from Ziklag against Amalekite territories; only by that time he already fought with, rather than against, the Philistines.

The comparison between the status of Keilah in the Amarna age and in the early days of David strongly suggests that the eastern confines of the Kingdom of Gath persisted through the centuries without considerable change. This conclusion, if accepted, may have far-reaching consequences for the history and culture of the eastern Shephelah. This important region, which after David's victory over the Philistines became part of the Israelite Kingdom (and is accordingly designated as the Shephelah of Judah), was an integral part of the Philistine realm before the 10th century. This should be taken into consideration in evaluating the material culture in excavations carried out in this region. The site of Keilah (Khirbet Qila) has not been excavated yet.[52] However, further south along the same fertile Senonian trough lie the mounds of Tell ʿAitun and Tell Beit Mirsim which have been investigated archaeologically. One may raise the question of the geopolitical status and the cultural character of these towns in the early Iron Age. Although these problems are beyond the scope of this study, it may be noted in passing that great importance was attached in the past to the finds from Tell Beit Mirsim for understanding the Israelite settlement. In recent studies the issue has been approached more carefully, and Finkelstein concludes, with good reason, that "it is still difficult to identify the origin of the inhabitants of Stratum B1–2."[53] The same conclusion may hold true in the evaluation of the material from the early Iron Age cemetery of Tell ʿAitun.[54] The remarkably rich Philistine assemblage found in one of the chamber tombs may indicate more direct Philistine involvement in this region than simply trade contacts with coastal areas. However, these are merely tentative remarks and the issue deserves to be thoroughly investigated.

Having dealt with the eastern borders of the Kingdom of Gath, we may now return to the opening observations regarding its southern confines. In this connection we have noted the remarkable fact that the distant town of Ziklag lay in the jurisdiction of Achish King of Gath. The explanation we suggested for this geopolitical reality was that the Kingdom of Gath dominated the entire realm of Philistia, south of Naḥal Elah. In this respect, there is a sharp deviation from the geopolitical map of the Amarna age, when the Kingdom of Gath was bordered in the south by the Kingdom of Lachish. Clearly, Lachish must have disappeared from the political scene at the time of the Philistine consolidation, and Gath must have taken over all its territories. This inevitable conclusion is confirmed by the excavations at Tell ed-Duweir, which have shown that after the destruction of Canaanite Lachish in the mid–12th century B.C.E., the town lay in ruins for about two centuries.[55] The combined territories of Gath and Lachish resulted in a considerably large Philistine kingdom, probably extending from Naḥal Elah in the north (bordering the Kingdom of Edron) to Naḥal Gerar in the south. This was indeed a strong regional power, which exerted its hegemony over the mountainous regions of Judah for a lengthy period, a situation duly reflected in the Samson stories. The defense of Ziklag, a "country town" (1 Samuel 27: 5) on the southern border of the Kingdom of Gath, was entrusted to David and his band of Hebrew mercenaries, who eventually caused its decline. Thus it is quite apparent why "Metheg-ammah," which David took out of the hand of the Philistines (2 Samuel 8: 1) was replaced in I Chronicles 18: 1 with "Gath and its dependencies."

Notes

1. This study was sponsored by the Yaniv Foundation for the Research of Jewish History and Jewish Philosophy.

2. See I. Singer, "The Beginning of Philistine Settlement in Canaan and the Northern Boundary of Philistia," *TA* 12 (1985): 109–122 (with a survey of different views concerning the date and historical circumstances of Philistine settlement.)

3. On the rise and decline of Philistine hegemony in Israel, see I. Singer, "Egyptians, Canaanites and Philistines in the Period of Settlement and Judges," in N. Naʾaman and I. Finkelstein, *From Nomadism to Monarchy* (Jerusalem, 1990), pp. 348–402 (Hebrew).

4. See I. Finkelstein, "The Emergence of the Monarchy in Israel, the Environmental and Socio-Economic Aspects," *JSOT* 44 (1989): 44–46 (with extensive literature).

5. See I. Singer, "The Origin of the Sea Peoples and Their Settlement on the Coast of Canaan," in M. Heltzer and E. Lipiński (eds.), *Society and Economy in the Eastern Mediterranean (c. 1500–1000 B.C.)* (Leuven, 1988), pp. 239–250.

6. See F. Pintore, "Seren, Tarwanis, Tyrannos," in D. Carruba, M. Liverani, C. Zaccagnini (eds.), *Studi Orientalistici in Ricordo di Franco Pintore* (Pavia, 1983), pp. 265–322.

7. This includes Ekron, which was earlier considered to have been founded by the Philistines. See T. Dothan "The Rise and Fall of Ekron of the Philistines, Recent Excavations at an Urban Border Site: The Late Bronze and Early Iron Ages," *BA* 50 (1987): 200f; idem, "The Arrival of the Sea Peoples: Cultural Diversity in Early Iron Age Canaan," in S. Gitin and W.G. Dever (eds.), *Recent Excavations in Israel: Studies in Iron Age Archaeology* (AASOR 49) (Winona Lake, 1989), pp. 2ff.

8. See I. Singer, "Merneptah's Campaign to Canaan and the Egyptian Occupation of the Southern Coastal Plain of Palestine in the Ramesside Period," *BASOR* 269 (1988): 6.

9. See I. Singer, "Toward an Identity of Dagon, the God of the Philistines," *Cathedra* 54 (1989): 17–42 (Hebrew with English abstract, p. 190).

10. B.D. Rahtjen, "Philistine and Hebrew Amphictyonies," *JNES* 24 (1965): 100–104.

11. For a history of research on this issue see H.E. Chambers, "Ancient Amphictyonies, sic et non," in W.W. Hallo, J.C. Mayer, and L.G. Perdue (eds.), *Scripture in Context I: More Essays on the Comparative Method* (Winona Lake, 1983), pp. 39–41.

12. Ibid., pp. 51–59.

13. Ibid., p. 50f.

14. See Rahtjen, "Philistine and Hebrew Amphictyonies" (see note 10), p. 102f.

15. R. de Vaux, *The Early History of Israel* (Philadelphia, 1978), p. 701.

16. Singer, "Dagon" (see note 9).

17. For the possible origin of the name see Singer, "Egyptians" (see note 3), p. 401.

18. "The Philistines and their Wars with Israel," in B. Mazar (ed.), *The World History of the Jewish People* III. *Judges* (Tel Aviv, 1971), p. 178.

19. Cv. also Pintore, "Seren" (see note 6), p. 297.

20. A.F. Rainey, "The Identification of Philistine Gath," *EI* 12 (1975): 63*–76*.

21. The political status of nearby Gerar, which plays a prominent role as a Philistine center in the Patriarchal stories (Genesis 21 and 26), is yet to be established. The archaeological excavations at Tell Abu Hureireh (Tel Haror), possibly identified as Gerar, will provide evidence on the size and importance of this city in the early Iron Age. For some preliminary remarks on this issue see Singer, "Egyptians" (see note 3), pp. 370, 381f (with refs.).

22. The territorial confines of Ekron are not discussed in detail. We may note in passing that it seems this Philistine city-kingdom first ruled over a limited area, between Naḥal Haʾela and Naḥal Soreq. After the Philistine takeover of Gezer and its realm, the confines of Ekron must have grown considerably. See I. Singer, "The Beginning of Philistine Settlement in Canaan and the Northern Boundary of Philistia," *TA* 12 (1985).

23. "Die Landnahme der Israeliten in Palestina," *Kleine Schriften zur Geschichte des Volkes Israel* I (Munich, 1950), pp. 89–125; English translation in *Essays on Old Testament History and Religion* (Oxford, 1966), pp. 133–169 (see esp. p. 136).

24. See, e.g., N. Naʾaman, "Historical-Geographical Aspects of the Amarna Tablets," *Proceedings of the Ninth World Congress of Jewish Studies* (Jerusalem, 1985), pp. 17–26; idem, "The Canaanite City-States in the Late Bronze Age and the Inheritances of the Israelite Tribes," *Tarbiz* 55 (1986): 463–488 (Hebrew).

25. Naʾaman, "Amarna" (see note 24), 18ff. For the archaeological aspects of these divisions see S. Bunimovitz, "The Land of Israel in the Late Bronze Age: A Case of Socio-Cultural Change in a Complex Society." (Ph.D. diss., Tel Aviv University, 1975), pp. 119–131 (Hebrew).

26. For a general survey on the history of Gath see A.F. Rainey, "Gath of the Philistines," *Christian News from Israel* 17 (1966): 23–34; idem, "Identification" (see note 20). For the Amarna Age see further N. Naʾaman, "The Political Disposition and Historical Development of Eretz-Israel According to the Amarna Letters." (Ph.D. diss., Tel Aviv University, 1975), pp. 119–131 (Hebrew); idem, "The Origin and Historical Background of Several Amarna Letters," *UF* 11 (1979): 673–684.

27. For references see Singer, "Merneptah" (see note 8), p. 5f.

28. The latter to be distinguished from ʿAbdi-Ashirta of Amurru. See Naʾaman, "Origin" (see note 26).

29. See A.F. Rainey, "The Administrative Division of the Shephelah," *TA* 7 (1980): 198.

30. Y. Aharoni, *The Land of the Bible* (revised edition) (Philadelphia, 1979), p. 174; A.F. Rainey, "Gath" (see note 26), p. 24.

31. "Political Disposition" (see note 26), p. 129f.

32. See also W.L. Moran, *Les lettres d'El-Amarna* (Paris, 1987), p. 597. It is perhaps worth noting the difference in spelling. Whereas the town in *EA* 290: 9 is spelled Gi-im-ti, all the occurrences of Gath-Carmel are spelled Gin-ti(-) (*EA* 288: 26; 289: 18; 290: 28 [?], see Moran, *Les lettres*, p. 520 n.4).

33. See Z. Kallai and H. Tadmor, "Bit Ninurta = Beit Horon: On the History of the Kingdom of Jerusalem in the Amarna Period," *EI* 9 (1969): 138–147 (with extensive bibliography); Naʾaman, "Political Disposition" (see note 26), pp. 104ff.

34. E.g., de Vaux, *Early History of Israel* (see note 15), p. 104 n.101.

35. Kallay and Tadmor, "Bit Ninurta" (see note 33).

36. According to A. Ofer's recent survey of Judah (personal communication). For the period of the Israelite settlement at Bethlehem see now A. Ofer, "The Judean Hill Country — from Nomadism to a National Monarchy," in *Nomadism to Monarchy* (see note 3), p. 202f (Hebrew).

37. Naʾaman, "Political Disposition" (see note 26), p. 108.

38. I. Finkelstein, *The Archaeology of the Israelite Settlement* (Jerusalem, 1988), p. 48 (with references to the excavation reports).

39. Naʾaman, "Political Disposition" (see note 26), p. 145ff.

40. See Naʾaman, "Origin" (see note 26).

41. The identification was already suggested by H. Clauss in 1907. It was later opposed on linguistic grounds, which were recently proven to be invalid. See S. Vargon, "El-Amarna *Muʾrašt* and Biblical *Moresheth*," in J. Klein and A. Skaist, *Bar-Ilan Studies in Assyriology Dedicated to Pinhas Artzi* (Jerusalem, 1990), pp. 207–212.

42. See M. Broshi, "Judeideh, Tell," in *Encyclopedia of Archaeological Excavations* III, pp. 694ff.

43. *Baʿalei Keilah*, "lords" or "citizens" of Keilah is a rare usage, which may be compared to the Amarna evidence on this city (see above). This usage of the word to denote the ruling class of a city is also found in connection with Jericho (Joshua 24: 11), Shechem (Judges 9: 22ff), Gibeah (Judges 20: 5) and Jabesh Gilead (2 Samuel 21: 12). See S.R. Driver, *Notes on the Hebrew Text and the Topography of the Books of Samuel* (Oxford, 1913), p. 185. Cf. Further B. Mazar, "The Early Israelite Settlement in the Hill Country," in idem, *The Early Biblical Period, Historical Studies* (Jerusalem, 1986), p. 42.

44. Whereas the Masoretic text has *el maʿarkot plištim*, i.e. "to/against the Philistine ranks," the Septuagint has something like "to the Philistine valleys/hollow places," which is more comprehensible. See P. Kyle McCarter, *I Samuel* (Garden City), p. 369.

45. On this and similar ostensibly decisive encounters between David and the Philistines see N.L. Tidwell, "The Philistine Incursions into the Valley of Rephaim (2 Sam. v 17ff)," in J.A. Emerton (ed.), *Studies in the Historical Books of the Old Testament* (VT Suppl. 30), (Leiden, 1979), pp. 190–212 (esp. 200ff.).

46. Caspari's assumption that it was the Philistines who had driven away the cattle of Keilah would necessitate unwarranted textual alterations. See H.W. Hertzberg, *I and II Samuel* (London, 1964), p. 190f.

47. E.g. G.B. Caird, *I and II Samuel* (New York and Nashville, 1953), p. 1,004; Hertzberg, *I and II Samuel* (see note 46).

48. J. Mauchline, *1 and 2 Samuel* (London, 1971), p. 159.

49. E.g. McCarter, *I Samuel* (see note 44), p. 371.

50. See ibid., p. 371.

51. It is worth noting that no conquest narrative is attached to this region of the upper Elah Valley. On the contrary, the story of Judah and Tamar in Genesis 38 reveals peaceful relations between Judah and the Canaanites in the area around Adullam. See Rainey, "Shephelah" (see note 29), p. 194; Singer, "Egyptians" (see note 3), p. 372.

52. The archaeological survey has produced Late Bronze and Iron Age pottery. M. Kochavi, "The Land of Judah," in *Judaea, Samaria and the Golan, Archaeological Survey 1967–1968* (Jerusalem 1972), pp. 48–49 (Hebrew); see also Finkelstein, "Israelite Settlement" (see note 38), p. 52. In the Shephelah survey conducted by Yehuda Dagan, a few Philistine sherds were also found (personal communication).

53. *Israelite Settlement* (see note 38), p. 55 (with previous references). A similar situation prevails in Beth-Shemesh (ibid.).

54. See T. Dothan, *The Philistines and their Material Culture* (Jerusalem, 1982), p. 44 (with references to publications).

55. See D. Ussishkin, "Levels VII and VI at Tel Lachish and the End of the Late Bronze Age in Canaan," in J.N. Tubb (ed.), *Palestine in the Bronze and Iron Ages, Papers in Honour of Olga Tufnell* (London, 1985), p. 222f.

The Changing Shape of Power
in Bronze Age Canaan

Shlomo Bunimovitz

In the mid–1950s, a graded scale of increasing difficulty of reasoning in archaeology was outlined by C. Hawkes (1954: 161–162). In this "ladder of inference," sociopolitical institutions fall near the upper limit of amenability to archaeological study, and climbing up beyond the initial technological and economic rungs was thought to be virtually impossible. This pessimistic view, shared by most archaeological writers in the 1950s (e.g. Childe 1951: 55), was replaced in the late 1960s and early 1970s by a more optimistic and ambitious program, claiming that the practical limitations on our knowledge of the past are not inherent in the nature of the archaeological record, but lie in our methodological naiveté (Binford 1968: 22–23; see also Klejn 1977: 3–16). Indeed, B. Trigger (1974), C. Renfrew (1977; 1986; Renfrew and Level 1979), G. Johnson (1972; 1980; 1987), J. Marcus (1973), J. Cherry (1978; 1986; 1987), and others, have shown that the archaeological record does contain varied information about past political structures and their spatial organization, but usually this information has not been gathered, nor dealt with systematically (Hass 1982: 87, 122). However, reading the archaeological literature about Bronze Age Canaan, one soon becomes aware of the fact that Syro-Palestinian archaeologists do talk liberally of kingdoms, city-states, and other forms of sociopolitical organization supposed to exist in Canaan during the 3rd and 2nd millennia B.C.E. What then are the most common methodological procedures, beside sheer intuition, which explicitly or implicitly lie behind these reconstructions?

Writing recently about the Middle Bronze II period in Canaan, N. Naʾaman gave a clear answer to our question:

> Trying to analyze inner relations in Canaan during the 19th to 17th centuries B.C.E., we have only meager information derived from archaeological excavations and surveys. Therefore, we also need to rely on analogy to neighboring

countries and on backward reconstruction from known situations in later periods. This last procedure is based on an assumption about continuity in the political organization of Canaan from the Middle Bronze II to the 12th century
B.C.E. (1982: 158)

Since direct historical documentation about sociopolitical organization in Palestine
during the 3rd and most of the 2nd millennia B.C.E. is still wanting, analogy and
"backward reconstruction" became the main tools for "political mapping" in studies
concerned with the Canaanite Bronze Age (e.g. Gophna and Beck 1981: 76–78;
Dever 1987: 164–165). However, the reliability of these procedures is open to question.

The proper use of analogy in archaeology has been scrutinized and debated in
recent years (Binford 1972a; 1972b; Gould and Watson 1982; Hodder 1982b: 11–
27). Clearly, in many instances the analogy is no more than an unconfirmed hypothesis. Quoting Na᾽aman again, the danger of sweeping analogies with neighboring
countries becomes obvious:

A comparison between the political, administrative and economical systems of
the Mesopotamian and Syrian kingdoms during the Middle Bronze II shows
that in spite of their superficial resemblance differences do exist; and in Palestine, which is southern to them and under Egyptian influence, quite different
patterns could have been developed. (1982: 158)

Here lies one of the main problems of a direct analogy — our interpretation of the
unknown past is *a priori* limited by what is already known.

Like analogy, "backward reconstruction" is a hypothetical procedure which needs
confirmation. To assume that a certain political organization, known to prevail in
a certain period, also existed before or after that period, and then to argue for continuity in the sociopolitical organization — is simply to beg the question. Furthermore,
the simplistic assumption that material correlates of sociopolitical organizations can
easily be transferred from one set of data to another, may lead to false conclusions.
For example: the strong fortifications which characterize many Early Bronze II–III
sites in Palestine, are traditionally interpreted as testifying to inter-city hostility and
to a political system of mini-kingdoms or city-states (Wright 1961: 81; de Vaux
1971: 234; Kenyon 1979: 85; Richard 1987: 29. For a different interpretation based
on the same data see, however, Lapp 1970: 112–114). Now, if we had no historical
information about the political systems in Palestine during the Late Bronze and Iron
Age II, then a mechanical application of the fortification criterion to the archaeological data from these periods could have produced some very wrong conclusions: On
one hand, the unfortified cities of the Late Bronze Age (Gonen 1984: 69–70; 1987:
97–98) — the paradigm of a city-state regime in Canaan — could have been easily
presented as proof of a peaceful period, obviously the result of a united political orga-

nization; on the other hand, the heavily fortified cities of the Iron Age II probably would have been interpreted as autonomous city-states!

The above discussion makes it clear that analogies and backward reconstructions, when applied uncritically and without further confirmation, tend to ignore the specific historical context of the case under consideration. As such, they may easily mask diachronic fluctuations in the political organization. It should be remembered, that every political system is a product of a certain historical environment, and this environment is not static but ever changing. As a result of our presently rough procedures, we lump together the political structures of the Early, Middle and Late Bronze Ages under the rubric "city-states" without further elaboration; but do we really mean that exactly the same political organization prevailed during these otherwise very different periods? and what about variations in the political organization during each of these long periods? Obviously, there were differences between the sociopolitical systems of the Middle Bronze IIA and IIB–C, or the Late Bronze II and III! Furthermore, analogies and "backward reconstructions" have usually been applied to the whole country en bloc; consequently, no synchronic (regional) variability in the political organization could be discerned. As exemplified by Finkelstein's contribution to the present symposium entitled "The Sociopolitical Organization of the Central Hill Country in the Second Millennium B.C.E.," one cannot ignore the possibility of regional differences in the Bronze Age political organization as a result of different environmental or historical conditions. Paradoxically enough, the "New Archaeology," rather than the traditional one, is habitually blamed for relying too heavily on noncontextual generalizations! (see e.g. Hodder 1982a, 1982b, 1986; Trigger 1984: 288–290; Kohl 1987: 4–5).

Some of the problems reviewed above were already noticed by other students of the archaeology of Palestine. Thus, referring to the "backward reconstruction" he himself practiced, Naʾaman comments that "such a reconstruction is inevitably schematic and unsatisfactory, and leaves many questions unanswered" (1982: 158, 169). Similar feelings of doubt, this time towards the helpfulness of a far analogy from Syria or Mesopotamia, were expressed by R. Gophna and P. Beck while trying to reconstruct the political map of the Coastal Plain during the Middle Bronze II (1988: 86). In another study, Gophna pointed out that during the Early Bronze II–III different patterns of settlement hierarchies — probably hinting at different patterns of political organization — existed simultaneously (1982: 113). However, as yet, they remain undeciphered, and are all embraced by the catchall term "city-states."

This list of references could be extended, but I hope that I have made my point: in order to study the full range of change in the shape of power during the Bronze Age we need to sharpen our old methodological tools, if not to bring in new ones.

Metaphorically, the problem can be described as a two dimensional graph. The perpendicular axis is composed of a continuum of sociopolitical structures of which the archaeologist has to choose the one corresponding to his or her test case. The horizontal axis represents the spatial organization of the political units, the "landscape of power" as Renfrew called it (1984: 10). As emphasized above, both the political structure and its spatial relations are ever changing; therefore, the procedures used for sociopolitical reconstruction must penetrate as deeply as possible into the specific context under examination. What this means in archaeological terms is that sociopolitical reconstructions should rely first of all on a careful and thorough examination of the archaeological material in its specific ecological, cultural and social environment. Only then may one confirm or negate analogies or pre-conceived models.

A few recent studies in the archaeology of Bronze Age Palestine seem to explicitly follow the procedure outlined above. Expectedly, some of the results deviate from the picture painted by the traditional procedures for sociopolitical reconstruction, and are therefore controversial. In what follows, I will briefly survey these studies and their implications.

The first study is T. Levy's social analysis of the Chalcolithic in the Northern Negev (1981). Though it is concerned with a pre-Bronze period, I would like to include it here due to its novelty at the time of its appearance. In this study, which is actually a whole research program, Levy proceeded from a comprehensive analysis of the archaeological remains: artifacts, ecofacts, architectural features, intra-and inter-site settlement patterns, burial customs, etc., towards a reconstruction of the local sociopolitical organization. Helped by the evolutionary framework developed by E. Service, M. Sahlins and M. Fried, Levy concluded that at the end of the 4th millennium B.C.E. the communities at the northern Negev were organized as low-order chiefdoms. This conclusion was actually reached by comparing the archaeological results with a "check list" of various features characterizing chiefdoms, which have archaeological correlates (see especially Levy 1986).

"Check list" archaeology has been criticized, especially in connection with the pigeonholing of societies into the Fried-Service evolutionary scheme (Hass 1982: 10–13; Kristiansen 1984: 72; Earle 1987: 280), and Levy was blamed for paying attention more to social models than to the archaeological record (Gilead 1988a; 1988b: 434–435). Nevertheless, denial of the methodological program underlying his research would be to throw out the baby with the bath water.

Two additional examples of sociopolitical reconstructions, based on a scrutiny of the specific archaeological, environmental, historical and social contexts involved, are I. Finkelstein's study of the Middle and Late Bronze "dimorphic chiefdoms" in the central hill country (in this volume), and his reevaluation of the sociopolitical role of Early Bronze Age Arad (1991). Concerning the first study, I would only point out that in addition to its methodological value, namely, its conceptual framework and practical procedures, the study makes one fully aware of the regional variability (lowlands vs. highlands) in the sociopolitical structure of Palestine during the 2nd millennium B.C.E. Though my own interpretation of the Middle Bronze-Late Bronze Age political organization in the central hill country differs from Finkelstein's (below), concerning the last point we apparently agree.

Finkelstein's second study challenges the traditional interpretation of Early Bronze Age Arad as a city-state. Instead of using simple analogy or formal criteria, such as the existence of a wall, inner planning etc., his renewed sociopolitical reconstruction, based on an anthropological oriented analysis of the site's architecture and economics, local and supra-local patterns of settlement, etc., seeks to understand the role of the site in its environmental, social, and historical context. According to this analysis, Early Arad was founded by the Negev nomads and served as their main center during the Early Bronze II. The rise and fall of this "capital" of the southern nomadic chiefdom are thus explained by the changing fortunes of that unique polity. Once again we see that a contextual approach enables both a better diagnosis of the sociopolitical organization and a closer acquaintance with the regional diversity of the sociopolitical system.

Finally, I would like to present briefly the main conclusions of my own recent study of Middle Bronze IIC sociopolitical organization in Palestine and its changes during the Late Bronze Age (Bunimovitz 1989: 47–74).

Since historical sources are silent on this matter, and the procedures currently in use for "political mapping" were considered methodologically deficient, a reconstruction based on an analysis of the regional settlement systems' rank-size distributions has been preferred. This method, which is much closer to the empirical data than the others, enables the sociopolitical organization in the examined region — whether in the form of a centralized government or autonomous polities — to be determined by detecting the level of integration in its settlement system (e.g. Johnson 1980, 1981, 1987; Kowalewski 1982; Paynter 1983). Utilizing this method, the Middle Bronze IIC and Late Bronze II settlement systems of three main regions in Palestine: Coastal Plain, Jezreel Valley and central hill country were examined, and the results compared with the current hypotheses of sociopolitical organization in the country during these periods.

In the Coastal Plain (south of the Yarkon), the Middle Bronze IIB–C rank-size distribution hints at the existence of a large, comparatively integrated urban system (which probably included the Shephelah). Additional data, such as that concerning the rapid urbanization and population of this very region in the Middle Bronze IIC (Gophna and Portugali 1988; Herzog 1989: 34–37), its economic prosperity and the high concentration of Hyksos royal-name scarabs within its confines (Weinstein 1981: Figs. 2–3; an indication for administrative integration?) tends to strengthen our conclusion as to its organization as a united polity (cf. Dothan 1973: 14–17; Seger 1975: 44*–45*; Kempinski 1983: 60–64, 210–211, 222–223; Herzog 1989: 37), and clearly exemplifies the "Pax Hyksosiaca" that prevailed there. This situation changed completely during the Late Bronze Age and the rank-size distribution, as well as evidence from the Amarna Letters, testify to a low degree of integration in the sociopolitical organization of the region — a cluster of semi-autonomous city-states. In the central hill country (especially the hill country of Manasseh), the rank-size distribution tells a diametrically opposite story: the Late Bronze II settlement system seems to have been more integrated than that of the Middle Bronze IIC. This conclusion concurs well with the locally clustered Middle Bronze IIC pattern of settlement that has been recently recognized in the Shechem Basin and in Ephraim (Zertal 1986: 188–190, 197; Finkelstein 1985: 164–165), and with Alt's concept of large territorial polities in these regions in the Late Bronze Age (1966: 153–155). Furthermore, they clearly contradict the hypothesis of an alleged Shechemite Hyksos kingdom (Zertal 1986: 198–200; Kempinski 1983: 64), and indicate that large settlement systems crystallized in the Hill Country only after its former settlement systems had disintegrated at the end of the Middle Bronze Age. It is obvious that in many regions of Palestine, the Late Bronze II sociopolitical organization was not identical to that which prevailed during the Middle Bronze IIC. Our analysis of the rank-size distributions of the Jezreel Valley also confirms these conclusion.

The above examples show that diachronic variations and synchronic diversity in the sociopolitical organization of Palestine during the Bronze Age were more common than has been estimated. Accordingly, it seems that the sociopolitical evolution in Palestine during the 3rd and 2nd millennia B.C.E. was highly punctuated, characterized by repeated crystallization and disintegration in addition to regionally differentiated evolutionary trajectories. As such, it fully corroborates the anthropologists' claims of flexibility and reversibility of political evolutionary processes (e.g. Yoffee 1979; 1988; Adams 1988; see also Coote and Whitelam 1987). Furthermore, the empirical richness of the archaeology of Palestine supplies valuable opportunities to study some neglected evolutionary processes, such as the formation of secondary states via historical succession (Price 1978: 161)(a processes that seems to have taken place at the transition from the Middle to the Late Bronze Age), and others. However, it is a truism that facts do not speak for themselves. So, as I have argued above, in order to make them tell us the full story of the changing shape of power in Bronze Age Palestine, we need to improve our methodological powers of persuasion.

References

R.McC. Adams, 1988. "Contexts of Civilizational Collapse: A Mesopotamian View," in N. Yoffee and G.L. Cowgill (eds.), *The Collapse of Ancient States and Civilizations*, pp. 20–43. Tuscon.

A. Alt, 1966. *The Settlement of the Israelites in Palestine. Essays on Old Testament History and Religion*, pp. 135–169. Oxford.

L.R. Binford, 1968. "Archaeological Perspectives," in S.R. Binford and L.R. Binford (eds.), *New Perspectives in Archaeology*, pp. 5–32. Chicago.

_____, 1972a. "Smudge Pits and Hide Smoking: The Use of Analogy in Archaeological Reasoning," *An Archaeological Perspective*, pp. 33–51. New York.

_____, 1972b. "Archaeological Reasoning and Smudge Pits — Revisited," *An Archaeological Perspective*, pp. 52–58. New York.

S. Bunimovitz, 1989. The Land of Israel in the Late Bronze Age: A Case Study of Socio-Cultural Change in a Complex Society. (Ph.D. diss., Tel Aviv University) (Hebrew).

J.F. Cherry, 1978. "Generalisation and the Archaeology of the State," in D.R. Green, C.C. Haselgrove and M. Spriggs (eds.), *Social Organisation and Settlement* (B.A.R. Supplementry Series 47), 411–437. Oxford.

_____, 1986. "Polities and Palaces: Some Problems in Minoan State Formation," in C. Renfrew and J.F. Cherry (eds.), *Peer Polity Interaction and Socio-Political Change*, pp. 19–45. Cambridge.

_____, 1987. "Power in Space: Archaeological and Geographical Studies of the State," in J.M. Wagstaff (ed.), *Landscape and Culture*, pp. 146–172. Oxford.

V.G. Childe, 1951. *Social Evolution*. London.

R.B. Coote and K.W. Whitelam, 1987. *The Emergence of Early Israel in Historical Perspective*. Sheffield.

W.G. Dever, 1987. "The Middle Bronze Age," *BA* 50: 149–177.

Dothan, M., 1973. "The Foundation of Tel Mor and of Ashdod," *IEJ* 23: 1–17.

T.K. Earle, 1987. "Chiefdoms in Archaeological and Ethnohistorical Perspective," *Annual Review of Anthropology* 16: 279–308.

I. Finkelstein, (ed.), 1985. "Excavations at Shiloh 1981–1984: Preliminary Report," *TA* 12: 123–180.

I. Finkelstein, 1991. "Early Arad — Urbanism of the Nomads," *ZDPV* 106 (forthcoming).

I. Gilead. 1988a. "Shiqmim and the Chalcolithic Period in Southern Israel," *Mitekufat Haeven* 21: 145*–150*.

———, 1988b. "The Chalcolithic Period in the Levant," *Journal of World Prehistory* 2: 397–443.

R. Gonen, 1984. "Urban Canaan in the Late Bronze Period," *BASOR* 253: 61–73.

———, 1987. "Megiddo in the Late Bronze Age — Another Reassessment," *Levant* 19: 83–100.

R. Gophna, 1982. "Eretz-Israel in the Dawn of History. The Early Bronze Age and the Intermediate Bronze Age (c. 3300–2000 B.C.E)," in I. Eph‘al (ed.), *The History of Eretz-Israel* I, pp. 97–127. Jerusalem. (Hebrew).

R. Gophna and P. Beck, 1981a. "The Rural Aspect of the Settlement Pattern of the Coastal Plain in the Middle Bronze Age II," *TA* 8: 45–80.

———, 1981b. "The Rural Settlements of the Middle Bronze Age in Coastal Plain," in S. Bunimovitz, M. Kochavi, and A. Kasher (eds.), *Settlements, Population and Economy in Eretz-Israel in Antiquity*, pp. 73–23. Tel Aviv.

R. Gophna and J. Portugali, 1988. "Settlement and Demographic Processes in Israel's Coastal Plain from the Chalcolithic to the Middle Bronze Age," *BASOR* 269: 11–28.

R.A. Gould and P.J. Watson, 1982. "A Dialogue on the Meaning and Use of Analogy in Ethnoarchaeological Reasoning," *Journal of Anthropological Archaeology* 1: 355–381.

J. Hass, 1982. *The Evolution of the Prehistoric State*. New York.

C. Hawkes, 1954. "Archaeological Theory and Method: Some Suggestions from the Old World," *American Anthropologist* 56: 155–168.

Z. Herzog, 1989. "Middle and Late Bronze Age Settlements (Strata XVII–XV)," in Z. Herzog, G. Rapp, Jr. and O. Negbi (eds.), *Excavations at Tel Michal, Israel*, pp. 29–42. Minneapolis.

I. Hodder, 1982a. "Theoretical Archaeology: A Reactionary View," in I. Hodder (ed.), *Symbolic and Structural Archaeology*, pp. 1–16. Cambridge.

———, 1982b. *The Present Past*. London.

———, 1986. *Reading the Past*. Cambridge.

G.A. Johnson, 1972. "A Test of Utility of Central Place Theory in Archaeology," in P.J. Ucko, R. Tringham, and W. Dimbleby (eds.), *Man, Settlement and Urbanism*, pp. 769–785. London.

———, 1980. "Rank-Size Convexity and System Integration: A View from Archaeology," *Economic Geography* 56: 234–247.

———, 1981. "Monitoring Complex System Integration and Boundary Phenomena with Settlement Size Data," in van der S.E. Leeuw (ed.), *Archaeological Approaches to Complexity*, pp. 144–187. Amsterdam.

———, 1987. "The Changing Organization of Uruk Administration on the Susiana Plain," in F. Hole (ed.), *The Archaeology of Western Iran*, pp. 107–139. Washington.

A. Kempinski, 1983. *Syrien und Palästina (Kanaan) in der letzten Phase der Mittelbronze IIB–Zeit (1650–1570 v. Chr)*. Wiesbaden.

K.M. Kenyon, 1979. *Archaeology in the Holy Land* (4th ed.). London.

L.S. Klejn, 1977. "A Panorama of Theoretical Archaeology," *Current Anthropology* 18: 1–42.

P.L. Kohl, 1987. "The Use and Abuse of World Systems Theory: The Case of Pristine West Asian State," *Advances in Archaeological Method and Theory* 11: 1–35.

S.A. Kowalewski, 1982. "The Evolution of Primate Regional Systems," *Comparative Urban Research* 9: 60–78.

K. Kristiansen, 1984. "Ideology and Material Culture: An Archaeological Perspective," in M. Spriggs (ed.), *Marxist Perspectives in Archaeology*, pp. 72–100. Cambridge.

P.W. Lapp, 1970. "Palestine in the Early Bronze Age," in J.A. Sanders (ed.), *Near Eastern Archaeology in the Twentieth Century. Essays in Honor of Nelson Glueck*, pp. 101–131. New York.

T.E. Levy, 1981. "Chalcolithic Settlement and Subsistence in the Northern Negev Desert, Israel." (Ph.D. diss., Sheffield University).

_____ , 1986. "Social Archaeology and the Chalcolithic Period: Explaining Social Organizational Change during the 4th Millenium in Israel," *Michmanim* 3: 5–20.

J. Marcus, 1973. "Territorial Organisation of the Lowland Classic Maya," *Science* 180: 911–916.

N. Naᵓaman, 1982. "Eretz-Israel in the Canaanite Period. The Middle Bronze Age and the Late Bronze Age (ca. 2000–1200 B.C.E.)," in I. Ephᶜal (ed.), *The History of Eretz-Israel* I, pp. 129–256. Jerusalem. (Hebrew).

R.W. Paynter, 1983. "Expanding the Scope of Settlement Analysis," in J.A. Moore and A.S. Keene (eds.), *Archaeological Hammers and Theories*, pp. 233– 275. New York.

B.J. Price, 1978. "Secondary State Formation: An Explanatory Model," in R. Cohen and E. Service (eds.), *Origins of the State*, pp. 161–186. Philadelphia.

C. Renfrew, 1977. "Space, Time and Polity," in J. Friedman and M.J. Rowlands (eds.), *The Evolution of Social Systems*, pp. 89–112.London.

_____ , 1984. *Approaches to Social Archaeology*. Edinburgh.

_____ , 1986. "Introduction: Peer Polity Interaction and Socio-political Change," in C. Renfrew and J.F. Cherry (eds.), *Peer Polity Interaction and Socio-political Change*, pp. 1–18. Cambridge.

C. Renfrew and E.V. Level, 1979. "Exploring Dominance: Predicting Polities from Centers," in C. Renfrew and K.L. Cooke (eds.), *Transformations. Mathematical Approaches to Culture Change*, pp. 437–461. New York.

S. Richard, 1987. "The Early Bronze Age" *BA* 50: 22–43.

J.D.Seger, 1975. "The MB II Fortifications at Shechem and Gezer. A Hyksos Retrospective," *EI* 12: 34*–45*.

B. Trigger, 1974. "The Archaeology of Government," *World Archaeology* 6: 95–106.

_____ , 1984. "Archaeology at the Crossroads: What's New?" *Annual Review of Anthroplogy* 13: 275–300.

R. de Vaux, 1971. "Palestine in the Early Bronze Age," *CAH* I/2A: 208–237.

J.M. Weinstein, 1981. "The Egyptian Empire in Palestine: A Reassessment," *BASOR* 241: 1–28.

G.E. Wright, 1961. "The Archaeology of Palestine," in G.E. Wright (ed.), *The Bible and the Near East. Essays in Honor of William Foxwell Albright*, pp. 73–112. Garden City NY.

N. Yoffee, 1979. "The Decline and Rise of Mesopotamian Civilization: an Ethnoarchaeological Perspective on the Evolution of Social Complexity," *American Antiquity* 44: 5–35.

A. Zertal, 1986. "The Israelite Settlement in the Hill-Country of Manasseh." (Ph.D. diss., Tel Aviv University) (Hebrew).